WHATEVER
HAPPENED
TO
JACY FARROW?

WHATEVER HAPPENED TO JACY FARROW?

BY CEIL CLEVELAND

University of North Texas Press
Denton, Texas

5   4   3   2   1

The paper in this book meets the minimum requirements of the American
National Standard for Permanence of Paper for Printed Library Materials,
Z39.48.1984

Permissions
University of North Texas Press
P. O. Box 311336
Denton, TX 76203

Library of Congress Cataloging-in-Publication Data
Cleveland, Ceil.
Whatever happened to Jacy Farrow / by Ceil Cleveland.
p.   cm.
ISBN 1-57441-030-X (alk. paper)
1. Cleveland, Ceil—Childhood and youth. 2. Archer City (Tex.)—Biography. 3.
Archer City (Tex.)—Social life and customs.
I. Title.

F394.A7C58	1997
976.4'543—dc21	97-22946
[B]	CIP

Design by Accent Design and Communications

For Daddy Joe

The rock on which we built our lives

Other people, so I have read, treasure memorable moments in their lives: the time one climbed the Parthenon at sunrise, the summer night one met a lonely girl in Central Park and achieved with her a sweet and natural relationship, as they say in books. I, too, once met a girl in Central Park, but it is not much to remember. What I remember is the time John Wayne killed three men with a carbine as he was falling to the dusty street in *Stagecoach*, and the time the kitten found Orson Welles in the doorway in *The Third Man*.

—Walker Percy

It is obvious that the values of women differ very often from the values which have been made by the other sex; naturally, this is so. Yet it is the masculine values that prevail. Speaking crudely, football and sport are "important"; the worship of fashion, the buying of clothes "trivial." And these values are inevitably transferred from life to fiction. This is an important book, the critic assumes, because it deals with war. This is an insignificant book because it deals with the feelings of women in a drawing-room. A scene in a battlefield is more important than a scene in a shop—everywhere and much more subtly the difference of value persists.

—Virginia Woolf

C·O·N·T·E·N·T·S

What we call the
beginning is often the end,
And to make an end is
to make a beginning.
The end is where
we start from.
—T. S. Eliot

P·R·O·L·O·G·U·E

AS ANYONE ACQUAINTED with contemporary American literature knows, Jacy Farrow was the blond, flirtatious, teen queen in
Thalia, Texas, who drove Sonny, Duane, and all the other boys wild
in Larry McMurtry's 1966 novel, *The Last Picture Show,* and in the
Peter Bogdanovich movie that followed in 1970.

Rumor has it, among old-timers, that the characters were based
on real people. In fact, a few years ago, with the cooperation of Cybill
Shepherd (who played the role of Jacy) and others in the original
film, actor Timothy Bottoms and filmmaker George Hickenlooper
made an award-winning documentary, *Picture This: Peter Bogdanovich
in Archer City, Texas,* which featured the "real people" on whom
these characters were supposedly based. I understand from my children that the documentary is aired a lot at 2 A.M. in Los Angeles.
Though I've never seen it on TV, I play a prominent role in it—
principally, as I recall, denying that I am the "real person" behind
the character of one Jacy Farrow and making it clear to the viewing
audience that I wouldn't *think* of behaving as she did.

But Jacy did misbehave in the 1950s, when misbehavior, especially in small-town Texas, was a good deal tamer than it is today,
before high school girls had become a miniseries of tousled hair, and
before sex traveled at the speed of fax. Cybill, nineteen when she
played the role, declared in the documentary twenty years later that
the film was "shocking for its time, in its language and nudity." She

never again, she claimed, took off her clothes in a movie. Randy Quaid thought it was "a Grade B, soft porn movie" when he auditioned for it and won the role of Lester Marlow, Jacy's rich boyfriend. The Reverend Deerinwater of Archer City, a real person interviewed in the documentary, allowed that "My wife and I are Christians, and we were just plain shocked."

Here in the nineties, these attitudes seem a little *retro*, but then, the film does, too. "It pissed the entire world off," said one Archer City man about the movie, "but it did tell the truth about local people."

"Naw," said another. "They didn't film the way we live, they filmed the way they think we live." But a man in the 1989 documentary tells, in alloyed English, about the time he broke a beer bottle on his own head and left the glass gouged into his temple until someone called his attention to it—beer-bottle breaking on one's head still being a manly sport in the region.

Texas is tall tales country, and I'm no better than anyone else at separating truth from legend. But I did grow up in Archer City, Texas (population 1,634)—the real little town McMurtry fictionalized as Thalia. The picture show people changed its name to Anarene so the actors could wear the high school football team's black jackets with the big gold *As* on them. That's *A* for Archer City Wildcats—or *Go Cats!*—as you can still see scrawled across the windows on nearly every structure around the courthouse square on every day that leads up to Friday night.

Today, downtown consists of a main street running in front of the court house, a post office, a couple of filling stations, and about ten small buildings ranging from the Wash Spot to the Texasville Cafe. Neither of these last two establishments was there when Larry and I were trying hard to grow up in Archer City. Then, the town consisted of a few little stores that leaned conspiratorially toward one another as if they too were passing on the local gossip. There were drug and dry goods stores, a five-and-dime, and a bank, along with the now-famous pool hall and diner, and The Wildcatter drive-in that became the Rig-Wam in McMurtry's book. On the Windthorst farm-to-market road stood the American Legion Hall, whose dances were the scandal of the First Methodist Church. And there was a picture show, until it burned down.

High school football was, and is, at the core of this small town's values. Signs, *Home of a Wildcat,* sprang up in the front yard dirt of the houses of boys who made the football team and stayed there until they graduated—or got hurt and limped off the field in disgrace. Cheerleaders' yards were often festooned with pompons. On Saturday mornings after a win, the boys swarmed the square in their black jackets, suffering hearty claps on their shoulders with modestly swaggering *Ah, twern't nothin'* shrugs. After a loss, the square rang hollow.

Today a lighted billboard, shaped liked a football, announces that the Wildcats won the state Class A Championship—in 1964.

Besides sporting a football stadium that doubled as a rodeo pen one month each summer, Archer City had a three-story, red-brick school, housing grades one through twelve. Nobody went to kindergarten in those days, and hardly anyone went beyond grade twelve. A lot fewer would have gotten that far, had it not been for the high school football and cheerleading teams. The school had a big front staircase with a shiny wood bannister that someone had nailed empty spools into about every ten inches, to discourage the sliding down thereon. And there was a flag pole up which many odd items were run by Archer City boys—a skunk, a pair of great flapping pink drawers, and, incredibly, an upside-down pelican.

There were five churches in Archer, but not a single library, unless you counted the few volumes in back of the study hall that grew even fewer as the school board took them home to scrutinize when people complained about their content and its possible damage to youthful moral fiber. What I remember about those books was that while there were plenty of Zane Gray westerns, there was not a lot to engage girls between the reading stages of *Nancy Drew* and *Little Women,* except *Elsie Dinsmore* and *Girl of the Limberlost.* American writers pretty much ignored the reading needs of young girls, and I had to scout my grandmother's bookshelves to find a copy of *Jane Eyre.* Then I was off and running with all the Brontes and several early and tormenting gothics, but they were, of course, British. The lesson I took from that was that American girls were not supposed to read and write.

Larry and I conjugated verbs in these halls of learning, and his family and my own were—and still are—close. We were in and out of one another's houses daily for twenty years or so. We left Archer City for college—he to Rice University, and I to what was then called North Texas State College. He soon joined me at North Texas, just as I was about to drop out and—what else?—get married. That's what girls did in those days. That, in fact, was why girls went to college in the first place—to find the right man to drop out for. Though my own dropping out story is a little different from most, I did marry soon after leaving college and lived in various parts of the country—the Northwest, the Midwest, and the Southwest.

For the past twenty years, I have lived in New York City and on the North Shore of Long Island. But Archer County/Thalia is my home as surely as Oxford, Mississippi/Yoknapatawpha County is home to William Faulkner's heirs. Steeped in that culture, both the real and the literary, I share with McMurtry the history and the social memories of a time and place that is past and passing. It is a culture within, without, and against which I fought to define myself. I carry its smells, its burrs and balls of dust in the lining of my coat, its residue in my resolute bones. It is for me a place with a soul, because it gave me my oldest, earliest stories.

For years I have had the urge to tell some of these stories. And as a fifth-generation Texan, I've wanted to write of a particular time and place that are a part of my pioneer family. I especially have wanted to write of my extraordinary mother, without whose influence and daily support I would certainly have gone stark mad in a culture so masculine that women were defined only in the ways they could serve men. I've wanted to write of the way she encouraged my intellectual abilities, while at the same time keeping in focus the reality of the life that I, as a Texas girl of the 1950s, was likely to live. This could not have been an easy juggle for her.

But as a writer, I have been a diffident poacher, this territory having been claimed and wrestled to a draw by my friend Larry, a fine writer, who produced a classic work of American fiction from much of the material of my youth. In mulling this over, I have sometimes wondered how another writer—a contemporary of Faulkner, say—would have approached this dilemma. Little Archer is not New York City, after all, where there are more than enough stories to go around. I recoiled at becoming a literary squatter in the country of my youth, a country that my childhood friend first scouted for possibilities, then claimed, settled, and populated with his own creations when he was very young.

It was not until the summer of 1989, when I went back to visit my family while *Texasville,* the sequel to *The Last Picture Show,* was being filmed there, that I thought perhaps I'd found a solution to the problem that had nagged me. Here I finally learned what seemed to be common knowledge to local people: That I—*I?*—was thought by many to be the girl on whom McMurtry's Jacy character was based.

This news astonished me. Jacy Farrow *c'est moi?* What likeness had I, a model high school girl, borne to this spoiled, catty, willful little flirt? How must I have appeared as a young girl to suggest to others the image of this tacky Texas teenager? This was not the way I had seen myself at all. I dismissed the idea.

I did recall that I'd been stunned by *Picture Show* when the author sent me one of the first copies in the mid-1960s. By then I was a mother of three babies and a "returning" college student living in Washington state. Reading the book was like being towed backward ten years into my stifling girlhood. Having myself escaped *death by small town* only by a little, I found the images McMurtry drew so disturbing that I rolled in my sheets several nights in a row, sleepless. I wrote him, saying that he had struck a deep chord with me, and he responded wryly that to date he'd received exactly two "fan letters"—one from me, and one from my mother. Mine was the only positive one.

But as I'd read the book whose setting and ethos seemed authentic, any resemblance between the major female character and myself had simply not occurred to me. As a high school girl, I had thought— as solipsistic adolescents have always done—that no one existed outside myself. I took little notice of all those rough-house boys who constantly hung out with my two brothers. In fact, I did a fair job of ignoring everyone who didn't fit into my fantasy life, a life more real to me than the one I actually lived. By my teenage years, I had decided that I would spend as little time as possible in this hot little town, where by some fluke I had been thrust from my mother's moist womb into an arid spot where nothing seemed to grow. As some insightful person from Archer remarked to me years later, "Even when you were here, you weren't here."

And clearly, I was too early vaccinated by a fancy grandmother and her book-learning ways to take to a place where high school coaches were drafted to teach history (since of course anybody can teach that), resulting in the odd pronunciations (*Só-crates. A-rís-tó-tole*) I brought home, where they were immediately corrected.

So what could prompt others to see a resemblance between me and the character Jacy Farrow?

That *Texasville* summer, when the actors and movie paraphernalia that the locals love to hate were again disrupting the somnolence of the little town of my childhood, I spent a good deal of time with an old high school buddy, the late Bobby Stubbs. McMurtry had years earlier identified Stubbs as the take-off point for his character, Duane, in *Picture Show*. Bobby teased me into reconsidering the rumor about myself. He thought it was funny and maybe just a little bit true, and after awhile, I did too. For one thing, I recalled a speech I'd heard Ted Koppel of ABC's "Nightline" give in New York City a couple of years before about the "Vannatization of America." Of the mute and fetching television alphabet queen, Vanna White (a big celebrity at the time), Koppel said: "Because nobody knows what—or even *if*—she thinks, we can project on her whatever we want to." I had been so struck by this comment that I had written it down at the time. I was especially struck by it because in my first semester in college, knowing not one soul in that fraternity, I had been elected—*on the basis of my mute and fetching photograph alone*—Sweetheart of the College Chapter of Sigma Delta Pi! Irony is a staple of a literary life, and here was a big one.

How I merited this tin title was a mystery to me then, but this did not keep me from accepting it. After all, I was busy racking up "honors" in those days. What was one more? So I went to the dance with a fraternity member—a blind date set up for me, since I knew no one there—and got photographed and crowned. Still, I could not imagine what they could be honoring. They didn't *know* me! My date, who had sent me an impressive bouquet of flowers that day, tried to kiss me in the cab on the way to the dance, and I jerked away like a perfect twit, answering haughtily, "I just heard your name for the first time ten minutes ago. What makes you think you can *kiss* me?"

Exactly like something Jacy Farrow might have done. It is this kind of behavior that *Picture Show* parodies so well. In small-town

Texas, expectations were set up by the boys. When the girls refused to play, we were thought to be strange and a threat to manly self-esteem. In the picture shows—as every director from Bogdanovich to Fellini knows—such behavior on the part of the girls usually produces humor.

After I left Archer and the *Texasville* bunch that summer and returned to New York to my work at Columbia University, something continued to haunt me about the disconnection between the character, the real girl then, and the woman I now know myself to be. Eventually, something became clear: *all* girls—maybe since Eve in the Garden—have been *Vannatized*, have been the repositories of the fantasies of the men around them. I recalled something that the playwright Arthur Miller, a major character in my own youthful fantasy life (more later), had said, not about his second wife, but about the "witches" of Salem: "When something is secret or unfamiliar, you're free to project anything on it." Throughout history, girls have been the *tabula* so *rasa*—nobody knew what, or even *if*, we thought—that men could project on us anything they chose.

I was startled, and amused, to hear Cybill Shepherd confirm my own thoughts on this subject as I watched the documentary. Of the Jacy role, she admitted to having been "afraid." Jacy "was everything people thought I might have been, but never was—heartless, walking over carcasses of men—'*Walk all over me, please.*'" Shepherd laughed and looked incredulous: "I was *Miss Congeniality* in the Miss Teenage America Pageant!"

Men see women not as we are, but as they think we are, or maybe want us to be. Throughout history, men have fallen in love with, married, and sired children with women who were merely projections of their own fantasies. No wonder so many marriages have crashed. And no wonder that in modern American literature this delectable package has become an archetype: A beautiful, flirty but calculating, gingham-clad blonde in a convertible. As someone in the documentary said: in everyone's life there is a Jacy—an unattainable girl who seems to have everything. That to some observers I once resembled this specific fictional character surprised me. But of course, as an archetype, there was a fairly obvious commonality: We were both conventionally pretty, naive girls, self-absorbed enough to be oblivious to everyone around us, intelligent enough to be manipulative, independent enough to be headstrong.

After a while, my presumed role in this creation seemed to me an interesting idea to explore. It was not wholly true, not wholly false. An American archetype had been created from my native soil. And here was a way for me to write about my roots in Archer County/ Thalia, a way not to *poach* on claimed territory, but rather to stand on the shoulders of a giant—not in order to see farther, but perhaps to look in another direction.

As everyone knows—but it bears repeating in this case, lest I give myself an importance it would not be altogether honest to assume—a fictional character is never based on a single person but is instead a composite of many people, one who takes on a life of her own through the imagination of the writer. A character can evolve for a writer from something as slight as a glance, as did Dante's idealized Laura, or from years of observation, as did James Joyce's multidimensional Molly. Actual people, for example, Agnes von Kurowsky, the presumed inspiration for Catherine Barkley in Ernest Hemingway's *A Farewell to Arms,* may loom small; the writer, as critics have said, often borrows an idea for a character from a person, then stands aside with a growing sense of wonder as the character takes over and speaks for herself.

McMurtry has always created his own characters, and for *Picture Show* he created remarkable ones from the raw material that, at age twenty-two, he had. He did not need to know what was going on in the minds of the girls in the little town he created to write his book. *Picture Show* is not a book about Jacy Farrow; it is the coming-of-age narrative of young boys and the fantasies they projected on the girls who stood between them and a fragile adulthood. Obviously, the girls in *Picture Show* have no life beyond what the author gives them— and he gives them life only through the eyes and gonads of adolescent boys. The girls go about their days, growing up in a bleak, limited landscape, being watched and lusted after by pubescent boys with nothing else to do. Boys of that era did stand around a lamp post, or a drug store, or on the courthouse lawn, whistling and leering at the passing girls in a way that most girls wouldn't put up with today. Cultural dictates during the 1950s demanded that young girls fairly sleep-walk through their adolescence. Boys were the *agents*; girls were *acted upon*. For girls, being "seen and not heard" was a reality, not a cliché. (This condition has been documented by a number of women writers since the seventies.)

Thus, it's not surprising that McMurtry's novel did not deal with what "the last picture show" meant to Jacy and the other girls of Thalia; this point was irrelevant to his story. But picture shows in general meant something quite specific and distinct to me and the girls I knew. Females in the films of the fifties and early sixties were the models we measured ourselves against, the influences that shaped our tastes. Since most of us in small towns were late in acquiring television, we had no other models except our mothers, and who wanted lives like *theirs?* What did we know of the macho passions of manifest destiny in *Red River*, which happened to be the last picture show shown in the last picture show in Thalia. That was men stuff, or more likely, little boy stuff. Women participated only as the love interest or sex object or some other impediment to male conquest of the forces of nature in the West. When we were not observing with horror the hardships of women's lives on the trail, or with stupefaction the brazenness of denizens of brothels—the most alert girls were absorbing the details of clothing styles that the women in the pictures wore, the way they shook a head or a hip, the flinty or come-hither looks they gave the men. We watched picture shows to find out what worked for women in *real life* since, clearly, it was not *real life* that we were living.

While the boys were projecting their fantasies on girls, I projected myself into every picture show I saw. I was *there*—learning how to act, to walk, to dress, to speak, to attract or dismiss men, to take care of myself. I could select or reject a certain setting for myself, certain behavior, a certain mate. In an isolated little town with no role models beyond those of domestic women, I had no other way of imagining my future.

But the boys' world—the *legitimate* world—of football, rodeos, learning to cuss, and dreaming about girls, was the world of Texas in that era. Girls had bit parts. We could play if we learned our lines and attempted no ad lib. We were allowed to be cheerleaders, jumping, squealing, shaking our hips and pompons—as in Hellenic games, the rewards of the boys on the field after the game was over. The booty. Or we could be majorettes in short skirts, pagan priestesses diverting attention from the snarling beasts waiting behind the goal posts to charge.

A few of the more reticent, like me, having found no more fitting role for ourselves, sang in church choirs and spent our evenings curled up with *Brenda Starr, Girl Reporter*, or *Antigone*, there being little distinction between the two to our untutored minds. Boys to us were definitely secondary creatures, necessary when there was a dance or a picture show in Wichita Falls, to which our fathers would not let us go without an escort.

McMurtry's satire was rooted in the minds of boys on the threshold of manhood, and girls were on their minds. But Jacy's story has never been told. What was going on in *her* life and in *her* head while Sonny and Duane saw a fantasy creature who would become an icon for boys coming of age in almost any size town?

A few years ago, after receiving nostalgic letters from both me and my brother (just a year younger than I) in the same week, Larry wrote me: "It was like the two of you lived on two different planets." *Exactly.* That is the point of this book. Amid all the changes the last four decades have wrought, it is important not to forget the two different planets on which girls and boys resided in mid-century of the 1900s—even when we shared the same culture, the same age, the same family. These differences were particularly clear in Archer City, Texas, because the culture was so limited, our lives so self-contained.

It may seem strange that two such intensely literary people as McMurtry and I could have emerged at the same time from Archer City, Texas, a spare and dust-blown speck on the Texas plains that housed not even the meagerest library. (Today, he is creating an international Book Town there—stocking the town with one million books.) "What are the odds of that?" some ask. "What was in the water there?"

Not in the water, but a wellspring in any case. We had the same early mentor: my mother, a talented, inventive woman of great depth and curiosity. Far ahead of her time, she questioned conventional wisdom. She was a reader and a writer, and a nurturer of both, and—like her earliest protegees—a kind of misfit in this place. The difference between her and us was that she could tolerate being a misfit there; it was imperative to us to move on. She provided the only intellectual backboard for the brilliant son of her closest friends, as well as her own curious daughter, to bounce ideas against. (Her initial shock on reading *Picture Show* was, she later admitted, that of recognition. On second reading, shock was replaced by admiration for McMurtry's talent. At the local celebration of his winning the Pulitzer Prize many years later, Mother—who else could have?—gave the major toast.)

My mother played the patriarchal game, as did the girls of Jacy's era, because it was the only game in town. Some of us are still playing it. I finally got fed up with it after a few decades, caused pain and angst to everyone who loved me, and turned my life around.

How ghastly that was; how sweet it is.

Perhaps it is, as author and scholar Carolyn Heilbrun has suggested, that only women who played the men's game and won a self *anyway* have the courage to face the pain bought by telling their own stories straight. And maybe only women of a certain age, say, in their fifties, can stop being what she calls "female impersonators" and can now do what they might have done much earlier had they not been born hostages to their gender.

I know about being a hostage: hostage to heart and hostage to head. I know about the conflict between biological creativity—the explosion in my body giving birth to new and precious little people; and artistic creativity—the explosion in my head giving me a strong and singular take on life that demands—*demands*—expression. The mother in me and the artist in me have been constantly wrestling bedfellows for three decades. Each has taken dominance in a different phase of my life. The mother is finally off the hook. The kids are grown and relatively independent, though I wonder every single night when I tuck myself in whether each of them in their various parts of the country has sufficient bedcovers. The writer, who has over the years made time during the hours after midnight to pen the millions of words I have published in short pieces, is clamoring to focus all that energy.

Now is a good time for Jacy to tell her story. Time to draw as clear a portrait of the mutating Zeitgeist as memory will allow—or to use the metaphor that Eudora Welty prefers, to lower the dipper into

the well as deeply as possible and bring up the clear sweet water—
and whatever bilge happens to float there. And yet, one can't but
wonder in approaching the writing of memoir how much of one's
past life is one's own? How much of it is one free to interpret? What
silence, what privacy, does one owe the people closest to her, her
family, her children? An artist has only her life as raw material, and
the urge to express it is strong; the stronger the artist, the more over-
powering the urge.

Someone please tell me that there's not always a catch.

"The upshot of all such reflections is that I have only to let myself go!" wrote Henry James in his diary in the later part of his life. "I
am in full possession of accumulated resources—I have only to use
them, to insist, to persist. . . . The way to do this is to affirm one's
self *sur la fin*—to strike as many notes, deep, full and rapid, as one
can. . . . "

Well, thank you, Henry. Somehow, gaining permission from a
man seems appropriate for a Texas girl of the fifties. In full possession of accumulated resources then, I am setting out in this book to
tell a girl's story—this girl's story—"Jacy's" story—of my time and
my place in the little Texas town of my childhood, and of those later
years when I shook off skin after skin and finally crawled out a woman.

I couldn't play football and have adventures in Mexico like the
boys in *Picture Show* did. But I did have a dress like the one Grace
Kelly wore to Prince Rainier's palace in Monaco for the first time. It
was blue and patterned and had a dropped waist with a full skirt and
a scoop neck. I saw it in a news reel at the picture show and copied
the pattern for my mother to follow. And I still have the poodle skirt
I wore to the sock hop as a high school freshman. And guess what?
I can still zip it up all the way! And guess what else? I finally did read
all those books that Dr. Mortimer Adler sent my mother for sending
a winning question to his newspaper column. I still have the books,
too, and I *still* read them. As my mother said, there are adventures,
and then there are *adventures*.

It was a long time ago, and it was not true, or only half true, or
only true in its tiniest kernel, or only true in the minds of the fanners
of the flame of local rumor that I am remotely suggestive of the girl
character called Jacy created by my childhood friend. But there is no

question that I am a girl who grew up in—and out of—those times and that thoroughly singular place.

So who was she—this Jacy Farrow? Whatever happened to her?

Some names of people and actual locations have been changed here purportedly to protect the innocent, but mainly to protect my own neck.

Acknowledgments

Memoirs are a special category of book. When the author dips into the well of her own memory, she cannot help bringing up other people, many of them still living. Their realities, their interpretations of the same set of circumstances, will undoubtedly differ. All I can say is this: if you think you find yourself here, and you disagree with any interpretation of events as stated, write your own book. I can't wait to read it!

For this book, I wish to thank one person above all—my childhood (and current) friend, Larry McMurtry, for his enormous generosity in giving me one of his own creations to do with pretty much as I pleased. Jacy Farrow is a character of McMurtry's imagination. He loaned her to me, and I have used her to narrate this memoir. I am deeply indebted to him for allowing me to build on his creation for my own purposes.

I am also grateful to Frances B. Vick, my publisher, for having faith in this idea, and this conceit, from the start, and for encouraging me to spend the two years it has taken me in odd hours of the day and night to bring the manuscript to completion. For helping me keep the narrative on track, and for unburying my prose when I piled remembered anecdote on anecdote, I am grateful to Charlotte Wright, absolutely the best editor with whom I have ever worked.

Beyond this, I thank my sister, Mary Ellen, my daughter, Wendy, and my friend, Barbara, for reading the manuscript in its early stages and keeping me honest—or at least trying to. I take full responsibility for any errors here, but I am grateful to them for knowing how literature works, and for indulging me. I also thank my two sons, Jay and Tim, and their father for being good souls and understanding that a writer must write—just as a teacher must teach, an actor must act, and a doctor must take care of his patients. I also thank my brothers, Jim and Joe, for letting me take their names in vain. They grew up to be really good guys, and I love them.

I thank my friends Cynthia and Robert, and Ryan and Jim for putting up with me and my mood swings for the last couple of years, and for their unswerving encouragement. And finally, I thank my mother, ME, who did not live to read this, for being my mentor and my guide; my father, Joe Donaldson Cleveland Slack, who has no idea what to expect from this book and is thus totally exonerated; and my husband Jerrold K. Footlick, whom I love inordinately, and whose name is only a little bit weirder than Marlboro's.

PART I

1

Time and trouble will
tame an advanced young
woman, but an advanced
old woman is uncontrol-
lable by any earthly force.
—Dorothy L. Sayers

W·A·T·E·R

I'M NOT BLONDE like Cybill Shepherd. My hair is auburn with natural highlights by Roberto that I wear sort of every whichway. Some days I pay immaculate attention to it with gels and sprays. And some days, even whole weeks, I stick on a gimme cap and go about my business. Hair is just one of those things like age, or wrinkles, or the crud under the refrigerator, that sit there all the time. If you focus on them they'll drive you nuts.

But like Cybill in *The Last Picture Show*, which was filmed in my hometown, I do drive a convertible—when my kids and grandkids are not visiting, at which time I have to resort to the six-seater. A comedown in cool. The convertible, in which I tool around my new hometown, a Long Island fishing village, is a throwback toy—the symbol of freedom and insouciance that I was not to find until I was in my fifties. Which is where I am now. Like child actors or others pressed too early into responsibilities, I never got to feel my oats— until today. And now, I guess, it's more like oat bran.

My mother has been dead three years, and I still miss her fiercely. I think of my mother, and in fact, of all the women in my family, as saxifrages—small brilliant flowers that manage to push themselves up through rocks, the power in their tiny forms creating cracks and crevices to nestle in. Their determination and fragile strength brought color and life to a hard joyless place. The men largely ignored the modest charms these women brought to the red clay of Thalia—that is, when they weren't outright mocking them. "Off to the Calamity Club again today?" they would snort, shaking what my mother called "the mud 'n worse" off their boots and onto the clean hardwood floor as they poked fun at the Amity Club, a clutch of women who gathered to hear a guest speaker or artist or musician amidst the white napery and gleaming cutlery of their dining rooms, which, once a month, shut out the smell of horse- and men-flesh.

For twenty years, my mother was the best thing in my life. Nothing else—the leather-faced men, the flatlands, the adenoidal singers wailing out of the radio from Clint and Del Rio, the hooves of cattle scarring the hard earth, the dust of rodeos, the raucous jokes, the football games, and in the evening the rattle of dominoes and poolsticks—made any sense at all. Sometimes I felt like my mother and I were the only human creatures in Thalia, a cowtown that, like all of Texas, had been settled by pioneer women as well as men. But the women had, finally, been outnumbered by their men, whose stubbornness matched that of the tough mesquite trees brought to the area as pods in the bowels of Mexican cattle and deposited in thick splats of cow dung that fertilized the striplings as they grew into dogged but lacy trees rooting in the thin soil and driving out every living thing around them.

If ever there were a symbol of West Texas for me, the mesquite was it—even more than the prickly clumps of tumbleweed that whipped through the fields when the wind-and-sand storms got up, as they did in every season but summer—when everything lay scorched and still—or more than the goatheads that clung to your britches' legs or embedded themselves in your heel. The men had taken over the environment, just as the environment had overtaken the men. And women were left to make beauty where they could. Mother painted endless fields of bluebonnets and hung the paintings around the house. "These and the red Indian Paintbrush are the only pretty things in Texas," she said, adding wanly, "and you have to grab a glance while you can since none of them lasts more than a minute."

Mother said that hanging the bluebonnets inside the house was a *blankety-blank-sight* nicer than the stuff she'd hung on the outside, such as diapers for four kids—three of us in the things at the same time—which had left the old wringer washer as gleaming as a good soak in Rinso White could make them, then after half-an-hour on the clothesline came back the color and texture of sandpaper. "These kids must have tough little heinies," she would say, fastening a triangle on one of us. "Yeah, Dead End Kids," said Daddy, passing through the room to hang his Stetson on a peg in the hall.

That was in spring. In winter the diapers came back in frozen white squares, which Mother stacked like a pile of large pale waffles on a bench in front of the fireplace, until they thawed and grew as limp as flour tortillas, the water puddling on the fireplace hearth. In the summer, the diapers came in off the line so hot you couldn't hold them. Mother would gingerly unclip the clothespins and let the cloth drop into the basket below. Inside, she would stick the diapers in the icebox to cool before she attached one of them to a kid.

One spring Mother put a diaper to more than one use. My just-younger brother was forever running away from home, toddling off down the street to visit the neighbors. Mother pinned a stout rope to the back of his diaper and tied the rope around a tree in the back yard. She gave the baby a bucket and spade to play with. Next time she looked out the kitchen window, though, she saw a diaper safely pinned to a rope lying under the tree, and the bare back-end of her son as he fled down the street.

Besides nurturing and corralling the children, the women gave hope a run for its money against futility by nurturing whatever twisted flowers could withstand the drought and heat. A marigold or two, with their acrid odor that supposedly repelled insects, might occasionally poke their strong little heads up in the parched ground, but the purple and yellow pansies Mother planted in her window box routinely panted and curled up their petals. One summer when the drought was so fierce and water so scarce that the county sheriff threatened to arrest people who watered their dirt lawns, Mother ran a hose from the upstairs bathtub, out the window, down the side of the house, and into the front yard, where the runoff from the family bathwater kept the pink crepe myrtle blooming feebly. It was the one spot of color in Thalia, if you didn't count the lone red traffic light blinking night and day at the intersection of Main and Center.

At age twelve, I was embarrassed by the tube snaking down the side of the house and told my mother that I was sure I'd never get a boyfriend if she made me live in a house that looked like it was taking a perpetual enema.

"Oh, pooh. You want to dip it out of the tub and water the lawn?" she said, dismissing me in the practical way she had. She did not care what people thought of her, and furthermore she considered a boy witless enough not to delight in a house taking an enema to be not worth a spitball anyway.

It was in Thalia that I realized once and for all that the earth was truly flat. I had no idea what would happen to me if I walked off the edge of it, but unlike most people there, I was bound and determined to find out. I practiced sometimes walking off the edge of a little hump in the ground that the boys called Old Tabletop, with only a couple of skinned knees and a twisted ankle to show for it. Edges didn't frighten me. And every once in a while, out at the family ranch in Jack County, where Daddy kept his cattle, I'd walk the wire when nobody was looking. The wire was actually two wires, one for your feet and one above for your hands that Doc, the hired hand, had strung to a tree on either side of the little trickle that once a year or so amounted to a creek. We called it "The Creek," whether there was water in it or not, usually not. When it was The Creek, your car stalled in it going across, and when it wasn't, you got stuck in the gooey red clay of its bottom. So Doc strung the wires to walk across it carrying two milk buckets in one hand, and with the other hand holding the wire above. Of course nobody was supposed to walk it but Doc, but sometimes I snuck off and did. It was just too suffocating keeping all that bravery down inside.

And on top of that there were so many words I couldn't say stuck down inside my throat like a bunch of chicken bones that I thought sometimes they would burp themselves up and strangle me in some public, embarrassing place. A girl couldn't do anything in Thalia except sit up straight like a lady, legs crossed at the ankles, and smile pretty. Even my mother couldn't help me on this one, since she used up all her bravery and words just surviving.

In a diary I'd bought at Mr. Wilson's five-and-dime I once wrote a line from Ovid, which I dipped into and out of, as I did with all my mother's *Great Books of the Western World* which she won for writing a winning question into a Mortimer Adler syndicated column in the *Wichita Falls Times*: "Why are the scales of justice represented by the figure of a blindfolded woman? Why is justice blind?" Dr. Adler wrote back that blind in this case meant "objective" or "fair," and as a prize sent her the works I planned to read from Homer to Freud—which was where the 54th book stopped, at Freud. These were the only *Great Books of the Western World* in Thalia, and clearly Mother was the only person who cared a hoot about the eyes of justice.

The line I wrote in my diary one night was: "I am a barbarian in this place, because I am understood by no one." This seemed an appropriately romantic and mysterious thing to write, and more or less true, though I couldn't quite see how my behavior was barbarian-like. Maybe it would come clear in the morning.

Mr. Wilson's five-and-dime was a funny place. All day long, it was dark inside. When you walked in the door a little bell tinkled, and Mr. Wilson got out of his chair way back in the rear of the store and walked toward the front, turning on lights all the way by pulling on long strings hanging down from the ceiling. He stood right by you smiling and bouncing and giggling *tee-hee-hee* while you were trying to pick out an autograph book or some fancy pink soap shaped like little pigs for a birthday present, and he always—every single birthday party—tried to get you to buy some awful perfume in a dark blue bottle called "Blue Waltz" that smelled like rotten pears. Mr. Wilson tried to lay that stuff off on some birthday victim for three years without success, until, I think, it finally blew up one day. After you'd finally selected the present—maybe some bright pink nail polish with a tall spire-shaped plastic thing attached to the top—you paid him, and started toward the door. Then Mr. Wilson walked toward the back of the store again, pulling on the dangling strings to turn off the lights as he went. My friend Janine called him Mr. Tee Hee Hee so many times that I usually forgot what his real name was. So that was where I found the diary to write down just why I was a barbarian in Thalia.

Now, I don't care who understands me, and my backyard is not a red clay desert but an old mill pond that feeds into the Sound. In its inlets live swans, mallards, herons and egrets, depending on the season. From the cantilevered deck where I often stand barefoot in the yellow morning sunlight, while the breeze flutters my hair and ruffles the flimsy batiste of my white nightgown, I am reminded of the way I stood on the hot tar surface of the balcony of my house in Thalia, a balcony my sister Ellie and I got to by crawling out our front bedroom window, since our long-dead grandfather who had built the house years before thought second-floor doors were the work of the devil, as most things not strictly utilitarian were to him, and who put the balcony on the front of the house only at the last minute when his wife offered to leave him immediately with the potatoes half-peeled in the sink if he did not.

As his revenge, he never finished the floor of the balcony. Instead, he left a black sticky substance that so soaked up the sun's rays that you couldn't bear to stand on it more than half a second. Nobody had ever fixed it, since it supposedly ensured that daughters would not be tempted to get half-clad and lie out on it to tan their legs. Ellie and I talked Daddy into letting us crawl out there every once in a while though, because he knew we were going to lie *somewhere* half-clad to get a suntan, and the balcony to him was a lesser evil than having us lie on a towel in the yard where the guys in cowboy hats and pickups would yell and whistle at us as they rounded the corner.

The stairway up to my room was another of those grinding compromises between my grandmother Mollie and grandfather Alf. Mollie had demanded both a fireplace with a carved mantel and a stairway with a carved banister. She got the mantel, but the stairway was, finally, gouged out of the middle of the house in such a way that you entered it by opening a narrow closet door and then climbed by placing your feet sideways on the narrow steps and stooping to about half size. Alf built a wider landing a few steps up, though, so he could get furniture up and down without having to make a pulley to heave it to the windows on the second floor—like Daddy had to do with the kidney shaped dressing table I just had to have after seeing one in a picture show. I drew it, and Daddy made it for me, but then he couldn't get it up the stairs for Mother to put the fluffy pink organdy skirt on it. All that sweating and swearing that Debbie Reynold's pink dressing table caused was all Alf's fault for not putting a normal staircase in to start with.

Later, after I grew up in the torturous way we all do, I began to think that house was a symbol of the generations of family that resided there: all spacious and gracious and sunny in its outer areas, but with an strange central core that sort of bent out of shape everything that tried to move around inside.

Grandfather Alf's full name, preposterously, was James Alfred Mills Logan Campbell Gowdy, Jr.—a list that fell thunderously upon most of his male heirs in adumbrated, reversed, or anagrammatic forms. He had Cherokee blood from his father, who in spurning Hungry Deer couldn't make up his mind how to go, so kept all the names that occurred to him, having a penchant for Scottish, such blood also flowing thickly in the family line. My grandfather, who shortened the catalogue of names to Alf, underwent one of those miraculous spiritual migrations of many Southwestern men and became a Bible-banger of the strict constructionist persuasion. He added to that the papers making him an itinerant Baptist minister. These being meager documents, they fit well in the pocket of his black topcoat as he sped across the plains saving souls on his choice of ministerial conveyance, a motorcycle. This, he explained to Mollie, was utilitarian because it carried the Gospel to the scattered heathen plainsmen faster than the old Model-T. Good with his hands when he wanted to be, he also operated the only lumber yard in Thalia County. But like every other man in the family, Alf's pride lay in his herd of cattle out in the dusty keeps of Jack County, where his parents had homesteaded on a place still recognized by the name on the cattle-guard: *Gowdy's Angus*.

His wife Mollie grew up in Indian territory around Duncan, Oklahoma, where her father was an Indian Agent. Isaac Newton Harper, called Newt, was son of Dr. George Harper whose ancestors reached back to Harper's Castle, Ireland, by way of Harper's Ferry, West Virginia. Colonel Newt had served in the Confederate Army, and was later a Texas Ranger, but he brought Miss Maggie Bateman Collins from the fancy Female Academy in Batesville, Arkansas—along with her hope chest filled with Irish linens, Battenberg lace, and silver epergnes—into stripper and Sooner territory and steadily gave her seven children. Like most of the men in Mother's family, he died young, of typhoid fever at fifty-six, and Miss Maggie, with her finery, her own brood of children, and four orphans she adopted, soldiered on.

Alf himself lived only thirty-eight years, being drowned in a well in a little town called Scotland, a few miles from Thalia, with his oldest son, whose name was—believe it or not—Hud, a name appropriated for another Texas-based book, in which, I am pleased to report, I have never been accused of being a character. My eleven-year-old mother, left alone above when her father and brother climbed down to inspect the damage done by a stick of dynamite they'd tossed in hoping to open up a deep water vein, heard them call to her and ran to the nearest farmhouse. When Mother returned with help, her father and brother were dead. From that day on, she was the resident grown-up and the chauffeur for Mollie, who, carrying to her grave the highfalutin mark of a lady as she defined it, forever refused to learn to drive.

Mother could talk about the death of her father and brother only up to their picnic of chicken and lemonade near the well site, where she and Hud snapped the pullybone before the men descended into the dark hole in the ground that emitted a fog of foul-smelling smoke. Mother got the short bone and made a wish: that she'd never have to come out to this awful-smelling well again.

She got her wish.

Mother had adored her stern father, and it was many years before she told me, in hushed tones, a puzzling story about him.

Once when she was about eight and sitting in church in Thalia, a group of Ku Klux Klanners marched in, approached the altar and presented a pouch of money to the preacher. The little girl, bored with the ritual goings-on, focused her attention on the Klansmen. "Look, Mommie," she pointed out, tugging Mollie's navy jacket with white piping. "That man has on Daddy's shoes."

"Shhh."

"But Mommie, they're Daddy's; they have that scuff on the heel. I know because I polished them the other night and couldn't get it off. He gave me a penny anyway."

"Shhhh." Pinch, pinch. "Such nonsense!"

Mollie would hear nothing more of this matter, even after they got home. But Mother kept all these things and pondered them in her heart (Luke 2:19). Later, after the death of her father, when she and Mollie went to clean out the attic of the house Alf had built, they found something that changed forever their view of Southern Baptists: the upstanding citizen of Thalia, the president of the school board, the hell and brimstone preacher, hid his Klan garb in a box up there. So *that's* where he went every Thursday night of his life!

Mollie was horrified when Mother reminded her of the scene in church.

"Oh, god," moaned Mollie. "Oh, god, forgive us all." She went into her bedroom and locked the door.

Shortly after, Mollie closed the house and went off to Baylor College, where an older son was in law school and where her husband had graduated. "The Gowdys have *always* gone to Baylor," she told members of the Roy Bedichek family who befriended her there, helping her find a home for herself and her daughters. Later, the Bedicheks helped her get established at the University of Texas, where Mollie stayed until she ran out of degrees to get. My mother went to college there, rooming with her mother and younger sister.

"No, living with my mother wasn't the best way to meet the opposite sex," Mother once told me, after I had screwed up my face at the thought of *living with your mother in college!* "Besides, Mollie talked for me at every social occasion, just like the cat had got my tongue. I had to marry and get away from her before I could phrase a thought out loud by myself."

This was something of an overstatement—a regular locution with my mother. After she learned to "phrase a thought out loud" by herself, Mother seldom did it without putting her own linguistic spin on it, and you learned by experience how much of what she said you could safely discount. Every story, every sentence, had a beginning, a middle, and an end—usually with a stinger. When the analogies were too clever, the metaphors too keen, the stingers too . . . well, stinging . . . you could begin to discount. She was a strange one who passed on to me her odd combination of opposites: strands of loftiness and earthiness, vanity and self-deprecation, lust for life and puritan restraint, intellectual curiosity and social reticence. These were wound within her, as in me, like a twisted helix of DNA. Hawk-faced Alf with his punishing Bible, and lyrical Mollie with her luminous skin, who read Robert Browning aloud on the porch, were a pair to daunt the most jaded geneticist.

Before that, according to Mother, her grandfather Newt playfully slapped his wife Maggie's ample bottom on the way through the kitchen as she stood at the crude counter on the reservation, a signal that this night another baby was likely to be made. In daguerreotypes Maggie holds her mouth in a grim slit. She called her husband "Mr. Gowdy" and blacked his boots for him every night until he died—called him "Mr. Gowdy," that is, except in those instances when he was out of earshot; then she called him *Himself,* as in, "What do you suppose *Himself* might eat for supper tonight?" Compliant but proud, Miss Maggie of the Female Academy, knew her place because she knew what was good for her. At the same time, she put on little airs. Her favorite line, as one of her children exited the door, was from *Mrs. Wiggs of the Cabbage Patch*: "Just remember, your mother was a lady, and your father was a member of the po-lice force." That warning was supposed to cover any questions of proper behavior a child might have.

Long before she had become my grandmother, Mollie studied "Elocution" at Kidd Key College for Girls somewhere in South Texas. The men in the family swore that she "damn near elocuted everyone to death." She was bent on bringing culture to the great unwashed, meaning, primarily, anyone who entered her sphere of influence. No one escaped the poems she carried in her head. No matter how many brain cells I may have vaporized over the years, still balefully clinging are those on which every line of *Hiawatha* and *Evangeline* are encoded. My brother, at about age five, was forced to stand before company and declaim: *"My pants all button on the waist; they might as well be trimmed with lace. If folks only knew just how I felt. Gee, I wish I had a belt!* After this, he was particularly terrified of the "elocution chair," in which one squirmed while having one's brains fried by Mollie.

But among the poems she taught me—including the now-appalling *"I'se G'wine Down to the Cushville Hop,"* which at that time no one thought to consider racist—was one that was actually useful:

"When I grow up and carry a stick and look very dignified, no one will know that it's only a trick, and I'm really myself inside." I used to repeat that poem to myself when I was a girl, for even then I understood that my outside gave wrong clues to my inside. That was the way it was with girls in those days. Even if you thought you knew something, you played like you didn't. You might look one way on the outside, but nobody knew what was going on in your head. It was good to learn early on that whatever preconceived ideas people might have of you, still *you* know what you really are. Even a silly little thing like a verse you repeat over and over can give you confidence and courage.

The women in my family were great storytellers. Mollie, Mother, even Aunt Celie told stories. Aunt Celie lived on the Jack County ranch most of her life, while the rest of us came and went, depending on the season. She actually ran *Gowdy's Angus*, tagged and branded her own cattle, and rode to the roundup virtually until the day she died at age ninety-five. She filled up the concrete stock tank for us to swim in, allowed us to burrow in the hayloft to read or drag the bales around to construct architectural fantasies, let us jump up and down in the oat bin until we were buried in oats up to our necks. Kids up north made angels in the snow; we made them in the oat bin—and we were very itchy angels. When she came to see us in Thalia, Aunt Celie sometimes sat on the porch in a white rocker, shoulders moving back and forth rhythmically as she watched the cars and pickups traveling the road in front of her, intoning with bemusement, "Cars goin' thisaway, cars goin' thataway. Lordy, lordy, people goin' everywhere, seeking satisfaction."

Aunt Celie was not really my aunt, nor was her name really Aunt Celie. She was actually Mollie's younger sister, my great aunt, and with her, as with most everyone else in the family, the opinion was that the name your parents saddle you with is not necessarily the label you wish to pack around for life. In our family, a name was added or dropped, or changed at will. ("Or at William," my mother was fond of saying. "He became Pete, you know.") If people were given long names, they made them short. If they were given short names, they made them long. If they didn't like their names, they created new ones—like Casandra and Vashti and Tiny and Parmelia. One even named himself Patrick Cleburne after a Confederate General. This was as ornery and independent a breed of human beings as you will ever want to meet.

Aunt Celie's name was actually Lucy Jane, which she naturally hated. She changed it to Lucille, and everyone around her changed *that* to Celie, which they tried to stick on me. She claimed she never learned how to spell either one, and sometimes signed her name *Cellie* and sometimes *Lucile.* How she spelled it wasn't nearly as important to her as getting to choose her own.

The sisters, Mary Ellen (Mollie) and Lucille (Celie) married brothers—Alf and Lee; their names are foreshortened here to match their lives. Both brothers fell on tragic times in their thirties, one into a well and the other off a horse. Aunt Celie, as rawboned as Mollie was dainty, was the only one of the family women who had no fancy airs outside of her fixation on her name. She wore boots and Levi's and shingled her dark hair like a man's when other women wouldn't think of doing a thing like that. But she got away with it because of her special circumstances: Her young husband was bucked off his horse, thrown over a barb-wire fence, and hit his head on a rock. He was never, as they say in Texas, "right in the head," after that. For years he was in the State Hospital in Wichita Falls. He left Aunt Celie with two little babies and a ranch she managed to keep running for sixty-five more years after his accident, with only the help of Doc, the hired hand. Every once in a while Uncle Lee would get to come home because of good behavior, but once when he did come on his birthday, he smiled sweetly, blew out the candles on his angel food cake, then tried to put his head through the hole in the middle. Aunt Celie sadly carried him back to the hospital.

Besides being a survivor, she was a woman of humor and pithy language. Once, when watching me walk toward her in a white sweater, snugly fitted, like girls wore them in the fifties, Aunt Celie said in mock awe: "My, my, girl. I guess I'd have me a couple of them jobs too, but I'd have to scoop them up from all the surrounding territory."

I loved to sit with the women and listen to the porch stories they told as they sewed, knitted, or shelled peas. These were usually long narratives they either remembered or concocted about their relatives.

The women told stories, and the men, if they happened past, refuted them: "Naw, look, that didn't happen thataway; you're making up half that stuff." There was a multigenerational fight to the death between female imagination and male literalness. After one particularly rank dispute about the accuracy of an anecdote, Mother told one of the men: "Well, if something is wrong with my way of telling things, how come everyone laughs at my stories, and nobody even listens to yours?"

Huckleberry Finn called them "stretchers"—those memories that hover somewhere between fact and fiction. If they were good enough for Huck, the women thought, they should be good enough for the men in our family. I mean how many trips did *they* take down the Mississippi for pete's sake? But the fellas had no sense, as Mollie said, "of the eternal fitness of things." The funny thing was, though, that the men had some really *dynamite awesome truly tragic* family stories to tell. But they wouldn't. You had to work to reel enough out of them to get a story going for the women to embroider on.

For instance, the story about Daddy's great grandpa, who shot a man point-blank dead for running grandpa's horse into a sweat up near Amarillo, then ran away from the sheriff to live in South America for twenty-five years. *He even kept a diary that none of the men had been interested enough to read!* As he was dying somewhere down there, one of his sons found out and went to see him. This was the bare bones of the story pulled out of the men. But lordy, wouldn't you know that he had a whole other family down there, little brown girls and boys running around, and goodness knows what all. The women made it lots more colorful.

I sat on the porch swing listening to these tales, awestruck by my heritage: I just couldn't help thinking it was *romantic* to have a *murderer* in the family, especially one that *got away to South America!* But the men didn't like talking about that. The women were sure that everything that caused pain and death, happiness and life, had its roots in love, which was riddled through and through with drama and romance. But the men thought talking about all this stuff was bunk and hooey and just reflected poorly on the family.

Mollie, who had grown up in the Indian territory of Oklahoma, liked to tell the story about her mother's pillowcases. Her mother, the Miss Maggie who had come from Arkansas as a bride bringing a wagon full of fancy things with her, found that her new home was to be a half-dugout, carved into the side of a dirt cliff with a shingle shack attached. Among the antimacassars and handhooked rugs in her hope chest was a pair of pillow shams embroidered in turkey red. On one was written: *I slept to dream that life was beauty.* Its mate declared: *I woke and found that life was duty.* One day Miss Maggie washed and starched these pillowcases and hung them out to dry. Hearing a noise in the back, Mollie looked out to see the first verse walking off on the back of a large feathered Indian, who had managed to steal it off the clothesline, rip arm- and head-holes in it, and, with the ruffle around his bottom, was swaggering off to the nearby reservation. "It wasn't that I minded his taking the pillowcase," Mollie moaned, "but why did he have to leave *me* with the *duty* one?"

Then there was the story about mother's sister Mary, who was a school teacher up near Cranfill's Gap and had to be on her very best behavior, as lady school teachers always did. So when that time of month rolled around, and she needed some Tampax, she called up at the local drug store and whispered on the phone to have them wrap some for her to pick up, so nobody would see what she was carrying out. Sure enough, after school she dropped by and picked up the package, but when she got it home and opened it, can you imagine what she had there that she didn't think would be very comfortable? Thumb tacks!

All the women thought this story was very funny and laughed about it, but I couldn't figure it all out the first time I heard it, sitting on the porch in my new June Allyson pedal pushers. I sat there chewing on my lip, trying to figure out why boys could buy something called "rubbers" over the counter in the drug store with a quarter and a snigger, and girls had to sneak brown-paper wrapped sanitary napkins out of the same store to preserve their dignity. Why were body functions and physical changes something for boys to show off and something for girls to be ashamed of? Why did even women speak in whispers: "Did you hear? She's *that way* again" about the condition that the world had clearly decided was the only important job that women could do?

In my mind, I tried to relate it all to church and the Virgin Mary, but all I came up with was that it was okay to have a baby if you didn't sleep with a man to do it, but it was shameful and disgusting to have one, if you *did*. And so far as I knew the Virgin Mary was the only woman in history to accomplish the first feat, and that was a long time ago and in another country. And anyway, having babies and taking care of them was all that women were *supposed* to do, it seemed like, so were women just all-round shameful and disgusting? And if so, why did we put up with it? Why did Mother put up with it? I couldn't put all these questions in words enough to ask my mother, and besides I thought that since she had *had* babies, and there was no news that she'd done it like the Virgin Mary, it might hurt her feelings if I let on that I knew it was shameful or something. Because I really didn't think my own mother was shameful. I just didn't know what to think.

A lot of it was confusing, but as a girl, enjoying the woman-talk, I thought it was the porch stories and the camaraderie among the women that made my family special. The women in other families in Thalia didn't seem as bright or funny or clever, and they certainly didn't sit around and laugh like we did. But it was years before I understood that some of the specialness drew its strength not only from my mother, but from a mother and father who had made a pact when their four children were born within six years of each other early in their marriage. "Your dad and I decided when you came along so fast that we could not do *everything*, and nothing else mattered in the world as much as you," she told me once. "So that's what we agreed to spend our lives on—you."

In later years, as I saw my own first marriage, and most of the marriages of people around me, fall apart—often over the difficulties of raising kids while trying to hone out some private space and a semblance of individual independence—this was humbling and flattering. To my parents, I had been the most important thing in the world. This commitment was clearly not the most healthy thing for them, I would learn many years later. But I cannot even now imagine another life for myself.

Daddy, not a voluble man, never once mentioned what personal dreams he might have put aside to make a decent life for his kids. And Mother, when I asked her once when I was about ten: "What would you do without me? Without all of us?" replied flippantly, "Lots more of some things, and lots less of others. Now go on outside until dinner." For her children, she had plainly limited her life severely and denied herself a multitude of options.

Age has taught me one overriding lesson: what counts is not where your body is—or even where your heart is, as any fool can tell you and many have. What counts is where your head is—something Mother always knew. Who was it said, "you think you're escaping and run into yourself," and "the longest way around is the shortest way home?" Leo, I think, Leopold Bloom. Mother and Leo were right about everything but the water. Leo should have known better, but Mother saw so little water she wouldn't think to address the subject. Thalia had no water except down at the little lake that stored the town's drinking reserves, where as kids we used to sneak off in the old pickup to swim. The drought of the fifties snakebit me, to mix a gritty metaphor, so that I can't live without seeing water every day. *Every day.* Even those dozen years I lived in New York City, I almost always had a view of the Hudson River with its ships, or the East River with its barges. Now, sitting at my desk, watching the water as I work, makes me think of the way life moves, slowly and inexorably, in smooth ripples that can turn almost instantly into torrential waves. I've seen it happen here in my own backyard. And I've seen it calm itself again and go about its business. I know, because at some point I read Heraclitis in Mother's *Great Books*, that you can never step in the same river twice. That's comforting—and scary.

I do want to set the record straight though: back in Thalia, no matter how I lusted after water, I never took a nude dive into Bobby Sheen's swimming pool like the Jacy Farrow you've probably read about. Trust me. With a daddy like mine, would I do a thing like that? And just as I was never blonde, neither was I wild. I count that a missed opportunity on both scores: if the reputation of blonde and wild was going to get stuck on me anyway, I might as well have had a little fun. But it wasn't until late in the fourth decade of my life that I let myself do that—go a little batty. If you put it off, I guess, you've got to do it sometime. Before that, all the fun was in my head— watching myself be the women in the picture shows: Is that *really* what you have to do to attract Marlon Brando—wear a slip around the house and talk silly? Or Gary Cooper—wear a big hat and hold your chin up? Or marry a millionaire—dress like Marilyn and stick your chest out? I tried all those tricks, of course, but only in the so-called privacy of my own room—when I could keep my brothers and all their friends from mocking me. They loved to stand at the door and make faces when I sat at my perfectly beautiful kidney-shaped dressing table with its pink fluffy organdy skirt and arranged my bottles on the mirror on the top—just like girls did in the movies.

And just for the record, I want it known that I never went to a motel room with Duane, let alone made disparaging remarks about his sexual expertise. How would I have known, for pete's sake? And I certainly did not participate in any activity on a pool table with a roughneck called Abilene. My father wouldn't let me go near the pool hall, for starters. No nice girls got close enough even to peer into its dingy old windows. And if Sonny and Duane had a fight over me, costing one of them an eye, I was totally oblivious to it. In fact, I was oblivious to a lot of things, but that was the way the world worked for girls back in those days. Girls weren't supposed to see much; they were supposed to *be* seen.

As to being seen, everyone in Thalia agreed—except my brothers—that I was okay to look at. But what bothered me was that everything I saw for myself with my own eyes I couldn't talk about—like the time I saw the daughter of the beauty parlor lady get in the car with the shingle salesman and stay gone all day while her mother was at work. I never told anyone, even after the daughter dropped out of school and disappeared for a long time, and then came home to live in the back of the beauty parlor with the baby she'd adopted in California. She looked worn to a frazzle though. That California's hard on a person.

So I tried to keep my eyes closed and my mouth shut. Boys liked girls better that way. And so did fathers. But mothers were to talk to. They were the only thing that could keep a girl sane in Thalia, if you had a good one. If you didn't, you were done for. Lots of girls back in Thalia were done for before they ever started.

Now, every time I hear a door slam on one of the houses around the Mill Pond, I think of Thalia. In a dry, dusty place, even the doors slam differently. More hard and shallow sounding. Kids ran in and out of the backdoor in Thalia, letting it thwak carelessly behind them, tormenting Mother, who was usually in the kitchen. "They have no more concern for other people than a billy goat," she would say of her marauding sons and their friends as they dashed through rooms, dropping hats and bats. Of the neighborhood boys who had teased some little girls coming home from school, Mother said, "The whole wad of them is full of sheer meanness." Once when Booter Jones, a neglected kid who seemed not to have any comprehension that meals were to be eaten at tables, stuck his head in the door and yelled at my brother, "Yeet, yeet? Squeet!" to the bewilderment of all present, Mother translated patiently: "That young man is asking if you have eaten yet. An understood part of that sentence is, 'if not—that is, if not, let's go eat."

My little sister Ellie and I especially loved to help when Mother was baking—making her specialty, Slam Bang Tannies. Ellie and I had a ritual: we'd come into the kitchen and dig our hands into the big bowl of pecans she was about to dump into the cookie batter. Each time, Mother would slap at our hands, shuss us away, and declare, fists on hips: "Your Mother's nuts! Begone!" This was the cue for Ellie and me to fall on the floor, clutching our sides, singing out, "Mother's nuts! Mother's nuts! She finally admitted it!"

MOTHER'S SLAM BANG TANNIES

3/4 c. shortening	2 1/4 c. flour
2 c. dark brown sugar	1/2 t. salt
6 eggs	1 1/2 t. baking powder
1 c. white sugar	1 c. pecans (or whatever is
2 t. vanilla	left)

Beat shortening and sugars until creamy, then push to side of mixing bowl, leaving center open. Adjust beaters to center and add whole eggs, one at a time with mixer on medium. Turn mixer on high until eggs are well-beaten. Gradually work the sugar and shortening stuff into the eggs. Add vanilla. Sift together flour, salt, and baking powder and add to above. Toss in pecans. Bake in 11x8x2 pan lined with waxed paper at 350° for 20 minutes.

Then reach in and lift pan. Slam bang it on oven rack to make all this fall. Repeat the slam bang activity in 5 minutes. Cook for 35 minutes in all, including slam bang time. Plop over on cutting board. Peel off waxed paper. Cool and cut into exactly 44 bars. These freeze, or you can eat them all yourself, if your kids don't get there first.

Mother seemed to enjoy the slam bang part of this recipe so much, and enact it with such vigor, that I sometimes wondered vaguely if she might wish she were doing something else, like maybe reading the book of Sara Teasdale poems beside her bed, or the pile of Edith Wharton novels she'd checked out of the Wichita Falls Public Library. And sometimes, I noticed, Mother would read standing up, stirring the potato soup, like when she couldn't put down *East of Eden*. There were books next to every place she might possibly sit down, including the bathroom, where I saw *A Tree Grows in Brooklyn* a good part of my junior high years, and even read it twice before it disappeared. In its place came a heavy one, *Kristin Lavransdatter*. I tried some of that too, but I must say it got a little hard to identify with once you got past *The Bridal Wreath* part.

When mother caught me reading *Forever Amber*, she spirited it away from my nightstand. It was a good year before I found it at the bottom of the ironing basket while looking for an old sheet to use for a costume for the school play. Later, Mother admitted to burying the book there.

"Well, that was the safest place, since nobody in this house ever got to the bottom of the ironing basket," she said. "Besides, I figured anybody who *did* finally get there must be grown up enough to read that book. I didn't count on you, Missy, to go plowing around in there for a costume."

With Mother we could be wonderfully corny. While making Christmas candy, she would slap our bottoms and say, "Be careful what you eat; as Shakespeare says, 'Tis divinity that shapes our ends." Then she would turn around and reverse her homilies: "But remember, a waist is a terrible thing to mind." She might actually like cooking, she once told me, "except it's so *blankety-blank* daily. Who can like anything you have to do three times a day that takes you four hours and disappears in fifteen minutes?"

Once when Daddy looked into the bare insides of the refrigerator and asked who had raided it this time, Mother told him, *"Et al, et vir, et ux, et peolla, et peurum, et everything in the pantry."*

Mother had a way of expressing herself that sometimes resulted in double takes, like the time I fled to my room screeching about some unforgivable action wreaked upon my precious teenaged person. According to Mollie, Mother turned to the rest of the family, my perpetually awed audience, and said: "I'm so sorry for Jacy. She's just as unhappy as if she really were."

Through the postwar years of Truman and Eisenhower, we grew bigger in little Thalia, a town in which there were no Jews and only one black couple—a pair who worked as servants for a local family. Their son had to be sent away to some mysterious place during the winter, because he could not go to school with us. This was a fact I do not remember questioning or discussing with my family, but when the boy was home for Christmas holidays, Mother invited him to supper. I found his presence strange and wonderful—like having Othello as a guest—and I remember pumping him about his life, then running to my room and writing a poem in my diary.

I wonder now how I came to consider such things as race relations as a kid. I didn't hear any talk of this subject at home or at school that I recall, except the vague rumor that Negroes were not allowed to stay in Thalia after sundown. And yet, I recall now that when I timidly showed my poem to my mother, she looked at me strangely and asked, "You liked having Jake here, didn't you?" I told her that Jake was different and not boring like most people in Thalia, and she had said, looking at me tenderly, "You're different, too, dear."

There was a Mexican family, too. They lived in a boxcar not far from my house. Stella, a daughter, was my classmate. She had a round, brown, scrubbed face and a beautiful singing voice. We sang duets at school programs sometimes. Stella was very much shorter than I and wore big fluffy white dresses to school with white anklets that had rosebuds on them. She had a big fluffy yellow dress, too, and shiny shoes. I thought her clothes were babyish, but she was so small they looked right on her, almost exotic. When Stella's mother died, I went to take food my mother had prepared for the family. I had never seen anyone live in a boxcar before. The place was so clean it smelled of bleach, and it had bunkbeds running all along one side. I was mesmerized by a huge statue of a bleeding Jesus hanging on the wall with his head turned to the side and holes in his hands.

Mr. Alonzo sat under Jesus looking very sad and saying, "What am I going to do with these children now? What am I going to do?" I felt sorry for Mr. Alonzo, but I thought living in a boxcar with a bleeding Jesus would be really interesting and asked Daddy why we couldn't move into one as well. There were several old vacant cars sitting out on the tracks. I was crazy to do something colorful and unboring, but here was Daddy making me live a pokey old life in a square old house like everybody else in Thalia. Now a boxcar. . . .

Thalia sheltered more than one really poor family, but the one I remember best is the Higgenbottoms, whose mother had a mental problem and couldn't keep track of her dozen or so children, one of them named Texas Centennial—T. C. for short—who seemed forever to be running away. Each time he did, the church ladies got together and prayed for his return, and the rest mobilized with deputies and flashlights to find him. I remember Mother and Daddy standing on the porch, watchful and concerned. "It doesn't seem right," Mother said, "to be praying about things and not doing anything about them." One time when T. C. was lost, Mother let me come with her to the Higgenbottom's house to take food for the people thrashing around in the fields with flashlights yelling, "T. C.! Texas Centennial! Texas Centennial!" You could hear it echoing all around like in church when you have choirs on both sides of the room and they haven't quite got the words synchronized. Mother turned to me and said, "I feel so sorry for that little boy and his mother, but I can't believe what I'm hearing. I'm just glad she didn't name him 'Constitution of the United States of America.'"

The house didn't have any lights or light bulbs and was dark and spooky, and Mrs. Higgenbottom sat there in the gloom in a rocking chair with big empty eyes, muttering, "My baby, my baby." They finally found T. C. down by the lake, and old Mr. Higgenbottom grabbed him by the collar and yelled, "Boy, I'm gonna whup you good!" and threw him down on the rickety old porch. T. C. looked like he wanted to get lost for good.

The Higgenbottoms were scary, but Pearl Ann Moose, who lived in a house made of tin over by the filling station and didn't have a husband, was sort of funny. At least I thought so. Her one child was about a half a bubble off, and Pearl Ann would walk the hulking kid to school each day and then pick him up afterward. Thalia school kids were accustomed to her voice: "Eddie Earl, Eddie Earl, where did you leave your yaller Crayola? We can't go home without it." It was every day with that yaller Crayola. Once Eddie Earl appeared after school with a test paper on which a teacher had written a big zero. "That's okay, Eddie Earl," his mother comforted, leading him away. "Zero's better than nothing."

The school kids picked on the most vulnerable, like Billy, the village idiot, and Joe Bob Blanton, the preacher's doofus son. Once they held Joe Bob down in the gym and painted his toenails bright red. And in church one time they somehow put firecrackers in the candle Joe Bob was supposed to carry down to the alter. There was always some big scene with Joe Bob that I couldn't get away from fast enough. My brothers loved to mock him and Eddie Earl, too, but Mother would have none of it at home.

"Now what if you'd been born like that?" she'd scold. "How would you feel if I had to come to school every day and count every last one of your little marbles?" The other kids and I would writhe in anguish on the blue leatherette of the kitchen benches at the thought of Mother appearing at the schoolhouse door for *any reason*. It was bad enough when the principal, shouting through the static of the loudspeaker going to every single room, announced that "Every one of Mellie's kids should please eat in the lunchroom today, because your mother has other plans." Hearing these crackling words shatter the torpor of another explanation of *pi r square* was sheer torture for me. Saying it like that made it sound like there were a million of us instead of only four, and being the oldest, I tried, without much success, to deny the existence of the others, at least in public. Elizabeth Taylor and Jane Powell never had a hundred little brothers and sisters dragging around after them. Why couldn't the rest of the family get it in their heads that they were just a part of the background scenery?

Thalia had its criminals too—one a nephew of a Congressman. Sometime in the sixties he was arrested as a peeping Tom. When I heard about it, what I couldn't believe was that I went out with that weirdo one time! My parents would deny it, of course, but they practically *pushed* me into the arms of felons and nitwits and guys who raised *hamsters*, for pete's sake! Any deviate would do, as long as he was from a nice family. One played the bassoon—*puleeze.* And another rode the bus to school. The bus! Oh, how can you be so dumb and live? One had feet so big you could build a sandbox in his shoes. But this one, the peeping Tom, wore a red and black lumber jacket to take me to Xavier Cugat at the Memorial Auditorium in Wichita Falls! I mean, die. The armpits of tackiness. He walked about three feet ahead of me, while I tottered along behind him in my brand new patent leather high heels, my very first pair, and I had to open my own car door and everything, almost getting killed in the traffic. By the time we got home I couldn't get out of that old white Nash fast enough. Creepsville! Deliver me! I know Sally Sullivan must have seen us and laughed all the way home. I could tell by the way she looked at me at school the next day. Anyway, I had seen this guy about every day of my life because he delivered the paper or the milk or something and was always looking in the front door when I came down to breakfast. Maybe that's how he got into his bad habit, peeping through that door. He just shifted to windows in later life, I guess.

Another guy from "a nice family" went to jail for stealing money from the courthouse, and later a fellow milked the bank dry and fled, seeming not to care that his very own grandmother owned the bank. Just your everyday small town felons.

Thalia also sprouted a few undeclared types that the kids called "sissies," "pantywaists," and "limp-wristed fellas." The high school coach, not one of your more refined creatures, called them "queers." To Texas men, not being an obvious "red-blooded man" was about as low as you could slink. They were pretty hard on anyone who deviated from their idea of perfect man- or womanhood. A guy could be called a "prevert" just from wearing high-water britches or cutting his hair an inch too long or short. The band director was outright run out of town when some ex-jock on the school board in a red Ford V-8 accused him of stepping just a little too high. I wasn't supposed to know this, but two guys were torn right out from one another's arms directly under the bleachers at the football field on a Thursday night after practice. I heard it but I never told a soul. What worried me was: what were they *doing*? I couldn't figure that one out for the life of me. I just knew from the way people whispered that it must have been *baaad.*

We had some funny-like women in Thalia too. One ran away from her husband, creating chatter in the koffee klatch. "Where do you think she's going, Mother?" I asked one afternoon after gossip had drifted down from the Calamity Club to the school yard.

"Well, if you ask me, I'd say she's going sane," she remarked, without looking up from her sewing. "But I don't know how my comments would go down in world opinion."

School in Thalia was one long snore. The teachers went over and over the same material every day, like maybe they were trying to memorize it themselves. We practiced our penmanship push-pull and ovals, were chastised by the old battle-ax Miss Hawkeye for fiddling with our pencils as we recited, "Friends, Romans, countrymen." After which the boys would whisper, "Lend me your beers," and snigger and put their heads under their desks. In a junior high play, I was miscast as the class smarty pants, who had nothing but these lines to say: "The square of the hypotenuse of the right angle triangle equals the sum of the square of the other two sides." I had no utter idea what these words meant, but I said them loud and clear every time there was a lull in the drama.

Outside school, Thalia girls graduated from listening to "Let's Pretend," on the radio to "Lorenzo Jones and his wife, Belle," to "The Romance of Helen Trent," and, later, in high school, to "Ozzie and Harriet" on TV, which I considered the nth degree of drivel.

"This is twaddle. Con-sum-*mately* boring," I told my mother. "Who would wear those drippy little dresses?"

"Con-*summet*-ly," she said. "And Harriet Nelson, I guess."

Television, besides creeping in to make a devious attack on my excellent taste, interrupted my parent's Saturday night bridge games with their closest friends, who had the first TV in town. "I am not going over there and watch that *blankety-blank* blurry thing," Daddy groused. "If I wanted to see a snow storm, I'd move to Canada. It's play cards or nothing."

A threatened Fred Allen agreed with my father. TV, he said, "is already conducting itself provocatively, trying to get radio to pucker up for the kiss of death." He also called it "a device that permits people who haven't anything to do to watch people who can't do anything." But, in fact, by the mid-fifties, twenty-five million TV sets sat in American homes, which meant about six in Thalia, and the scandal of the day was that Lucy was pregnant. Pregnancy not being in good taste, CBS would not let "I Love Lucy" use that word. The station did, however, let Lucy look rosy and rotund and sit around smugly knitting amorphous things. Again it was brought home to me, in my very own living room, *that what the world expected of women—all women—was in fact unspeakable.* The appearance of TV was already making me more sophisticated.

Cities around the country began to report a drop in picture show attendance long before the old Royal burned down in Thalia. According to my primary source for everything, *Life* magazine, fifty-five theaters closed in New York City, and I figured I'd have to hurry and get there before all the Bijous closed down—Bijous being what they called picture shows in Gotham. My family, full of sit-down-dinner values, began to abandon the dining table for portable trays. Actually, this came less from the encroachment of television than from all of us growing into teenagers who splintered off into different interest groups—football, basketball, band, play practice, lessons of all kinds. And dating.

The boys could get away with murder, but the girls had to be models of virtue. I remember the day my parents wrote a will and made my younger brother, Mills, executor. He was always getting into mischief, coming home late, turning over Daddy's Chevy. For all my efforts to behave myself, I thought, this is what I got. An insult! How could my parents have selected my errant brother to trust more than me? My feelings were so hurt that I fumed up to my room and pouted all afternoon, until Mother finally came up to see what was wrong. When I told her, she laughed. "Oh, is that all? I thought it was something serious. That's just the way things are done, you see. The older boy oversees the family's will and estate. Girls don't do it because when they marry, their husbands take over these duties, and not being a part of the family, they may not have the family's best interests at heart."

It was nice to know it wasn't personal, but it still struck me as odd. Most frequently, Mother encouraged me, saying, "Jacy, you can do anything you really *want* to do," emphasizing *want*. But she was a product of her times, and she didn't get around to analyzing the strange rules of primogeniture until many years later. By this time, she'd been married forty years, and patterns were a little hard to break. But Mother did balk after Daddy—who taught school after the drought made it unprofitable to cowboy anymore—retired. The very day Daddy retired, she decided not to get out of bed at six o'clock and fix breakfast. Daddy was stunned.

"I'm retiring, too," Mother said haughtily as she sauntered downstairs all combed and powdered about ten o'clock. "I've been working just as hard for just as many years as you have. I'll fix breakfast on days I feel like it; but for other days, I'll be happy to teach you how to use the coffee pot."

From then on out, Daddy fixed breakfast every morning of the world.

While the boys were getting away with mischief, about the raciest thing Ellie and I did was drive around the courthouse square on weekends looking for boys who were riding around looking for us. We hardly ever got out of our cars, but great flirtations occurred as we leaned out the windows of the old Plymouth and chatted with the cute guys in pickups—usually guys from Olney, which made the local boys jealous. Sometimes the more sophisticated boys from Wichita came around in their cars, and occasionally a local's grandson from Dallas would gun the motor of his chartreuse convertible under the red light to give the girls a thrill.

In Thalia, everyone knew everyone else's business. What I knew was that I could get away with nothing. I was accountable to dozens of parents, friends of parents, teachers, neighborhood busy-bodies and the various preachers whose homes were never far enough away. Still, I lived in mortal terror that I would get myself into some situation that would embarrass Mother and Daddy.

All that was left for me to do was daydream. At least Daddy couldn't read my mind—though I thought sometimes that Mother could. I held there an image of the perfect man, who looked and dressed in no way like anyone in Thalia. Even when the ragged ends of my days were punctuated by lonely Hank Williams songs to go to sleep by—"Why doncha luv me like you used to do? Why do you treat me like a worn-out shoe?"—and my romantic options consisted of bow-bellied farmers and beer-legged cowboys, roughnecks with oil rig fingernails, and sweaty football players who had to cheat real hard to make a C in social studies taught by the coach, even then I fantasized the perfect man. The perfect man was as important to me as I was to the fantasies of the horny boys of Thalia; that is, if you believe the seminal book about this area.

My perfect man had nothing to do with sex. Sex I would not have known if it rose up and bit me. But I was sure there was a man somewhere for me—one who dressed in the black turtleneck of the artist, not the boring plaid shirt of the cowboy, and who did not ride bucking bulls, but read *War and Peace.* In fact, I had seen a picture of this very man in *Life* magazine, and I even knew his name: *Arthur Miller!* I was sure Arthur Miller could talk about great works of literature, and would know better songs than "Hey, hey good lookin', whatcha got cookin'?" Arthur Miller might even take me—*sigh*—to "Green-witch" Village, where romantic Bohemians lived deliciously in garrets practically starving.

2

When memory takes
over, corrects fact, it
makes things tolerable.
—Claire in
Edward Albee's
A Delicate Balance

F·L·E·S·H

CLEARLY, I WAS STUCK IN THALIA, no matter what. Daddy
wouldn't let me take the car outside the city limits, which gave me
all of a good square mile to carouse in, and so far Arthur Miller
wasn't burning up the phone lines from New York. After Duane went
off to Korea, and half-blind Sonny went off to wherever he went,
what I did was just exactly what was expected of me: finish high
school.

Like a lot of girls in the fifties, I excelled at sitting quietly, taking
good notes, and saying little. I also excelled at writing fanciful essays
derived from my readings in the *Great Books*, using many big words,
so I had no trouble graduating high in my class. I sang at graduation,
a sappy song my mother picked out, "Beyond the Blue Horizon."
The only line in it I liked was, "Goodby to things that bore me, life is
waiting for me!" I sang that one out with more feeling than I think
the principal thought it deserved.

My ambition was to read all the *Great Books* in Mother's library
before I started college. But by June, I was finding *Hippocrates and
Galen* a heavy plod, and that still left forty-two books to go. Would I
ever finish? Somewhere I had got the idea that if I didn't actually
understand everything I read in the *Great Books*, the words would
remain in my mind anyway, just waiting to pop up when I was ready
to use them. I thought information was sort of like vitamins; if you
put enough in your head, what you needed would stay there and

make you strong, and your body would just eliminate what it didn't need. I think I may have got this idea from Hippocrates himself, though I'm not sure that's exactly what he intended.

Basically, I just wanted to travel more than anything—goodbye to things that bore me—and talk to people who knew something new; to go to fantastic places and study mysterious cultures. From the time I was a kid there was a series of books in our shelves, *The Land and Its People*, which I would pore over, taking in every detail of the Tarajans who live in bright colored houses shaped like ships in the middle of tall grasses on an orchid-shaped island in Indonesia, and who hang effigies of their dead in niches in the sides of mountains. My stomach ached to climb up those rickety ladders and stare at the Tau Tau dressed like the real live dead—grandmas and babies all leather-faced hanging up there for centuries. And the city with a hundred statues of Buddha all covered over with tangled growth that some explorer uncovered sometime during my childhood. I wanted to go there. How could a whole city be covered up with vines? The only thing I ever saw Thalia covered up with was dust.

Then there was the book of Greek myths that Aunt Celie had out at the ranch. Nobody knew where it came from, that little old leather-bound book that smelled like mildew when you turned its brittle pages, but I loved it from the time I could read at all. When I was about eight or nine, I'd take it to the hayloft and burrow in for hours with Pandora opening that box and letting all those evils out, which made me think of Eve, who brought down Eden with her curiosity. Then there was that poor guy Philoctetes with his festering wound and his bow, and Proserpina, who suffered the first joint custody case, and Orpheus who lost Eurydice when he looked back, who reminded me of Lot's wife who got turned into a pillar of salt from looking back. Looking back over your shoulder seemed to be a dangerous thing to do whether you were a Greek or not.

Once I asked my aunt if I could take the book home with me, after reading it for about six years there, and she said, "My lord, yes, child. But what would you want with it? There's new magazines there on the coffee table." What I wanted were the wonderful stories. Here was a literature where women could *do* things: start and stop wars, bring lovers together, reward people, get in black moods, create themselves from the foam of the ocean or the head of Zeus. These were fairy tales where women were not sappy like Snow White, who just waited on a bunch of dwarves day and night; or Sleeping Beauty, who just waited around for a man to wake her up. These women didn't wait; they had fire and passion and could sink ships and turn themselves into flowers and stags and tears, and tell true stories that no one believed. These women were *players*. I loved this cast of characters so much, I was dying to live in Greece, rather than in a western cowboy town where girls couldn't do anything.

I knew the feeling of longing long before I even knew what it was, and I was very sure there was life after Lefty Frizzell. I knew this from spending my high school years listening to the radio every Saturday afternoon as Texaco's Star Reporter brought into my bedroom the Metropolitan Opera from New York City while I lay on my bed and read *Life* magazine. From *Life* and *Look* I got the inside dope. Here I was introduced to the secrets of the real world in a cartoon advertisement for sanitary napkins captioned "Are You in the Know?" The girls in these ads had careers, and dates, and they didn't live in pokey little towns that thought *Stormy Weather* was a fine picture show because Ginger Rogers stripped down to her slip, and where the boys were obsessed with football, and the Quarterback Club gave the coaches .12 gauge Marlin under-overs, or sometimes a new Cadillac or diamond ring, after a winning season. The girls in these ads didn't have silly neighbors sticking noses into their business, and preachers telling them they needed to get themselves saved. These girls didn't have porch lights on when they came home from the picture show with a boy, and little brothers hanging around, and fathers who told them when to breathe. These girls had a life!

From ads in magazines, as from the picture show in Thalia, I took my image of fashion and glamour. *This* was what life ought to be. Unlike my mother, who wore a flowered housedress made from a McCall's pattern, a career girl in New York wore a trim little suit and shoes with Cuban heels. A girl could have a desk and a rolling chair, and she could store in her desk drawer tasteful accessories to dress up her work clothes when she wore them to an after-work party. A girl could add them discreetly, just after five o'clock, to prepare for her exciting evening of dining and dancing with the wonderful new man in her life—who looked just like Arthur Miller!

I often lay awake at night planning what I would keep in my desk drawer when I became a career girl in New York City, the best place for writers for *Life* magazine. My fantasies were so vivid and detailed that I knew I must be rehearsing for real life. I could, in fact, make things happen with my fantasies. Some days went just exactly as I had daydreamed them the evening before, because I would deliberately station myself in the right place, and say just exactly the right thing, and this would make others say just what I wanted them to say! I often felt that the only control I had over my life was to perfect my fantasies, for I could frequently make them work out to be real. Mother told me that philosophically you had to do only one free thing to be free, so my free thing was moving people around by thinking about it.

Thalia people seemed so dumb they didn't even know that I was making them do and say this and that sometimes. Once I asked Mother if she thought people could make other people do certain things, and she said there was an awful lot of power in simple concentration. I never forgot that, and when I was bored I'd try to make someone turn around or scratch his nose or something just by staring at him and concentrating very heard. Strange to say, it often worked, especially in church. I could make that silly Joe Bob Blanton turn his head and stare at me every time just by focusing my eyes on the back of his neck.

I saw in my daydreams how I would look (like Audrey Hepburn in a black dress with a bateau—that means boat—neckline); where I would work (for *Life* magazine); what kinds of friends I would have (witty like Dorothy Parker and the Round Table crowd at the Algonquin, but nicer, and not so fat and repulsive as some of the men); and the exact sound of the perfect man's voice (like Arthur Miller's). And in my desk drawer in New York City, I knew I would stash a short black velvet jacket, a double string of pearls, a velvet clutch bag, and a pair of black high heels. With these handy, I could dress up on the spur of the moment any old thing I had worn to work that day. I was definitely going to be in the know!

I was so excited by my fantasy of working as a writer in New York City that when I saw an ad promising to send a kit telling me how to become a "Life Underwriter," I walked all the way down to the post office and mailed the card back that very day. I thought it would be good experience to learn how to write those captions under the photos in *Life,* surely that's what a Life Underwriter did. I watched the mailbox for days. Then what a let-down when all I got back in the mail was a big packet of material instructing me in the techniques of insurance sales! I wrote and told the *Life* people that was not what I had in mind at all and to please send me the caption-writing kit. But they never wrote back. How was I going to be a famous writer if they kept sending me the wrong materials?

I also drew the head of the girl two and one-half times the size of the model in the magazine and sent it to the Famous Artist's School. Mother helped me block it out in little squares so I would get the dimensions exactly right. The Famous Artist's School sent it back with a grade of 97 and said I definitely had talent and could enroll with a one-hundred-dollar discount, but the school was in Connecticut or New Jersey or some place far away, and of course I couldn't go. They did write me a lot after that though, and I still have the picture of the head of a girl I drew.

Next to reading books and practicing caption writing and drawing, I liked singing best. Singing was my "talent" in the beauty contests that threw North Texas girls of that era into a tizzy. I sang because, well, you could hardly stand up there and read a book to the judges! But I was always scared to death. I hated to perform. Ellie was really a much better musician than I, and she would often play the piano while I sang, but she was still too young to enter in the contests.

Businessmen sponsored us in these contests, hoping to pick the winner so their name would be linked with hers in the post-contest folderol. Then the merchant might even get his picture with the winner on the front page of *The Thalia Times*! I am proud to state that I was already several Miss Somethings by the time I finished high school, but every once in a while the thought crossed my mind that standing up and being looked at was not the way a writer, artist and world traveler ought to be spending her time. And Mother discouraged this activity fiercely as undignified, but she allowed it, since this seemed to be the only thing I could do that people in Thalia really appreciated. She seemed to understand that this was my ticket out of town as surely as being the star football captain was for boys. This realization sometimes brought a wry look to her face. But I often came away with a little college money and some crowns and badges for my bulletin board, which let me know I was good for something. Girls didn't seem to be good for much in Thalia. Sometimes I wondered how it must be for girls who didn't look so hot, so nobody called them for contests. I thought they must *really* feel worthless.

I could certainly stand up straight. Mollie had seen to it that I had excellent posture. And I could sing pretty well. My brothers joked that I jumped up and sang every time three people congregated anywhere in town, which wasn't true of course, although that *would* have made a fair-sized audience in Thalia. I did sing most of the solo parts in the church choir. Sometimes I sang duets with the handsome male high school teacher who had a beautiful voice. When I did this, Mother said they sounded more like simultaneous solos to her—like Kathryn Grayson and Mario Lanza in the picture show— words I should have taken to heart, for they became emblematic of a difficult relationship later on, one that did not end until I finally declared unilateral independence and freed myself to sing my own solo. But that was years later.

So from age fifteen to seventeen I stood up on that stage singing my heart out in a cloud of organdy courtesy of Brown's Dry Good Store. One particular dress of midnight blue, flecked with rhinestones, always smelled like a Christmas tree, and I kept it for years in the big closet in the north hall in my family's house on South Center Street in Thalia, even after I had left and gone off to reinvent myself a dozen times. Every time I came home, I couldn't wait to run into the closet and sniff it.

The merchants gave contest girls dresses of organza and net and tulle and crystalline. They gave us swimsuits too, which I wore in a contest only once, because seeing me up there "flouncing around," as he said, made Daddy embarrassed. After that contest, he took me home and said, "Don't do that again." So I didn't. I always did what Daddy told me to do, even though he always seemed to think I was up to some mischief, when I truly didn't even know what kind of mischief there was to be up to.

For instance, one day when I was really young, maybe ten, Sonny and Duane and some more boys were out in the vacant lot behind my house building a fire to roast weenies, and I was standing around trying to get myself invited. Wearing my blue Margaret O'Brien school dress, I reached up to one of the lower branches of a mesquite tree and hung on the branch by my hands, swinging back and forth as I talked to the boys. Just then, Daddy drove around the corner, saw us, and screeched on his breaks. He jumped out of the car, grabbed me and threw me into the car. "What do you mean," he yelled, "hanging out there on that tree so all those boys could look up your dress! What could you be thinking of?"

I was flabbergasted. I wasn't thinking of anything but asking Sonny and Duane if I could join the weenie roast too. Sometimes Daddy didn't make any sense at all. It was like he never knew what was inside my head, and he always thought something else was. I wanted nothing more than to make him proud of me, but I never could get it right. He was just hard to please, even when I brought home straight A's.

Once the school principal came to see my parents to tell them that my brother and I had made the highest scores on some test. I heard the principal talking, and I watched from behind the door. Just as he was about to go, he said to Daddy, "Well you've got to make sure that boy gets a real good college education because he sure can amount to something one of these days." Then he said, nudging Daddy, "And you've got to keep an eye on that girl; she's bound to get too big for her britches, if you know what I mean." Chuckle, chuckle.

When things like that happened, I wanted to go out and throw rocks at the water tower. Sometimes I did. And sometimes I got in Daddy's old pickup and drove it to the courthouse square to park in front of the drug store and watch the old people go in and out. I decided then and there that I would never, *ever* be an old person going in and out of that drug store in Thalia. Now, every time I go back to Thalia I can't look at that drug store without thinking about the vow I made to myself forty-some-odd years ago. Somehow, seeing old people going in and out of there horrified me, scorching an image on my brain. I remember asking myself then: Wouldn't it be terrifying to be born and die in the same place? I mentioned this to Mother, who said, "Well, I can see how that might not be appealing to some people."

Mother had carved out a room of her own on the first floor in Thalia by converting a large closet into her retreat. She called this space—outfitted with a desk, chair, typewriter, her paints and canvases—her "hidey hole," the temperature of which, in summer, could climb upward of 110 degrees. It was to this room she would retire in the evenings after the dishes were done and sometimes stay all night. Even after all the kids left home, and she had an entire house in which to create a proper office, she kept her tiny closet space because "when I can get in there and close the doors it's the only place in the house that I can't hear that *blankety-blank* TV with its *blankey-blank* ball games blaring." I'm sure my pathological abhorrence of football on TV stems from the same root as my mother's: for a long time in the Thalia house, there was no way to get away from the sound of it.

When Mollie, who hated football too, came to stay with our family in the summers, she arrived with six flowered hat boxes and lots of "afternoon" dresses. Her husband Alf had put all these fancy airs to the fact that she'd gone to a finishing school. And it was true that Molly had made a career of being a lady while Alf was alive, but later, after he was killed, and she'd gone back to school and become a teacher, she was well known all over West Texas for being as smart as she was elegant. She wore white gloves and big hats everywhere, even to the grocery store.

I still have a mental picture of the two walking in front of me, Mother striding along pushing the shopping basket, quickly snatching bran flakes, beans, milk, and catsup off the shelves, stocking up on necessities as fast as possible because she loathed shopping and was eager to get out of there. She used to say that every time she picked up a pencil and paper, her hand automatically begin writing "bread, milk, toilet paper." Beside Mother minced Mollie in her black pinwheel hat and white gloves, gingerly plucking capers, green gage plums, slivered almonds, and bing cherries off the shelves, laboriously reading their ingredients and placing them daintily in a little mesh shopping bag she carried to "keep them separate, since I plan to purchase the extras." For Mollie, food shopping was a social event, as was most any occasion when she was bound to run into someone she knew. And "one must always be prepared," she instructed. "One must never leave the house without looking one's very best, because one never knows what might turn up."

In actuality, what might turn up was a greasy roughneck coming in from the rig to slug down a couple of Orange Crushes while standing bowlegged in the aisle. This would have to hold him until he could get over the state line and buy a six-pack, since Thalia was in a dry county. I suspected it was dry precisely because Mollie would have thrown a hissie fit to see beer consumed before her very eyes in Thalia—and right across the street from the First Methodist Church to boot. That nothing ever turned up worthy of Mollie's hat and gloves and floral pastel dresses of purest lawn seemed not to daunt her. Beautiful clothing was every lady's birthright.

Mollie had, after the death of Alf, left the Baptist Church and joined the Methodist—her choice all along. Mother "crossed over" the day she had her car filled with kids taking them to Baptist Sunday School and was hit by the Baptist minister, who never got around to fixing her fender.

The women in my family loved two things above all: books and clothes. You could disappear into a book and make up your own world, blotting out the straggly, parched mesquites and the tumbleweeds that blew up on the porch to the front door in the Spring, attaching themselves to the screen, so you'd have to pry the stickery things loose to get inside. And creating pretty clothes—and reasons for wearing them—was about all you could do to put something beautiful in your life, since clearly there was nothing in the landscape worth looking at.

Establishing beauty and order in the harsh environment was done chiefly by learning how to be a lady. My grandmother was the resident maven of ladyhood: "Good carriage, good carriage; that's the secret of good breeding." Mollie would walk across the room imperiously and hold her pointer finger out: "Now, let's see that again. Shoulders square, head back, chin high . . . no, no, no, no, don't swing the arms . . . there you are. Now, step, slide, step, slide, step. Tighten your backside. Feel those cheek muscles. Now, hold them in." According to Mollie, one of the prime qualities of ladyhood was seeming unavailable. "Now," she would say to me when a boy called on the phone, "now, you don't want to sound too *available*, remember."

I found out pretty soon, though, that there was almost nothing a lady could do that was much fun. I used to dream up things in my head that I might do to shock people when my great posture and unavailability got so completely boring that I thought I'd lose my last little chalkie. But I was too chicken to try anything outrageous. Ellie and I did pull a prank one night, but we didn't intend for it to turn out the way it did. We were sitting around in our bedroom upstairs trying to smoke Kents without letting the smoke seep under the door into Daddy's room. While one of us puffed and coughed, the other stood at the door flapping her arms to clear the air. After a while, somebody—well, don't look at me—called up Sonny to come get us. I guess Duane was working, because Rooster Coleman came with him, but instead of throwing pebbles at our window to get our attention, as we'd instructed, Rooster decided to climb the back porch trellis to knock on our window.

The thing was, though, Rooster got the windows mixed up and happened to go scratching on the screen of the bathroom window where Mother was taking a bath. She had the blinds pulled down and all, but Rooster's scratching around on the roof scared the bejabbers out of her, and she started yelling for Daddy.

"Help, help, someone's peeking in the bathroom window! Someone's on the roof!"

Giggling, we hightailed it out the window and down the trellis, and met Rooster on the way down to the car where Sonny was gunning the motor. As we zoomed around the corner on the way to town, we saw Daddy standing in the bright light of the front porch hopping up and down with a shotgun in his hand.

Uh-oh. Big trouble. We looked at each other. "Let's just drive around on the back roads for a while, until he cools down," somebody said. After an hour or so, we crept back to the main drag and were coasting under the red light, when Daddy screeched up in his pickup. He jerked open Sonny's car door and yanked Ellie and me out.

"Get in the car, and I don't want to hear a word out of you. You scared the living daylights out of your mother!" He turned to Sonny and Rooster: "And you. Which one of you was scratching on the bathroom window?"

Silence. Sonny sat with his hat pulled down over his eyes. Rooster paid a lot of attention to chewing on his thumb and then looking at it. Daddy jerked Rooster out of the car. "You!" he shouted. "You have the stickers in your thumb, don't you?" Rooster kept chewing and looking.

"Don't you know those are rose bushes on that trellis, young man?"

Rooster quit chewing and looked at Daddy with wretched eyes.

"You boys go home, and don't let me see you around my house again!" Daddy shouted, as he got in the pickup and slammed the door. Ellie and I sat with our heads down, looking at one another out of the corner of our eyes. We hadn't meant to scare Mother. We were just bored and wanted to have a little fun.

"Get to your room," Daddy said when we reached home. "And I don't want to hear a peep out of either of you again." In those days, nobody had thought up the word "grounded." So what we got was just evil looks and a lot of "You know better than to ask for *anything, young lady,*" threats for a couple of weeks. It was awful, and it was all because of Daddy's bad temper.

My two brothers were perfectly capable of coming up with their own ideas for getting into trouble—like putting a dead skunk in old Miss Hawkeye's brown paper lunch bag and leaving it under her desk. Or holding a boy by his legs outside the second-floor window, while dumb old Coach Popper, supposed to be monitoring study hall, was asleep at his desk. Cute things like that.

I just tried to stay out of their way and disown them when I could manage it. In a small town, it was hard.

The things I loved most to do—like read, write, and sit around listening to porch stories—were not what normal Thalia school kids did, which led to some of them thinking I was stuck-up. But I wasn't. I just knew more about unavailability than they did, and I didn't know how to respond to some of the things they said. I thought that, by and large, people in books had better ideas to think about, and mostly I preferred them to live people. I knew the boys thought I was distant, except for Sonny and Duane, who at least tolerated me.

I had a nice, manageable boyfriend that I went out with in high school. He was tall and intelligent and sweet and was going to make something of himself in later life. I thought a good boyfriend was one who was not boring and who wanted to leave Thalia as much as I did. But Daddy kept telling me that I should look for "a Texas boy who is going to amount to something." Mother said he should respect me and keep his hands to himself, which I added to the mix, and then I had this extra thing to consider: Mollie kept telling me that if I wanted to find the right kind of young man, I had to seem "unobtainable," which went right along with being unavailable. When I asked her what this meant, she said, "Well, for one thing, gloves, flowers, and candy. These are the only appropriate gifts for a young man to give a young lady. Beyond this, a young lady should accept no gift that touches her body."

I thought about how to put those things together. This was nothing like what any other girl in Thalia had to listen to. This was all just too weird for words. It was like being on the moon, when everyone else lived a normal life in Thalia. Being a girl was just confusing. Besides, one day I got my feelings hurt real bad: I heard some boys talking, when they didn't know I was there, and one called me "a little refrigerator," and the other said, "Yeah, built like a brick outhouse."

This horrified me; I couldn't get these images out of my mind. I couldn't visualize what being built like an outhouse, brick or otherwise, might be—square? a half-moon for a mouth?—and I didn't think I acted liked an ice box. I was nice to people and smiled in the hall. When I was invited to parties, I went. Never mind that I spent most of the time tending to the record player and reading the names on the labels of the 78s so nobody would ask me to dance. The boys sweated a whole lot and got awfully close.

The one thing I loved to do that seemed normal to people in Thalia was ride a horse. Daddy kept horses out at the ranch, and I liked to ride fast as the wind, feeling the horse run almost out from under me, while my hair streamed out behind me. It was the only time I felt free at all. But riding a horse fast worried Daddy. Horses were for boys. Besides, he didn't like to see his daughters in those tight Levi's. Furthermore, Mother and Mollie didn't think riding horses fast as the wind was very ladylike.

They didn't think playing basketball was ladylike either, but I made the Thalia High School team one year. I wasn't very good at dribbling down the court, and the ball would get away from me sometimes and go off whomper-jawed in another direction. Then my brothers made fun after practice: "This is Jacy dribbling: plop, plop, plop; this is Jacy with her famous slam dunk, kerplunk, kerplunk." I'd

Flesh

bang off to my room with Daddy shouting: "And that uniform's too short, too!"

Next season I didn't come out for the team. Mollie consoled me by saying that ladies didn't play basketball anyway, and just wait and see who remembers all this in five years.

"You must always remember to hold yourself above the crowd, Jacy," she said. "You are better than any of this nonsense that surrounds you. Things that are important when you're a teenager are not important at all when you're a grownup. And you stay a grownup much, much longer than you stay a teenager."

I tried to remember this each day. The only problem was that the more I tried to be mature and ladylike and hold myself above the crowd, the more I didn't fit in with everyone else in Thalia.

While Mollie was instructing me to hold myself above the crowd, Daddy was embarrassed when his daughters stood out from the rest of the people in Thalia. He wanted us to know our places and stay there and not attract attention to ourselves.

Being a pretty girl was supposed to be a good thing, I thought; at least everybody said so. And singing was supposed to be good and ladylike, too. But Daddy didn't like it when I sang the kinds of songs my teachers told me to. He thought I was putting on airs, and why couldn't I just sing "Tumbling Tumbleweeds" and get it over with? I thought people were pulling me in all directions, and I hadn't a clue about what was right to do.

Sometimes I'd meet Sonny and Duane in the drugstore for a cherry coke and try to tell them about how depressing it was living someone else's life instead of my own. But they just looked at me like I was weird, and it didn't matter anyway, and went on with their plans to run off to Mexico and have an adventure. Of course, they never asked me to come along. Girls couldn't have adventures, they could just sit and look pretty. All the women in my family were pretty. Except maybe Aunt Celie, who just didn't try. Every once in a while Mollie would say, "Lucille, let me pick you out a cool little voile dress." But her sister would say, "Lord a mercy, Miss Mollie, what would I do with something like that? I'd get saddle sores for sure." And Mollie would drop the subject.

Mollie had all these funny little vanities. Much later, when she was eighty, she died in a hospital in Lubbock, but not before she sent

Mother out to buy her a padded bra. Lying in her pink bed-jacket with mimosa branches embroidered on it, she made a final request: "I'm so embarrassed when that nice young doctor comes to see me, because I'm so flat and scrawny." Mother headed to the lingerie department of Hemphill Wells, and Mollie died a proud 34C.

Mother seemed always to understand about people, even when she couldn't do much about them. But Daddy had a talent for getting on my case. One time a lot of the girls in high school were asked to be models for the clothing stores in the area. The style show was supposed to raise money for polio children. I selected a white dress with a bright red duster to model and finagled a way to be the last one in the show, since I thought it was the prime spot, and nobody else seemed to care. I loved the outfit so much that when I stepped out on the stage, I twirled around and flared the duster out to show how full and dramatic it was. I got home feeling good because the people said I'd done fine with my first modeling job. But when I went to their bedroom to kiss Mother and Daddy goodnight and say my "Now I lay me's" as Ellie and I did every night until we left home, Daddy said, "You didn't have to pour it on so thick, did you? Everyone was looking at you."

Now this truly bumfuzzled me since I thought that was the *point* of being in a style show. Daddy had a way of taking the air out of you. Maybe he just didn't want us girls to get too big for our britches, like that principal said.

But there was another episode that even *Mother* didn't understand. It was at the Miss Thalia County contest. I'd just learned that one of the other contestants had leukemia. The rumors were that doctors had told her she didn't have long to live. Standing on the stage in my strapless blue Leslie Caron dress, I prayed hard that the sick girl would win the contest. When I was supposed to be singing and curtsying, all I could think of was praying and crossing my fingers:

"Please God, let Maxine win. Please God, let Maxine win."

When the winner was being announced, I squeezed my eyes tight and prayed as hard as I could, and the leukemia girl won! I was sure I'd made it happen, and I burst into tears.

"Thank you, God! Thank you!"

When Mother and Daddy came backstage to get me, I was crying my eyes out in a dramatic way. "Shhh," they said. "Stop it this minute. You're a better sport than that." I sniffled harder and tried to tell them why I was crying, but they made me come home because "in our family we don't cry after losing." For that, I couldn't go out for cokes with the rest of the girls!

Three months later when Maxine died, and I took Mother to the funeral, she finally believed that I hadn't been a bad sport. But Daddy was never quite sure. As a sort of apology, he did take me to the Fat Stock Show in Ft. Worth, though. I never figured out how that was a stand-in for a ruined beauty contest, but I guess in his mind it was.

It was years before I sorted all this out, or thought I had. I came to suspect that I'd been receiving double messages all my life. On the one hand, I was being groomed to be so unavailable that no boy in Thalia County would be good enough for me, and I'd have to go elsewhere to find a mate where my vast worth was more appreciated. On the other hand, I was being groomed to stay in Thalia and live there in the most conventional *girl* way forever. How did you "hold yourself above the crowd" and still fit in?

It seems clear that my mother and grandmother would prefer that I have a life different from their own, but neither could imagine what that might be. Nothing in the culture gave them a clue. The life I imagined for myself in the privacy of my room—what I would do in New York City—I never mentioned more than once. They pooh-poohed the notion immediately, since they knew no one who lived that far away, and were not quite sure New York existed outside of books and magazines. Where did I get such fantastical ideas, anyway?

"The thing is, Jacy, that you stay in Texas and go to college here, because the people you meet will be those you'll be living among the rest of your life. It's important that you know people here like you—like us. It is not safe to bolt one's culture, especially for a girl."

Well, that *sounded* okay, but there was no one *in* Thalia like me—like us. I hadn't met anyone *anywhere* like that. Our family was just too weird for words.

A reporter from the *Wichita Falls Times* came to the high school in Thalia one day and asked a couple of other girls and me to go home and put on shorts for a photo he wanted to take for the news-paper. I went. I thought it would be a ball to get my picture in the paper. Maybe that would make Daddy proud. But just as I was about to leave the house, he came home from work and said, "What are you doing going outside in that riggin'? It doesn't even cover your backside!" When I told him I was going to be in the newspaper, he turned bright red in the face, and said "Get in this house and stay there; no daughter of mine is going prancing around like that!"

So I didn't get my picture on the front page of the *Wichita Falls Times* like my girlfriends did, over the caption: "Wichita Falls girls have curfews and can't wear shorts on the street in order to cut down on tempting the service men stationed at Sheppard Air Force Base, but girls in rural areas wear what they like, as you can plainly see here, Hubba, Hubba!"

My girlfriends looked cute, especially the one with white shorts and ruffled blouse and spaghetti sandals that tied with criss-crosses up the legs. I huffed to my room and cried because of my father's cruel actions. He was always getting in the way of me being a star and making him proud of me.

Some years later, I asked Mother why my father was so much stricter than those of the other girls in Thalia. She said that first, he wanted to raise nice girls, and second he didn't know how. He was terrified of the responsibility of having pretty daughters; he felt his primary goal was to keep us from getting pregnant before he could get us married off. This stunned me. I thought that if Daddy had just told me that, I could have made him feel a whole lot better. I was not *about* to let a boy get close enough to do something like *that! Gross*! I just *assumed*—like I just *assumed* I was going to college, and *assumed* I'd get out of Thalia as soon as possible, that I'd be a *virgin* when I got married—whatever that meant. It was still pretty murky, the whole thing. But I was going to be one, anyway.

Daddy was such a scaredy-cat. He didn't realize that the closest I let a boy get to me was to clutch my hand during the scariest part of *The Spiral Staircase* when Dorothy McGuire was on the phone saying into the receiver, *It is I, Helen,* when everyone thought she was a deaf-mute. And later I did let the nice boy from a good family who was going to make something of himself in later life kiss me goodnight sometimes, but it was never very much fun, because the porch light was always on with about a thousand watts beaming down, and my brothers were peering over the railing of the balcony making wise-cracks.

Besides, I didn't think he kissed right anyway.

One day, I approached my father: "Daddy, don't you trust me? I'm not going to do anything bad." And Daddy replied, "It's not you I don't trust, Jacy. It's those boys. I was a boy once myself, you know."

This was a real puzzle. I couldn't figure out why if Daddy couldn't trust *himself* as a *boy* he was taking it out on *me* as a *girl*. Not a lot of stuff made any sense about Daddy.

I loved the picture show almost as much as I loved *The Great Books* and *Life* magazine. I had a dress like almost every girl in every picture show that came to Thalia. While the boys were outside noisily pretending they were Doak Walker and Kyle Rote, I'd get bored and lock myself in the bathroom for hours to wash my hair. I would soap it into a big white froth and arrange it in various glamorous ways in front of the mirror—pompadour, pageboy, French twist, gamin. I fancied I could make myself look like Elizabeth Taylor or Gloria DeHaven or Leslie Caron just by the way I arranged my soapy hair and held my face. In the summer, while the guys were being Micky Mantle and Ted Williams, I'd lie out in the sun and get golden; then I'd wear long skirts and thong sandals like Ava Gardner, and let my hair blow wild. And in winter, I'd get very, very pale and suck my cheeks in. Then I'd wear black turtlenecks like Jean Seberg. I could be anything I wanted.

One day my brother, who'd played Stan Musial all day Saturday, asked at Sunday dinner: "Why does Jacy sit in the choir with her cheeks all sucked in like she's sick? That is just dumb looking." Everyone laughed, even Mother, and I huffed away from the table and slammed the door to my room, dislodging the picture of Rory Calhoun on the wall beside my Debbie Reynolds dresser. *Nobody* understood me. I *must* be a barbarian, just like Mr. Ovid said.

One night when I was Audrey Hepburn, I went out on a date with a rich boy I'd met at the Wichita Falls Country Club. He invited me to the picture show, but he took me to his house instead, and his father and mother weren't at home. I was getting nervous because I was not allowed to be in a house without a parent present. The rich boy told me his parents would be home in a few minutes and that he'd invited people over for a party. While they were on the way, he suggested that we take a swim in his pool. Of course, I'd brought no bathing suit, which the rich boy said in kind of a greasy way was just fine with him, but I made such a noise about it that he said, "Here dammit!" He tossed into the room, where I sat on the edge of the bed fully dressed and refusing to budge, a white one-piece Esther Williams suit he said someone had left there.

Not being a quick study in those days, though I must say, I *was* a straight-A student, I took a while to deduce that nobody was actually coming to that swimming party but me. Starving, I ate another cube of yellow cheese on a toothpick and went upstairs to dress. "Take me home!" I demanded importantly about a dozen times, and finally he did. I never saw that weasle again—at least during that life—and good riddance to bad rubbish is what I told all the girls the next day in the restroom. When I walked into my house after that date, who did I see sitting there drinking ice tea and playing bridge with Mother and Daddy and Mother's friend Hazel, but the teacher I sang simultaneous solos with at church! This was weird. When I told them my date had been a big washout, and he was short to boot, the teacher said, "Oh, I could have told you about him. That guy has a terrible reputation with women."

Then while Daddy squirmed, Greg went on to say that the reason the rich boy's parents had not been at home was that he had no mother, his father having shot her dead on the front staircase—*just where I'd stood and eaten a piece of cheese on a toothpick that very evening!*—in a scandalous event a few years before that rocked all of Wichita County and sent the father to the penitentiary. *The penitentiary! The rich boy lived in that house all by himself! Maybe it was even his murdered mother's white bathing suit I'd worn! Wow! This was almost like living in "Green-witch" Village! My heart pounded. I had nearly been raped!!*

From then on I considered this the closest thing to getting raped that I'd ever hope to witness. Though I had to admit, when pressed as I was by my father, that getting raped would have been a little difficult, since every single moment I'd had on every stitch of that *murdered woman's* white one-piece Esther Williams bathing suit, and the rich boy never touched me. But this was what I considered my narrow escape from rape, anyway. It was a few years before I came any closer.

For all the raunchy boys running around Thalia in those days, if we are to believe the literature on that subject, I'd had no bad experience with boys beyond this one, which, as a matter of fact, I told over and over in the girls' restroom at Thalia High to the accompaniment of squeals and oohs.

I really could not imagine anything more dramatic than that. After the scare in *that murdered woman's house* in Wichita Falls, I buried my nose even deeper in a book. And after my best friend, Janine, had to move away to Wichita Falls because her family wanted her to be a debutante, I spent a lot of time alone. Janine was the only girl in Thalia who'd read as many *Nancy Drews* as I had in junior high. She got jokes that nobody else got. We exchanged our *Cherry Ames, Student Nurse* books and our *Brenda Starr, Girl Reporter* books and talked their plots to death every day after school. I had put all my energy into this one friendship, and, in fact, I think we had been a little snobby about not needing anyone but each other. But then I was bereft. What was I going to do? I didn't know how to start over making girl friends that late in life.

Besides there were some really weird girls in Thalia. There was this one girl who got married to a rodeo cowboy and dropped out of school. When her husband was away calf-roping one time, Shirleen invited some girls to a pajama party. I was a little bit scared because all the girls had talked in the restroom about how excited they were because they were going to get Shirleen to tell them what it was like. Just in case, I took my secret notepad that I ordinarily wrote in while scrunched under the covers at night holding a flashlight with my knees. That night we all sat around hardly breathing, leaning forward in our pastel baby doll pajamas, drinking Dr Pepper and eating Peanut Patties. I had my pen poised, but Shirleen would only look mysterious and say, "Oh, it's so beautiful, it's so indescribable. I can't describe it in words; you'll have to find out for yourselves."

So it was all a big bust, as far as I was concerned, and I got no information about it at all. But I did make friends with Peggy Sue who was Church of Christ and didn't know anymore about this stuff than I did. She was my first friend since Janine. We went home and talked about it and crept up and got the book that Mother kept hidden on top of the secretary about *The Miracle of Life*, or something, but it just showed little pictures of tadpoles and things, and said *penis this, penis that*. We knew what a penis was, of course, but it wasn't very exciting, especially on brothers who ran around the house naked flipping towels at one another. We thought this was supposed to be thrilling, and so secret nobody would even talk about it, but it looked just absolutely disgusting.

It was almost as boring as when the Kotex people came to the school to show a film in junior high health class. All the girls were herded into the auditorium, and Mrs. Beard got up there and said, "Now, girls, many changes are about to go on in your bodies, and these nice people have come to prepare you for this by showing this film." Then somebody pulled down the map rack and put a sheet over it and turned the film projector on, and we saw all these cartoon characters of a girl growing up, standing by the door while her father marked her height on the doorframe with a ruler and pencil. She grew and grew, and then when she got to be about our age, we held our breath, because we were going to find out something really important. But what happened was a voice said, "And one day you will wake up and be a woman!" And just then Tinker Bell flew in with her wand and touched the girl on the head. Little sparks flew out, and the girl got up and smiled real big and danced around her room, and a voice said, "Be prepared! Buy Kotex *before* you need it!" Then there was some music and stuff, and that was the end.

I figured I was never going to learn about it.

Another time when I was sitting on the front porch, a boy from Dallas I had a crush on, who visited his grandparents in Thalia a lot, pulled up to the curb in his chartreuse convertible. There was another boy with him. Normally Mother wouldn't let me go down to the curb like that; the boy had to come up to the door to get me, being that I was thoroughly unavailable. But Mother wasn't home, so I strolled down to talk to the boys as they sat in the car. As we did some flirting, I spotted something shiny in the gutter and reached down and picked it up. It was what looked to be an aspirin tin, but a little different, and as we chatted I flipped the lid open and shut, open and shut. The Dallas boy kept looking at the box in my hand, then at the other boy, then back at me.

Finally he said, "What's that you got there?"

I looked down at the little tin. "I don't know. Looks like an aspirin box to me."

"Are you sure?"

I examined it more closely. "No, I don't know. Not aspirin, I guess, something like that." I could not have been less curious about the dumb thing I'd picked up and wondered why the boys were making such a big deal of it.

The boys were smiling: "What's it say on the lid?"

"It says, I dunno, 'pro-phyl-lactics' or something."

By now, the boys were beginning to giggle and snort. "Do you know what that means?" One of them asked.

"Well, not really," I said, examining the object closely, "but *lactic* means milk or something in Latin, and I think *pro* means before, and *phylax* or something like that means a protection. So I guess it's a pill of some kind to guard against milk before you drink it or something. Maybe it's medicine for babies . . ."

By the time I'd finished, those disgusting boys were laughing their heads off and hooting.

"Jacy, why don't you just throw that thing back down where you got it," the Dallas boy said, after he'd calmed down a little.

"Yeah, and then go ask your mother what it means," chortled the other.

Then they roared off down the street, practically dying of laughter and slapping at each other.

Stupidly, I didn't go ask my mother. I was embarrassed enough by being laughed at as it was. I went in and looked it up in the dictionary and found I was pretty close to being right, and I couldn't imagine what was so funny about that.

I also found out that *lactic* means milk in French, too. *So there!*

The boy from Dallas never asked me out after that, and I couldn't figure out why, since I'd showed him how smart I was and all. Boys had no sense.

If I'd just *asked* Mother, she would have told me about the word on the box. But when she tried to tell me about stuff, after I got my first period, which scared me out of my wits because I thought my insides were falling out for sure, I'd just continue washing out my underwear and not look at her, and say *Uh-huh, uh-huh,* like I knew about it all the time. I knew just enough to be embarrassed to talk about it with my mother, which left me about two-thirds in the dark. And, well, I must say it was always a little hard to tell me something I didn't know in those days. This, Mother often said with a little exasperation in her voice, was her older daughter's most defining feature. I did think I knew an awful lot, and if I didn't, I was a good pretender. You had to be a good pretender to live in Thalia and not go just flat out, raving mad.

I did learn some lessons though. When a girl in high school, Cassie, didn't get picked as drum major for the band like her older sister had, Cassie quit school and married a roughneck and had a baby just like that. This was scary. It was then I decided that I'd never go out with any local boys again because I definitely did not want to have a roughneck's baby and be stuck in a really run-down little house in the projects. Seeing what Cassie did, just from not getting picked to be drum major, taught me a lesson for sure.

Another thing that taught me a lesson was going down to the courthouse for the trial. One day after school, a bunch of kids sneaked in to hear how B. L. Pink had shot his wife Bonnie Lou when he came home from the Fat Stock Show in Ft. Worth, and Floyd Pratt was sleeping right there beside her *in his own damn bed.* He kept saying that over and over: *"In my own damn bed!"* like he wouldn't have shot her if she'd been sleeping with Floyd Pratt any place else. Anyway, Floyd got away without even his best boots and ran across the goathead pasture hopping on this foot and then that one, B. L. chasing him while poor Bonnie Lou just lay there bleeding in his own *damn bed.* It was a pretty exciting tale, but I didn't get to hear the end of it because one of my brothers ratted on me, and Daddy came down to the courthouse and huffed all the way up to the balcony to pull me out and take me home. I had to stay home for a whole week just because B. L Pink shot Bonnie Lou, and I didn't think that was a bit fair, which I let Daddy know in no uncertain terms.

Later, when I was supposed to be asleep, I heard Mother and Daddy talking about the trial, and Mother saying, "You mean B. L.

Pink actually got off after killing his wife?" And Daddy saying, "Well, of course, she was being unfaithful, and that's the law of the land in Texas."

"'Well, I'd like to know what would have happened if it had been the other way round, if Bonnie Lou had shot B. L. under the same circumstances in her own blankety-blank bed?'"

"Well, they'd probably have hung her," Daddy said.

"That's the law of the land, too, I guess," Mother said, and gave a bitter little snort.

"I reckon so," said Daddy.

This made me think that maybe all the girls I knew were sort of being taught to lose, and when I asked Mother about that, she said, "Well, Jacy, there's losing and then there's losing. Sometimes you can win by losing, which is the way women have to do it a lot. But you have to figure it out, and it's not easy." Mother looked a little sad when she said it, but then she told a story of how when she was a little girl Grandmother Mollie would take her to church and make her sit down in the pew in her white dress and sailor hat. Mother couldn't see when she was sitting down, and she would bounce up onto her feet and look around, and Mollie would push her back down. One day this happened about three times—Mother jumping up in the seat, and Grandmother pushing her down again—until finally Mollie leaned over her and whispered,

"If you do that one more time, you are going to be a very sorry little girl when you get home. Very sorry."

So Mother slowly slid her small backside down the back of the pew one little vertebra at a time, ve-ry, ve-ry slow-ly, and finally she sat down, plop! real still for one second. Then she looked at her mother out of the corner of her eye and yelled out loud right there in church:

"But I'm standing up insiiiiiide!"

That, said Mother, was how girls had to do a lot of things: just do as you are told, but then *stand up insiiiiiide!*

With Janine gone and Peggy Sue always having to do something at the Church of Christ, which had so many meetings I thought God must get really tired, I felt depressed and had to find something to do, so Mother suggested we shop for fabrics and draw patterns based on dresses I'd had seen at the picture show and sketched out on a pad. Then she would make the dresses. Mostly my clothes were based on those of Audrey Hepburn and Grace Kelly, but sometimes I drew patterns of the big skirts and peasant blouses of Sophia Loren. Once my mother made me a halter dress of white linen with little blue polka dots that I'd seen Marilyn Monroe wear in a picture show.

"Wouldn't it be cute to make little polka dot gloves to match?" I asked Mother, and she rolled her eyes a little, like *where did I get this child?* but she drew around my hand and made the gloves to match my outfit, which I wore to church. Nobody had ever seen anything like that in the First Methodist Church in Thalia.

The most beautiful dress of all, though, was one with many skirts and petticoats of white tulle that I saw in a picture show about Queen Victoria. It had a tiny, tiny waist that came down to a V with lots of gathers all around, and Mother worked hard with wire and pleated fabric and starch and whatnot to make the ruffled collar stand up high around the neck. It never stood up perfectly, being prone to droop limply on one side or another, but it worked long enough to create a dramatic effect when I walked into the junior prom. That was the important thing, the entrance.

For my senior picture in the yearbook, I saved my babysitting money and bought a black jersey scoop neck top with a full black organza ruffled skirt at McClurken's in Wichita Falls, because that year I'd seen a picture of someone in the Stork Club in *Life* magazine sitting at a table smoking a cigarette in a long holder with someone named Sherman Billingsly in just *exactly* this dress. This woman and Sherman looked like the kind of people I wanted to be, and I decided if I had a son sometime I would name him Sherman, that is if I didn't name him Arthur for his father, Mr. Miller.

Daddy despised that dress and said, "This is not what I had in mind for any daughter of mine to wear. In this outfit, you look like you've been kicked out of the back door of a honky-tonk! I hate this picture and will not put it in my house."

Well, Daddy had never been to a honky-tonk in his whole life, so I knew he didn't know what he was talking about. I pleaded with my mother and then went over to see Claudia, a neighbor about ten years older than I. I thought she was very stylish, because she was tall and slender and wore simple black dresses like Audrey Hepburn, so I asked her to talk to my parents about this. I was not about to wear another lavender *georgette* dress like everyone else, especially as a *senior*! I would stay home first and not go to the prom or get my picture made at all!

Claudia talked to Mother and Daddy, and I don't know what she said, but Daddy calmed down, and Mother said to me, "I'm beginning to understand that you are different in a lot of ways, and that includes your tastes, too. So as long as you continue to behave yourself, your father and I will not monitor your dress so much as in the past—at least not much."

When I did my Grace Kelly stroll into the prom, a casual entrance perfected in the full-length mirror of my parents' bedroom, I could see from the corner of my eye that my black Stork Club dress was having the desired screen effect: To the boys, I was more than ever the Queen of Unavailability; to the girls, I had become Miss Upstage, basically demoting their old-fashioned pastel dresses to *underclassmen* status. *Puff sleeves! to die! Satin bows. geek! Shoulder corsages!! don't even think it.* Some girls flew over to the corner avoiding me, probably gossiping meanly. Others gathered around twittering. Where did I get my different ideas? they asked.

Simple: You just paid attention to the picture shows instead of kissing in the balcony all the time, and you studied photos in magazines, and held your mouth just right—and never, *ever*, wore anything at all like *anyone* in the First Methodist Church in Thalia.

I was too self-absorbed for it to occur to me at the time, but in later years I came to think that maybe Mother put so much energy and thought into making beautiful clothes for me during that period because she was bored out of her skull in Thalia. There was, truly, nothing for her to do there, after she took care of her kids and her house. She didn't drink alcohol, like a lot of Thalia women, or even coffee. She didn't go to Wichita Falls to the country club to play tennis or sit around at the pool; she hated to shop, and she didn't hang out at the drug store, or park her car on the main drag so she could watch people come and go every night so she could gossip. This last move was the major entertainment for the women of Thalia.

Mother read, and wrote, and tinkered, and sewed. Having produced her own Barbie doll, she found a creative outlet in dressing it. She was a brilliant woman with little in the immediate culture to engage her. Playing dress-up with her daughters, analyzing what she read and concocting large theories to answer the first question that always occurred to her: *Why?* and rambling on philosophically about ideas and books with anyone with an attention span of more than five minutes, these activities filled a gaping void in her life.

Mother didn't take up painting until her kids left home, and then she was very modest about her work and about the poems she wrote. After she had published a few things, the comments began: "We didn't know you were so talented. Why did you hide your light under a bushel for so long?" She only smiled and said, "My children were my lights for many years . . ."

My own plans to study, travel and write were, like everything else around us, reduced to dust by the drought in the mid-fifties. The cattle that Daddy had raised to sell for his kids' college tuition died of a terrible disease, or, being scrawny, brought little money at the market. He'd already sold off three large plots of land around our home to keep us going, a sale that must have hurt him terribly, since owning land was a primary source of pride for the men in and around Thalia. Again, I was too preoccupied with my own adolescent needs to notice his distress; either that, or he never talked about it. This was a home in which difficulties, or anything unpleasant, were never acknowledged aloud. A polar bear could have died in the middle of the living room floor, and if this incident were thought to be in poor form, no one would ever mention it; we'd all just walk around it. Small things, yes; these were quickly pointed out and corrected. Big issues were not.

So I took the best scholarship offered me, one which promised to train me to become a singer. I had no real ambition to be a singer, but I went along with the plan. Clearly, Daddy had enough problems without me complaining—though I almost had to mind-read to know this.

Mother put a Toni Home Permanent in my new poodle cut and sewed for weeks. Daddy drove me to Denton in a car he described as having a backseat filled "with the biggest wad of net petticoats you've ever seen, and an ironing board hitting me in the back of the neck at every stop light." On the first day of college with my music scholarship, I wore a brown and black plaid dress with a white collar. Mother thought that no school year could begin without a plaid dress with a white collar, a new book, and an old one. So I took a brand new copy of *Bulfinch's Mythology*, and an old copy of *A Child's Garden of Verses* in English and Latin that Mollie had given me on my eighth birthday and helped me memorize in both languages. So far, I have never found a conversational opening in which to introduce, "Oh, how I like to go up in the swing" in Latin.

To my surprise, since I hadn't knocked myself out with school work in high school—meaning I'd paid little attention to the books I was *supposed* to be reading—I mean how long can it take you to read three short stories by Guy de Maupassant (pronounced *guy day maw pissant*) and bake a pineapple upside-down cake?—I tested out of Freshmen courses except for biology and French. I didn't know a thing about science because back in Thalia the boys took real science with Miss Amelia, whose lab room always smelled like rotten eggs, while the girls took Domestic Science and learned to make pillow cases and Bundt cake. I abhorred this class, except for the part when we got to decorate play-like rooms. It was fun picking out fabric and gluing it onto little couches and chairs, like building a doll house. But the cooking part I despised. "How many colors of Jell-O can you make and cut up in little wiggly squares?" I asked Mother once after spending third period making Broken Glass Salad. "I guess as many as Jell-O makes," she said with a sigh.

This was what I learned in four years of Domestic Science:

BROKEN GLASS SALAD
Take one package each of lime, lemon, orange and strawberry Jell-O. Follow instructions as directed on the back of package. After Jell-O is set, cut into 1/4 inch squares. Toss together in a large bowl, and top with whipped cream.

In college I faced biology with fear and enormous insecurity—both my own biology, as it turned out, and the more theoretical kind. And French was new too, but necessary if I were to become a famous singer like Renata Tebaldi, but not so fat—my new favorite ambition, since my career as a writer in New York seemed to have gone down the tubes with the cattle market. (My parents, which just shows what they knew, thought I was studying to be a music teacher, in case I "had to have something to fall back on." Nobody mentioned what one might have to "fall back" *from*, but then nobody had to.)

Mostly, I put in my time on English courses, which I loved. My teacher made us subscribe to *The Atlantic Monthly*, and I'd never read a magazine so fascinating. *Life* was filled with pictures, but *Atlantic* had writing in it—really *good* writing. I longed to be able to write like that—wry, dry, witty, erudite, informed. Though I don't recall the name of the teacher, I recall a word that she kept using: *hyperurbanism*. My teacher, a young woman with straight brown hair who wore the same black skirt and sweater to class every single day, said it meant saying things like "between you and I," that were incorrect, but showed that you were trying so hard to be correct and citified that you overdid it and got it wrong. To this day, I have never heard anyone else use this word, but from that time on, I have thought it was a good idea not to try things so hard you get them wrong. Better to make an honest mistake and get corrected. Or better yet, ask questions. So I've passed the idea on to my own students.

In my first semester, I got to sing a role in *Carmen*, wearing a short, Ava Gardner-like olive skirt with a cream peasant blouse, and very high-heeled sandals. Mother and Jean, my Thalia music teacher, came to applaud. After I sang, Jean cried and said, "Thank God, I didn't hurt your voice!" This astonished me, because I was very sure she knew exactly what she was doing all those years with running scales, and arpeggios, and *mi mi mi's.* Finding out that she, like the rest of us, had doubts too, was a surprise.

The lead singer, Jody, a beautiful senior girl from La Porte, who surprised me by knowing my name, told me that the makeup on my legs was too shiny, and people in the audience had complained that it made me stand out too much. I wiped it off between the acts.

The boys at college were different than those in Thalia—for one thing, they had cars instead of pickups, and were a lot more forward. The boys in Thalia just leered and flirted with girls. The boys in college had graduated to more advanced moves. Unlike the boys in Thalia, they did not understand that I was the Queen of Unavailability. My father was not there to tell them, and I had no idea how to deal with them.

I had barely gotten settled into the dorm, when I walked across campus one morning to see a large photo of myself on every other tree. I couldn't even figure out where the photo came from. Who made it? It looked like my ID photo. Fraternities were selecting queens and announcing this with posters. The sight of my face nailed to a hundred trees startled and embarrassed me. It seemed immodest and a little silly, and I didn't think this was what Grandmother Mollie meant by holding yourself above the crowd. She would say with pursed lips, *"This is just a little common, don't you think?"* And I knew Daddy would hate it. I could just hear him: *"Your FACE on a HUNDRED TREES??? What are you doing down there? I thought I was paying for you to go to school, not run around down there like a wood damn nymph!"*

I had thought contests were just a silly Thalia thing and I would be rid of them in college. But somehow they were big here, too, and I fell into it again—waving from open cars wearing off-the-shoulder gowns. But *any* attention, I guessed, was better than none at all, so I waved and smiled as if sleepwalking, wondering when real hard serious college stuff was going to begin to happen. I was ready to grow up and move on, but how did you do it? No one in the dorm seemed to know: the older girls were busy getting themselves pledged to sororities, and the rest of us just walked around with blunked-out eyes like Little Orphan Annie. My roommate sure couldn't tell me. First semester, I got stuck with a piano major from Tulsa, Oklahoma, who wore lace-up shoes and knew even less about real life—meaning, mainly, boys—than I did. Poor thing.

Mother refused to sign "blanket" permission—*"What a term!"*—she said, for me to go off campus on the weekends, so I was often stuck there. But she did, miraculously, sign permission for another outing: Splash Day in Galveston! I still have the letter to prove it. My date was an ROTC cadet, who was so handsome and toothsome that my brothers, when they finally met him, called him "Pearly-white."

Dearest One,

Your letter asking for formal permission to go to Galveston has just come. Yes, you may go, and I do understand about the coming and going and where you will stay and having met Colonel Waggoner and his wife, I feel that they are certainly acceptable chaperones . . . oops! there's that word again. Please forgive, even now that you've reached the age of (shall we say?) unaccountability, we are still apt to let that horrible word creep up now and again. I also received a letter asking permission for you to go on a week-end retreat with the Theta Chi's, but this is *not* that permission. So far, it has not been discussed in family conclave, and I personally am very short on information concerning the Theta Chi's in general and one Bill Smith in particular, and the idea of fraternity house parties is not in itself exactly appealing to me. So that one will have to await further consultation with the authorities. Yes, I know we make an issue of everything, but that has been the wail of children, especially oldest children, since the beginning of time, so be patient with us, we certainly are with you.

Love, Mother

Shortly after that, another permission request was issued from Dean Bentley's office. This one, too, received grudging attention:

Dearest One,

Yes, I have signed and returned the permission for you to go on the weekend Jag—what a lovely expression—not because we approve, for we do not, but because we realize that our approval or disapproval is not the immediate concern with you, simply the signed permission, and that from now on out we can act only in an advisory capacity, if at all. All we can do is offer our ideas, and the small amount we have gained by experience, and hope you will try on a few of them for size and find some of them to fit. Frankly, I think you are too involved with out of town trips, dances, parties, fraternity la-de-da, and boys to really anticipate, appreciate, or enjoy any of them. You are spreading yourself too thin, and that may mean the difference between a pancake and a crepe-suzette, but for a steady diet the corn meal hoe cake will stand you in better stead.

Love, Mother

Those outings that caused the Thalia "family conclave" so much grief were relatively benign, being heavily patrolled by chaperones to start with. And secondly, any electric ideas I might have were quickly short-circuited by my terror of doing something to cut off the hard-won permission current. The young man I dated my first semester in college was so attractive he scared me, and I think I had the same effect on him. After one evening when the air seemed particularly charged between us, and neither of us knew what to do with it, we decided not to go out anymore. He returned to his nice, safe church youth group, and I to my drama club where most of the men were more interested in each other than in me.

By now, I've raised several children, and I try to recall whether I wrote similar Mother-letters to them after they left home. I may have, but mainly because I thought I was supposed to. I knew part of the parental role was to set boundaries, but I'd had so many set in my own youth—needlessly, it seemed to me—that I was loathe to repeat the past. I do know that finally, cautiously, I encouraged some of my kids to move in with their loves-of-the-moment to see how things worked out. This seemed to me preferable to going through the charade of getting married to find out whether they could stand one another in bed.

I often refer to women of my own generation as having gone through "the obligatory first marriage," which for many of us in the fifties was like sticking a toe in to test the waters and having our ankles grabbed by a force that kept us for many years in a maelstrom not unlike the Bermuda Triangle. One could disappear for years. I've seen too much of that, and I don't want that for my own kids. But they did—and are still doing—whatever they please anyway, so I might as well have saved my Mother Agonistes for something else.

Flesh

Sometimes I wonder, though, how I moved so effortlessly from my own timid traditional dealings with boys and sex to the point where I encourage my own kids to break new paths. The mores of the fifties seem to me so silly now—making such a to-do about womanly virtue and chastity. What was that all about? Male aversion to the thrift shop, maybe. Most guys balk in their tracks and can't be dragged into the things, whereas most women love consignment shops and can plow around forever among the dusty objects looking for that treasure with just the right degree of patina or vertigris, the more pre-owned, and the more you know about the previous owner, the better. But men lust after being the *first* owners of everything, whether a golf club or a Corvette. Maybe it's a power trip. They want it when it's new and shiny and untouched—like Prince Charles with Diana. And we now know the end to that sorry story of the Princess and the Peahead.

In this mood, the low point of my dating life in college occurs to me. An older sorority girl campaigning for a new pledge had set me up with a date to the BMOC dance with the Biggest Man On Campus. Stupidly, I let the older girl, Alison, convince me that this was a "fabulous opportunity" for something or other. But she hadn't bargained for me. The fellow was pleasant enough at the mixer and seemed to know everybody, which made me—a Freshman afraid to say Boo if the pigs ate me—feel important. But he did drink an awful lot of beer. I didn't drink, but smoked lustily and with great pretension, since alcohol tasted to me like perfume, and I needed something sophisticated to do with my dangling hands. (I had learned how to smoke from Marlene Dietrich in *The Blue Angel*.)

Later, after the dance, Big Man guided me into a long, dark building that inside looked to be an infirmary, lit only by a faint blue light. When my eyes adjusted, I saw bed after bed of couples doing extremely complicated things, and I bolted as my date tried to lead me toward a cot. Outside, he took off his class ring and offered it, then his fraternity pin. Stupefied and hurt, I lit out for the dorm alone, running through shrubbery that scratched my legs until they bled. I fell into bed in my brand new pink angora sweater set and cried myself to sleep.

Next day, Alison caught me in the library, shook me angrily and hissed: "Don't you know who he is? You humiliated him, and you will never be pledged to any sorority on this campus as long as I live!" I was hurt, and called my mother, who said that being a sorority girl was not a noble goal in life and that black-balling people was cruel and unworthy of me. "Jacy, clubs that get their jollies from excluding people are not the kinds of places you want to put your energies into. This stuff is beneath you. You have better things to do." If I did, I didn't know what they were. This was like holding yourself above the crowd again, and where had *that* got me? *A misfit everywhere*, that's where. Now I wasn't even *college* material.

The following week, though, I made a comeback. At semester assembly, Mr. Brown read one of my poems to the audience, and I was asked to stand along with the other honor students. Stunned, Alison and the BMOC looked at me as they sat in the C-average section. Of course, I stood up a little longer than necessary to make sure they saw me, and I was glad I'd worn my bright red Cyd Charisse dress. This was my finest hour in college.

But boys were still a puzzlement. They either asked too little of you or too much. I wanted someone I could talk to like a grown-up, have fun with, and go to the picture show with, but who would keep his hands to himself. Once I went out with a boy from Levelland who had a red Thunderbird that all the girls in the dorm wanted to go out in. I was really honored that he asked me out, when I didn't think he even knew I existed. But once I was in the car, he drove like sixty and drank beer even while he was driving! He picked up another couple who were drinking Bourbon out of a bottle, and the guy said, "Let's see if we can make eighty the rest of the way to Dallas!" I was terrified. I kept thinking all the time we were driving: *what if we have an accident and Daddy finds me dead with all these bottles and beer cans around? He would be so ashamed, I just couldn't stand it!*

After a lovely evening in the spring in which I was crowned Queen of the Military Ball and walked through a pointed arch of swords, then danced to the strains of Harry James's Orchestra in my blue lace Debbie Reynolds dress, I decided that this was the best that college had to offer, and I was not coming back.

I had topped out at eighteen.

I went back to Thalia that summer and took the only job I could find—one in a business that repossessed cars. I didn't tell Mother, but I was secretly saving money to move to New York City, though I didn't know a soul there and had only been out of Texas to go to New Mexico to visit Uncle Hank, and to San Francisco on an un-memorable senior trip in a bus with Sonny and Duane and the rest of the graduating class. (Mostly, everyone in the bus acted like babies, and that's a long way to drive with a bunch of babies. I couldn't wait to get away from them and go off to college where there were grown-ups. *Huh. What did I know?*)

Back in Thalia, I began going out a little with the high school teacher with the beautiful singing voice, who was working on a gradu-ate degree and could discuss the finer points of *King Lear,* even with the wailing of Lefty Frizzell in the background. He had a brain that was amazing! He knew *everything!* All the Houses of the British Kings and Queens and who they were married to and how they were all related to each other, and all the bones of the body, and all the words to Rudolf Friml and Sigmund Romberg songs—I mean *everything!* I was really flattered that an *older man* with all that worldly knowl-edge was interested in me. And he wasn't even a cowboy, though he did coach some sports. Oh, well, in Texas you might as well forget it; you're not going to find any man without the football disease. Col-lege was just a bust as far as I was concerned; it was nothing but contests and clutching boys. Back home, even the rules of Daddy—after the more bewildering ones of college life—looked good.

But I hated repossessing cars. I hid the little payment schedules in my drawer when I was supposed to follow up with threatening phone calls to people. I watched late-payment people come in to other desks, and they looked so miserable and pathetic, I knew I could never yell at them that I was sending someone to their homes to take their cars away.

This job was beneath the dumps. Going to see Elvis at the Me-morial Auditorium didn't even help. He didn't strike me as very in-telligent, and I hated songs about Hound Dogs anyway. Mollie turned her nose right up at him, and even Daddy said he had a weak chin. But Elvis aside, I couldn't seem to figure out what I might be cut out for. Mother wasn't much help. She was irritated with me for dropping out of school to start with, and she was also worried about where the tuition money for her next child was going to come from. Besides, neither she nor Daddy seemed overjoyed to have me and my stack of Four Freshmen 45s back home, though I played them on low and kept my door closed.

Duane was off in Korea or somewhere, and god knows where Sonny was. Janine had married some boy she'd met at her debutante party. The girls from high school had moved to Wichita Falls or had kids by now. Everything was depressing, and I felt liked a jerk. You come back to Thalia and you're not in high school, you might as well be dead. You walk around seeing people you've known all your life all around you, and they simply don't see you. You're not in any contests, or at the pep rallies, or in the band any more. Being out of high school in Thalia gave you the feeling that you were invisible. Life just wasn't the way it was supposed to be at all.

One night on a date with the teacher, after seeing a picture show about the circus with Gina Lollabrigida flying on a high trapeze looking so free and happy in her little pink tights and curly black hair, which just made me feel sad and empty, we were driving home, and Greg said, "Look, the moon is on fire!"

I told him, "Don't be silly; it's just an old shed burning," and we alerted the firehouse. Standing by the car watching the fire, Greg told me that he liked to think the moon was really on fire, and that he wanted me to marry him—a declaration that astonished me, for I had no idea of marrying anyone for years, let alone someone in Thalia. But he was several years older than I, so I sputtered, "Not now, I mean I don't know, I mean I don't know what I mean. . . " I was so miserable what I basically wanted to do was cry, or just plain whine.

But Greg said sternly: "What kind of answer is that? I thought I'd get a better reply out of the only girl I ever asked to marry me!"

I felt just awful to have hurt his feelings, and the tone of his voice sounded a lot like Daddy's, so I muttered that I'd think about it. From then on, Greg considered it settled and went off and bought a ring. When he gave it to me a few weeks later during dinner at a steak house in Wichita, I put it on, upholding in that act my unbroken record of doing exactly what every man, from father to teacher, had told me to do. Besides, Arthur Miller had just married Marilyn Monroe.

The next few months were surreal. I'd never thought it would come to this. I thought Mother would beg me not to marry, or that Daddy would forbid it. All the protective mechanisms I'd depended on for eighteen years were crumbling. Mother and Daddy had never let me take such a drastic step by myself before. I called my grandmother as a last resort, hoping she would tell me not to do this. She said, helpfully: "Marriage is very difficult, dear, but then, so are all relationships. However, in whatever circumstance one finds oneself, one must learn to be content."

Confused, I threw myself into plans for dresses, and cakes, and teas, and parties. At a shower, someone brought me a white organdy apron with purple flowers on it placed in the outline of a woman's pelvis and ovaries. Everyone laughed, but I was horrified. I hated aprons, and, for some unaccountable reason, this one in particular made me shudder.

It was not until many years later that my mother confided in a letter to me that she shared my repugnance for aprons, since they were, she wrote, "the symbol of the kitchen's defining women's lives." She'd never said so before, "because I guess I was afraid it would sound 'unpatriotic.'"

I am still puzzled about how long it took my mother to divorce aprons from patriotism. Clearly, with her gift for language, and her knowledge of the roots of words, she understood what she was saying: rebelling would not be giving the proper honor to patria, family; pater, father. It had nothing to do with patriotism, as in country.

Or, on second thought, maybe *all*. As usual, she was ahead of me all along.

And yet . . . yet . . . She had allowed me, too young and clearly too naive, to leap into the same role that had for so long controlled her own life.

"Mother, how could you *let* me get myself into the same fix?" I asked her years after I married and was feeling the pinch of life in a strait jacket.

"Let Smet! I let the wind blow, too. The more I tried to discourage you, the more determined you were to do what you wanted. What was I to do with you?"

God knows.

The week before my wedding I would awaken in the middle of the night and murmur, "Why am I doing this? What will happen to me now? What will I do after this?" I had no idea. Picture shows always *ended* with weddings. They never *started* there except for one—*The Father of the Bride*—and that was a picture show about the *father*, not the *bride*.

When I went to my mother asking "What do brides do for the rest of their lives?" she gave a short laugh and said, "You'll find out soon enough," but even then I noticed a sadness in her eyes. I remembered some questions that Jo March had asked her mother in *Little Women*. I looked them up and tried them. "Mother, do you feel, like Mrs. March says, that you are angry every day of your life, but you try hard not to show it?" She looked thoughtful: "No, I am not angry every day. I have everything a woman could want. I just learned many years ago what was appropriate for a woman to want. I love my children very much, so I've chosen to decide not to want any more than that."

This answer mystified me; I longed for a life of travel and adventure. I wanted to learn everything there was to know. "Mother, am I doing right?"

She whispered into my hair: "I don't know what's right for you, dear. I'm not going to try to talk you into or out of this marriage. I can just tell you that you always have a home here, and we love you dearly."

I pulled my head back to look at her: "Even Daddy? Does he love me?" She nodded: "Of course he does, but he doesn't know what to make of you. Your wedding will be the happiest day of his life: He can turn you over to another man."

When I reflect on that conversation, I half wish my mother, for all her smarts, had been less supportive and more brusque, like the mother of a Thalia girl you may have read about who told her daughter pretty much the truth: Life is monotonous, and marriage often makes it more so; living in the Texas plains is too damn hard, where the land has so much power over you; there's nothing to do there but spend money, so you have to be rich even to go insane in Thalia; and a girl ought to go out and have a little fun and find out that boys aren't the magic creatures they're cracked up to be *before* she settles down with one of them.

But that would have made mine a different kind of mother. So I, like millions of girls before me, was offered up in an ancient tribal rite, by good women, kind women, loving women, even by women who didn't much believe in those rites anymore but found the truth too harsh and could not imagine any other way for a woman to live.

I had begged Greg to move out of Thalia, so he made plans for a teaching exchange to Europe the following year. At least, I told myself, I had this to look forward to.

I was already starting on an adventure: The first time I was allowed to drive a car out of the city limits of Thalia all by myself was to go to Wichita Falls to have my wedding portrait taken at Olin Mills. It was Greg's new Chevrolet, and in my nervousness, I ran it into the side of an underpass. He was good about the fender.

In the First Methodist Church of Thalia, I was a vision in bridal illusion, wasp-waisted, in satin high-heels and a fluttery little net cap and veil, just like Elizabeth Taylor in *The Father of the Bride*. I took my wedding vows amid tall banks of white candles and gladiolus. Afterward, I turned, holding my bouquet of white roses and baby's breath to my side, as I stretched to kiss the groom—an act of bald courage with my father standing right there. I wasn't sure what he would say later: *My daughter kissing a man in church right before God and everybody???*

My best friend, Janine, was Matron of Honor. She took me aside while I was dressing in the pink cotton dress with pleated skirt modeled on the one that Marilyn Monroe wore to stand on the air-shaft, and told me:

"I know you don't know much about all this stuff, so I want to tell you. Don't be afraid. There's nothing to it. It doesn't hurt much, and it's all over in just a few minutes."

Zipping my skirt, I turned to her, puzzled: "What doesn't hurt?" A wedding was about wearing a gorgeous dress, being queen for a day, and then getting out of Thalia as soon as possible. What's to hurt?

That night my high school friend, Peggy Sue, ran off to a justice of the peace in Altus, Oklahoma, and married a cowboy from Megargel. Intent on impressing my college suitemates with my big production, I had forgotten to ask Peggy Sue to be in my wedding.

A car with boots and cans dangling drove me and my brand new husband to another car to elude prankster brothers who were up to their usual mischief. After that, we drove and drove in the dark. It seemed weird to drive in the middle of the night wearing a Marilyn Monroe dress, a round black hat, and white gloves, sitting by a man you didn't know very well. I kept stealing peeks at him, like I'd just seen him for the first time. I wanted to keep driving forever. After all, I had on a new dress and was getting farther and farther away from Thalia with every mile. This was the way I had planned it in my fantasies. This was the place in the picture show where I was supposed to be happy out of my mind.

But the groom was getting tired, he said, and needed to stop. When we were in a hotel room, I insisted on calling Mother and Daddy to thank them. I hoped they would tell me that the wedding was over, and it was time to come home now. But they didn't.

Being in a hotel room with a man was embarrassing. This was something I was not supposed to do. So I decided that we should go swimming. Running nervously to the pool, I fell and skinned my knees, which continued to bleed as, later, I locked myself into the hotel bathroom to put on the lacy gown that my college friends had given me; it was cut like the slip that Rita Hayworth wore in the famous photo on the bed.

My bleeding legs made me flash for an instant on the incident in college when I had scratched my legs on shrubbery as I ran away from the blue-lighted fraternity house. It occurred to me that maybe I was not cut out for blue lights and hotel rooms—I wasn't college material or marriage material, and if that was the case, then what *was* I cut out for?

But I tried to assume Rita Hayworth's pose because I knew Greg liked that picture. My knees hurt too much, though, and finally I fell back on the bed, defeated.

3

B·L·O·O·D

COMING HOME FROM DALLAS was not as much fun as going. I had been bleeding every night and was afraid to put on the white halter dress when we went out to the hotel for dinner. Maybe Greg was right. He hadn't wanted to go to Dallas for the wedding trip in the first place; he had made plans to go to a cabin on Lake Kickapoo.

I had gone to Mother: "*Lake Kickapoo!* Mother, *Yuk!* Greg's so proud of his plans that I don't want to hurt his feelings, but I have these new wedding clothes, and I don't want to wear shorts on a honeymoon! I always dreamed I'd go somewhere elegant if I got married. Everything is going wrong." I started to cry, then stopped: I was supposed to be grown up now. Brides don't cry. Or do they? Frankly, I had no idea what brides do. "Fishing is boring, and the water is muddy, and what is there to do out there anyway? Lake Kickapoo! This is not the way it happens in *Life* magazine. You go to the *Stork Club*, or something."

Mother listened to me, her eyes wandering from ceiling to floor, from wall to wall. "Do you want me to discuss it with him?" she asked finally.

"Please. Like with Daddy, I don't want to go against his wishes, but Mother, it's *supposed* to be *my* wedding, and everyone seems to think it's *Greg's*. . . ."

It was odd, I think now. Why did Mother offer to intervene? Today, if she were alive, she would say with a shrug: "Don't tell *me*, tell *him.*" She would say that making your wishes known *directly* to your fiancé, or husband, was the only way to survive marriage. She would say that marriage serves children first, men second, and women third, if at all. Mother had become much more direct in the twenty years before she died—after she'd raised her children. After I was grown, she'd told me once that when her kids were at home, she never felt free to express what she *really* thought, because she had to keep us uppermost in her mind; *we* were her first responsibility. Later, she sent me a book she'd come across, *The Yellow Wallpaper*, about a woman's descent into madness because of her lack of freedom and self-definition.

It's hard to believe now. The wedding trip was the least of undiscussed subjects between us when Greg and I married. We had never discussed *anything* about our future together. Why? Why hadn't we talked about what each of us wanted, where each of us was at that point in our lives? We had not discussed values, or ambitions, or dreams. We had not discussed having children. All I told Greg was that I didn't want to live in Thalia, and he'd said okay, he hadn't planned to live there much longer anyhow. And I knew, because he'd told me, that he loved me because I had the auburn hair of his long-dead mother. And, of course, I knew I loved him because he could talk about subjects that no boy in Thalia knew anything about: books, language, history. He was the smartest man I'd ever met.

When you deconstruct that, what do you get? He married me for my looks; I married him for his brains. A typical fifties marriage.

The next day after Mother had talked to Greg about the wedding trip, he'd come in saying he had a great idea. "Why don't we go to Dallas for a few days after the wedding, and then end up out at the lake for the weekend?" I thought that was a fine idea, and thanked him for coming up with it. But coming back from Dallas, I sat in the car thinking: I don't want to go to the lake. I want to go home. My wedding trip days had been fun, but the nights were confusing. I'd been programmed to put on the brakes with boys; now I didn't know how to switch into reverse on demand. Everything was too new, and it hurt. Maybe that was what Janine had meant.

I wondered if I were normal. Maybe there was something wrong with me that I didn't have a "beautiful experience." Back in Thalia, everyone looked at me funny. I knew why they were looking. I'd heard in the girls' restroom that after you'd done it, you walked different. I knew people were looking at the way I walked, so I just tried to walk like I always had. When I finally got to talk to Mother, she hugged me and said things would get better; she understood this was all very new, but soon I'd get used to it, and maybe even learn how to enjoy it. Don't worry.

I had taken my mind off these things by beginning to plan our move to France, where Greg had found work as an exchange teacher for a year. I was going back to college, this time in Paris! and this time I could focus on studying without the interference of boys and sorority girls and contests. I was a grown-up woman now and never wanted to hear about those juvenile things again. I'd never been abroad before. My grandmother had offered to give me a trip for high school graduation, but my parents, worried about the drought, decided this might set a precedent for the younger children that neither Mollie nor they would be able to keep up, so they said no. But this time I was going. I would study hard, meet different kinds of people and keep a journal so I could write about my experiences. I was so happy that finally, *finally*, I was going to find something worth getting serious about.

When I went back to my job for a few final months, the guys at the car repo place gathered around asking how I liked married life. I said, "fine, fine," waving them off. But I saw them watching me so I tried hard to walk normal. One salesman came over and leaned on my desk, leering. "Well, how was this one, honey? Doing it was nothing new for you. How about you and me go out; I could show you something you won't forget." I was flabbergasted, and told him to leave me alone.

The guy hooted and said loudly, "You can't tell me a gal looks like you didn't get some before tying the knot. Now, c'mon." All the men hanging around laughed, and I slunk behind my desk humiliated. I couldn't think of anything to say, and my stomach felt queasy. I had to hold on to the edge of the desk to keep from getting dizzy. I was so upset that I marched in a few days later and quit. They knew I was leaving soon, anyway. Girls didn't work after they got married. I went home that day relieved, back to the little house we'd rented near the high school. I didn't make much money anyway, and I hated it. Now I could focus on making plans to move to France.

A few weeks later, I discovered it was a good thing I'd quit my job. When I went to Dr. Horn about the headaches and dizziness, he told me I was pregnant. Counting back, we found it had happened on the honeymoon. The honeymoon! What a cheap shot! My brother laughed and said, "Hey, Jace. The first rattle out of the box." And Greg did a little jig around the room.

I didn't know what was happening to my body. It started pudging out all over, and I didn't help things by eating graham crackers all day. I felt sluggish and couldn't figure out what to take to Paris to wear if I was going to keep getting fat. Leslie Caron didn't look like this in Paris!

Furthermore, I was supposed to be matron of honor in the wedding of my college roommate, and when Kay sent the dress it was a gold crystalline number with a dropped waistline. I looked like a bundle of soiled laundry in it. The waistline didn't drop above or below my belly, and I just looked dopy. I just couldn't go to the wedding looking like a fat hag. Besides, I didn't like the word *matron*. It sounded so old and frumpy. What was wrong with my life anyway? I told Kay I was "expecting" and sick and was sorry, but she'd have to get someone else.

Even worse, I started bleeding. Did bleeding just *go* with marriage? It seemed that's all I'd done since I got married. Marriage was one big period, except when you wanted one. Dr. Horn put me to bed for a month and said I had to stay put. Then the next week he said I couldn't go to France either, because "the health of this baby is more important than whatever it is you want to do, young lady. That's what being a woman is."

Having to stay in Thalia was agony. I had almost escaped, and then I got stuck there, fat as a pig in a tacky little house with a husband who brought football players home with him after he'd coached them. I didn't see why he had to tell them that I'd fix them something to eat every night. Why didn't he just go to summer camp or join the Boy Scouts if he needed all those boys around all the time? Every single time I wanted to do something—*really* wanted to do something—there was a catch.

And yet, I keep telling myself, and my students, and every group that will listen to me that *nothing is lost. Nothing.* Even if the only past you have to build on is negative, you can build from that. And even those things that seemed negative at the time can turn out to be a positive. You never can tell. You think timing is all, and it is at the time.

But I remember the dead-end of those days: I felt like—what's the Eliot line?—a bug pinned and wriggling on the wall. I was nineteen, married, pregnant, fat, stuck in a place I devoutly wished to be rid of. Life was unfair: I'd been a good girl, done everything my father, and now my husband said; I'd followed all the rules and tried to please everyone, and here I was tethered, just like Cassie or another classmate who hadn't planned any other life, to a run-down house in an icky place. I would never be an American in Paris. I'd be in Thalia forever! Why? Why should I have to shrink myself to its shrunken possibilities?

Already Greg was strutting around telling folks he wanted three or four more kids, and I was afraid to cross him. We'd just come back from his father's home, where we'd gone for Christmas Eve, and it was one big crazy mess. One stepbrother chased another with a shotgun, and people were crying and breaking things. When we got back to Thalia, Greg had gone upstairs and sat on the floor of my old bedroom with his head in his knees, and moaned "I want a *real family*; I want my own *real family*, not one like that," over and over again. I didn't want to see him hurt more. I wanted to make things better for him. But I didn't want three or four more kids, and I sure didn't want to live in Thalia!

I have to sigh a little at the odd way lives stack up. In retrospect, I understand that Greg had come from a wildly dysfunctional family and wanted something traditional and orderly, while I had come from a traditional family and wanted wildness and adventure. Ah, the perversity of things. I recall the time my father proudly brought me a bicycle for my birthday. I thanked him and rode it, but what I really wanted was a pony. Later my father told me that he'd always had to ride a horse to school in West Texas and envied the kids who had bikes, so he was going to see to it that *every last kid of his* had a bike.

Mother did her best to make me feel better about the thwarted trip abroad and my awkward body, but she was distracted, worried about the younger children coming along ready to go to college. Another had gone and returned, finally joining the army, and who knew where he'd be next year?

The whole thing I came to think of as a family plot. It caught you in a death grip and wouldn't let you go until you cried Uncle or went to your grave. I remember something Robert Frost said about poets in socialist states, who either had to write party-line propaganda or fear for their lives. It was "death or Pollyanna," he'd said. That was often the way it was for women in a democracy. Death or Pollyanna. Mother had opted for Pollyanna, and, for a long time, I had too. It wasn't until the seventies that I said death *to* Pollyanna, dammit, and ran away from home. I've often wondered why my mother hadn't done the same.

I remember a couple of funny times when Mother rebelled. Now, when I look back at them, they seem more poignant than pointed. Daddy had gone to an all-day ball game somewhere, and Mother was angry with him for leaving her by herself with the kids on a weekend. After all, she had them all week by herself. She bundled the kids up and went to see a neighbor. The two sat at the white metal kitchen table drinking Jewel tea, trying to figure out a way to show Daddy a thing or two. Mother's vice was tea with lots of sugar and lemon; any kind of alcohol "made bubbles" in her nose. Daddy seldom took a drink either, and in fact had liquor in the house only when one of his brothers came to visit.

As it happened, one of his brothers had just left, so Mother and her friend Martha devised a plan: Martha would come to our house and help Mother put the kids to bed, then they would go into the kitchen and get the bottle of Bourbon from under the counter and sprinkle it all over themselves. Mother would pretend she'd passed out on the sofa. When they heard Daddy coming home, Martha would stand over her, trying to revive her, all the while sobbing incoherent and vile things about men, principally Daddy. When Daddy came home he'd think they'd been on a drinking binge. That should fix his wagon! But Daddy, shot through with remorse, came home a little earlier than they expected. When he banged in the back door, what he saw was Mother and Martha standing in the kitchen passing a Bourbon bottle back and forth, Martha laughing and pouring the liquid down Mother's collar, wiping it on her cheeks and lips; Mother hooting as she sprinkled Bourbon in Martha's hair.

Daddy stood there with his jaw hanging, thinking they'd both lost their minds. "What is going on here!" he shouted so loud that he nearly tumbled me off the stairs, where I had been huddling in my owl-and-pussy-cat nightie, watching this act with round eyes. At the sound of Daddy's voice, Martha stood petrified, but Mother turned around with eyes crossed, and a goofy expression on her face. She held out the bottle to Daddy with a big grin. "Here, have thum," she said. "It'll take your mind off killing yourthelf, tho I can do it for you!" Then she and Martha burst into giggles.

Daddy surveyed the scene. A great cloud of judgment hung in the air. Then Daddy stomped off to bed, hitting each stair extra hard, just three steps behind me as I skedaddled as fast as I could. Oddly, I never heard a word about this strange occurrence.

Nobody ever talked about anything unpleasant or strange. But I took it all in anyway—like the time Daddy whipped the newspaper from under my nose while I was reading the most horrifying story about a little girl named Suzanne Dregnan who was kidnapped, murdered and cut into small pieces and put into a sewer in Chicago. I was not yet in the first grade, but I was riveted to the story in the newspaper I'd spread out on the living room floor.

"Let's go bake cookies, girls," Mother sang out, and led me and toddler Ellie off to the kitchen.

Another time, Mother got so irked with Daddy that she went off to see her sister in Lubbock, leaving Daddy to take care of the kids. A week was a long, long time without Mother. Daddy couldn't cook popovers, or braid hair, or iron blouses or anything.

POPOVERS DADDY CAN'T COOK

1 leveled-off cup of flour	Dash of nutmeg
1 tablespoon soft butter	1/4 cup granulated sugar
1 cup milk	1/4 cup powdered sugar
1/2 teaspoon salt	

A good supply of brown paper bags, some big, some little. Turn the big ones inside out to lay on the counter, so the clean side is up. Keep the clean side on the inside of the little ones.

Blend first five ingredients together. Then drop the batter by teaspoon into heavy saucepan of deep-fry oil. Watch the little balls until they look brown on the bottom. With a wooden spoon pop them over, so the top half becomes brown too. Be careful not to splash the hot oil when you pop these critters over, because it will pop up on your wrists and burn little round circles and bring tears to your eyes. Your arms will itch, and you'll want to scratch them all the time, and they'll get infected, and you'll have to wear gauze on your arms up to your elbows and look like a freak.

When browned all over, the popovers should be placed on brown paper bags laid on the counter, which will soak up the oil. While popovers are draining, take two small paper bags. Put granulated sugar in one and powdered sugar in the other. Put two or three popovers in each bag at a time, and shake the bag gently, to coat them with sugar. Shake off excess sugar and place popovers on plate for breakfast or a treat.

When it was about time for mother's return, Ellie and I decided to bake a cake and decorate it for her. We spent all day in the kitchen making a vinegar chocolate cake from scratch, icing it in white and writing on the top with blue frosting: *Welcome Home, Mother*! But Mother was a little late, and the natives got restless. First, the boys took little slices from the edges of the cake. Then they took a little more. Then, since Mother wasn't there yet, they started eating backwards into the message: *Mother* went first; then *Home*. I told them to stop there, because it was okay to leave just *Welcome*; Mother'd get the message. So we put it under the cake cover and went off to play, leaving the pans and cups and beaters and things to soak in the sink. When Mother came home and we started to show her the cake we'd made for her, we lifted the aluminum cake cover, and thanks to the boys—who'd snuck back in and helped themselves—all it said on the top was *We*, and there was only about one bite of cake left. Little rivulets of blue frosting ran down the front of the kitchen counter.

Mother took off her hat, hugged us, closed her eyes for a moment like *I don't believe what I'm seeing,* and went off to her bedroom, ignoring Daddy, who was sitting in his chair reading the Ruidoso racing form. I never heard any more about that welcome home surprise, but then, I knew better than to bring it up.

Probably my mother hadn't really been overjoyed to have four kids in six years. Once or twice, I'd heard her say, "I might as well not have a name. I'm nothing but your father's wife, and the mother of you four children. One day I'm going to make up a name for myself that is just *mine!*" In a sneaky way, she did. She dropped her first and middle names, Margaret Ellen, and began using her initials, ME, which she wrote in capital letters. Later, she published a book of poetry under that title, *The Best of ME.* She never made a big statement about changing her name, she just did it.

During my pregnancy, my family tried to make me feel better about being fat and ugly and stuck in Thalia. Mother made a stuffed baby doll to sit on the window sill, and Mollie made a charming quilt and curtains with pictures of old fashioned toys for the baby's room. Daddy painted a little chest and bed white, and strung colorful toys across the bed. I thanked them, but I became more and more depressed. I didn't know what a baby was; I couldn't remember the last time I'd seen one up close. It must have been when I was in high school and baby-sat with Mother's friends' kids sometimes for fifty cents an hour. But basically I liked to baby-sit with one family, the man who owned the bank, because he had a whole roomful of books different from those at home. I would rock the baby and read all night. That's when I read *Red Flannels and Green Ice,* all about how Eskimo men give their wives to any guest who comes into the igloo, and *The Wayward Bus,* and *I the Jury,* and *Sironia, Texas*—a story so long and shocking it took two books to tell it. These were books Mother wouldn't have been happy to know I was reading, and Daddy—well, he would have popped out in three different colors.

I always got myself very busy if someone called who had toddlers. You couldn't read and watch toddlers at the same time.

And that was all I knew about babies, except that they were something grown-ups had after they got tired of doing everything else they wanted to do. It had never occurred to me that I'd have a baby at all, much less before I'd done all the things I'd planned in my fantasies. I'd never even played with dolls much.

Greg and I hadn't had a single conversation about babies before we got married. It hadn't occurred to me even to think about such a thing, and later when I asked Greg why he'd never mentioned it, he said, "Well, I wanted to have children as soon as possible, and I just assumed you would too. Men need to make sure they can, you know, and besides you know how I like the little devils."

I just knew I wasn't normal. Greg kept telling me that I should be thrilled to be fulfilling myself as a woman, but I didn't think I'd even fulfilled myself as a girl yet. He just said "Grow up, then." I figured that about eighty percent of the time, being married was miserable. I said this to my mother one day, and she retorted absent-mindedly, "Well, I wouldn't put it quite that high." Did she mean put the percentage quite that high? Or rate it quite that high? I got busy with my journal and forgot to ask. In my journal, I tried to write poems and stories to tell myself how I felt about what was supposed to be such a monumentally satisfying event in a woman's life. Once I decided to write a poem about having a baby, so I wrote down "Having a Baby," then I couldn't think of anything at all to say. I scratched through it and wrote:

GOING TO PARIS

I won't be the first
American in Paris, and I will not
dance in the street, but I will
climb the Eiffel Tower in my ballet shoes
and eat strawberries on the Champs Elysee
and leave one perfect red rose for Paris
to remember me by.

I felt guilty because what I really wanted to do was be thin again, and not throw up all the time, and eat strawberries in Paris. Once when I told Mother that I felt guilty, she sat me down and put her hands on my shoulders: "Guilt is a coward's defense," she said. "*Never* feel guilty. Do the best you can with what you have. Take the hand you're dealt, play it the best you can, then forget it. Sleep well at night, and *do not feel guilty*. Guilt can destroy you. And furthermore, don't ever try to make someone *else* feel guilty! That's the worst trap there is."

This was about as heavy a sermon as I had ever got out of my mother, and I still remember the passion with which she gave it, along with a few other mini-sermons about how the words *ought* and *should* had no business being in the English language since they caused more grief than not.

After Mother's speech, I tried to write a poem about guilt:

GARAGE SALE

All that moldy accumulation
of conventional wisdom
is gone now.
And my clean house now
leaves me room
to grow
my own.

I wasn't sure this said what I meant, but maybe I could fix it later, as the idea I wanted to convey came clear.

I could no longer fit into anything I had, and my new husband, in a gesture of kindness, went and spent too much money on a fine maternity dress that I had no place to wear. I couldn't figure out what you do with skirts with big holes where the stomachs should be. Maternity clothes were droopy and looked like aprons, just the kind of things I'd vowed I'd never climb into. They were not at all like little black velvet jackets to put in your desk drawer in anticipation of a night on the town in New York City or black turtle-necks to wear in Greenwich Village. I knew this was the end of my life. Everything had gone downhill so fast, and I didn't even know why. Every once in a while I saw Sonny on the street, and he just looked at me like *what happened to you*? I wished I knew.

Pushing my heavy body down the aisle, I preceded Greg into the picture show to see *Breakfast at Tiffany's*. On the screen before me, larger than life itself, was the person I wanted most of all to be: Audrey Hepburn. As Holly Golightly, Audrey had a trim figure, a black dress, and lived in New York City. Throughout the picture show, tears ran down the sides of my face and formed little puddles on the pillow of my stomach. At one place in the picture show, a man wants to marry Holly and says to her: "You belong to me." But Holly says back: "People don't belong to people. You can't put them in a cage." When Holly let her little cat go to run off into the city and be free, I began to sniffle so loudly that I had to leave the theater. Greg thought I was crying about the runaway kitty that would probably starve or get run over without anyone to take care of her.

By the time I was three weeks overdue, I'd gained fifty pounds, and my ankles were so swollen I could hardly walk. "Strutted," offered Mollie helpfully. "That's normal. Don't worry." I weighed one-hundred-and-seventy pounds! *Nobody weighed one-hundred-and-seventy pounds who wasn't a halfback*! Even Daddy had a startled expression when he looked at me. Mother and Mollie said it was okay; with the first baby you always gain weight, and so on and so forth, just wait until the second. This was not a cheering notion to me. I thought it was about time to slit my fat little wrists.

Greg kept telling me how disappointed he was in me. "You're supposed to be ecstatic. Girls are supposed to love this," he said over and over. "What's wrong with you?"

"Well, I *am* ecstatic," I spit out at him one day. "Ecstatic means 'beside yourself.' Go look it up!"

In desperation, I drank castor oil, which I'd read in *McCalls* would make the baby come. In the lobby of the hospital, the interns put me on a gurney and rolled me toward the elevator. My hands reached back over my head for Mother, but no one was allowed to come with me. Later, Greg could come to the labor room, they'd said. But as I lay flat on my back, looking back over my shoulder watching my family recede, first Greg, then Daddy, then Mollie, then Mother, I was terrified. This was the very first thing in my life I'd had to do all by myself. Nobody could help me, and there was no turning back. I thought of an old church camp song: "So high you can't get over it;

so low, you can't get under it; so wide, you can't get around it; you have to come in at the door."

This door was the elevator to the "prep room," whatever that was, and only I could go through it. Tears squeezed out of my eyes and rolled into my ears. Giddy with anxiety, I gave a pitiful little laugh and started humming a song they used to sing on the bus in high school: "I get tears in my ears from lyin' on my back in my bed while I cry over you." This was not at all the way I had planned to have my courage tested. *Pooh, pooh, pooh!* It wasn't supposed to be this. Any girl could have a baby; I had planned to do something special.

Labor was long and terrifying. Sometime during the tenth hour, Greg leaned his head against the bed-rail to rest and inhaled too much of the ether tied in a packet to my wrist. He fell off the chair and crumpled onto the floor in a dead faint. I called the nurse to scoop him up and send him back to the waiting room.

Sweating, screeching, and railing at the gods, I thought the violence to my body would never stop. I hate it! I hate it! I hate it! Stop Stop Stoooooooopppppp!

After fifteen hours, I expelled from my bruised body a perfect six-pound baby girl. And little Carrie did exactly what Mother had promised: she brought love with her when she joined the world. Carrie was the first baby in our family in a long, long time. She was not an ordinary baby; she was special. And everyone agreed that I had finally done something important. After the first week, I was taking care of her by myself, and I could not believe that anyone could love a baby as fiercely as I loved Carrie. When I was too tired in the night and knew I couldn't possibly get up to nurse her, I did it anyway. When Carrie cried with colic and I couldn't stand it another single minute, I stood it anyway. I did a lot of things anyway—things I was sure I wasn't up to, and I realized that never again—*never again in my whole life*—could I think only of myself.

Back in Thalia, before I married, I used to lie in bed just before going to sleep and repeat a particular conversation of the day, rolling the words and ideas around in my head, trying to make sense of them. Like the time Mollie said that a sign is a reference to something definite, and then Mother said that a symbol was a reference to something indefinite. So a sign would be like a stop sign; seeing it means *stop*, which is something definite. Then what would a red light be? It's not exactly a sign, but it means something definite: *Stop*. So would the red light at the intersection of Main and Center Street be a sign or a symbol? If it's a sign, then what would a symbol of *stop* be? Maybe red, but does red always mean stop? Is that what they mean by indefinite? Maybe signs and symbols are different things depending on how you use them. . . . .

Mollie called such maunderings "brain sit-ups," and they were a way to keep my head muscles a little exercised even when Thalia was so terminally boring I didn't know whether I could stand it one more minute. To help me, Mollie came bearing books like a Greek, meaning that my acceptance of them carried the condition that book reports be delivered to her. It was under her tutelage that I learned the penalties and rewards of intellectual curiosity: when I casually asked the meaning of a word, she sent me directly to the enormous dictionary, which sat on an elevated turntable and held the position of respect that family Bibles held in the houses of my friends. I was instructed not only to report what *that* word meant, but what the words just above and below it meant as well. That usually carried me off in a half-day orgy of reading, for who could stop with *Pott's disease*, when there were *potwalloper, pouchy, poud, pouf,* and *Poughkeepsie* to go? And what was a *pouncet box? A pomander?* An *Ezra Pound? A pousse-cafe?*

My head swirled with words. When all I could see from my bedroom window was flat, cracked, red clay and tortured mesquites, words became exotic dancers before my eyes, the sensation of forming them in the back of my throat could evoke a spine-shiver, and my heart would beat a little faster as I discovered layers of sounds and meanings leading back to Greece and Rome, Phoenicia and France, the sounds of the word before me echoing behind. Words could be dazzling dancers or birds on the backs of which I could ride, like Thumbelina, to a fantasyland far from the desert outside my door. Standing on the little stool, I would roll words around in my mouth: beautiful words like azalea, saltcellar, mellifluous. Ugly words like slug, grunt and scrofulous. Funny words, like gabble, bumptious, troglodyte, lop. Besides falling in love with the music of words, I learned, in writing the book reports for Mollie—a critical grandmother when it came to books, ladyhood, and posture—that actions have consequences and are seldom pure. Mother, too, frequently argued that there was no such thing as a purely unselfish decision:

"If you do something, it's because you want to do it above all alternatives, even when it appears to be an unselfish act. You like to *see* yourself doing that unselfish act. Or doing that act makes you *like yourself* better. There's nothing pure; all motives are mixed." From her I learned, with many examples, the seven (at least) types of ambiguity, and the inescapable paradoxes that riddle our lives.

It was years before I considered that my mother talked to me as an adult because there were so few adults around for her to talk to. But these confabulations tended to complicate my thinking and give me a severe case of suspended judgment. They also made me appear a little odd in Thalia. On the outside I was all convention, thanks to Daddy; on the inside, all imagination, thanks to Mother. Classmates sometimes told me that I didn't live in the "real world," but this made no sense to me. I thought living in the real world meant transforming it—at least it meant that in Thalia, a place you couldn't stand to be in unless you transformed it. Transforming was a simple process: if the real outside world was not to your liking, then you just dipped inside your head and made it into something that was. If the iris bulbs you planted, chipping away at the hard earth, didn't bloom, you figured out a way to make them do so. You just looked out the bedroom window and made something up:

IRIS

The messenger of the gods is
asleep, buried in the earth
under my window sill.
Someday soon she will awake smiling as in a miracle—
her purple wings reflecting
off my deep blue eyes.

When I read my poem, I could see my iris in living color and didn't need it to be blooming outside my window. Mother had told me that just as you can have great adventures by sitting in a chair reading a book, you can also have exciting things happen by just lying around thinking. Nobody could put hobbles on your mind, even in Thalia, she said, and she demonstrated that every day.

Being different on the outside than you are on the inside makes you feel like you're in drag all your life. It's like having a split self—cleaved down the middle. Once, when I finally made it to graduate school, I overheard one professor say to another: "Jacy looks like a girl, but she writes like a man." I'd never quite known what to make of that remark, except that on paper I'd always felt honest feelings and observations could be legitimated, whereas in everyday, walking, talking life you pretty much had to hedge your bets for fear of shocking the heels off even those closest to you. *Especially* those closest to you. When writing articles, you could say things like "Madame Bovary *c'est moi*," but you'd better not confront your husband and kids with that, if you knew what was good for you. But, like a gay person, you sooner or later have to come out of the closet and say *to hell with it. I will be what I am no matter how complicated that is or how raw it rubs.*

Tonight at dinner on the Mill Pond, for example, I'd found myself having contradictory feelings, and forced to declare myself on a delicate subject. The conversation had turned to children, as a dinner guest, only a dozen years younger than I, mentioned her five-year-old son, born after six miscarriages.

"He's so very precious because we didn't think we'd ever have him," Chris had said. "But in retrospect, it's good we waited. I see so many young women at Stevie's playschool who are struggling not only with children, but with bills, and unstable husbands."

I told her that it's hard for me to believe now, but when I was her age I had kids in their twenties—one married, a couple in college.

Chris stared at me. "My god, how did you do it? *Nobody* really understands what that means until you have a kid of your own."

"I know," I said. "I remember writing a letter to my mother years ago, telling her I saw her in a whole different light after I had my own kids. And I did; I was astounded. I had no idea what she had to put up with. Four kids in six years? How could she do it?"

"That's what I just asked you," Chris laughed.

"Well, I had no choice—nor did my mother. You do a lot of things when you have no choice, I guess. You find out what you're made of, too."

Then Chris asked the tough question: "Would you do it that way again? Have kids when you're that young, now that women have a choice?"

I looked off into the distance. "Well, if you'd asked me then— especially during the first ten years—I would've said *you've got to be out of your mind to have kids when you're that young!* You soon *would* be anyway. It was such a wrench, you know, going from a naive, spoiled girl to being a mother overnight, from thinking of yourself as the *principal star, the major player,* to becoming a part of the *background scenery.* My own childhood had been built on daydreams, rehearsals for the future. But in my mid-twenties, with three young children, I came to find that even my daydreams had dried up. All my talents for transforming the world had fled. I couldn't imagine a life different from the one that was making me so miserable. I felt sick, blind-sided, depressed. But I had, for better or worse, the same kind of tight control my mother did. I remember her saying to me about her kid years, 'Sometimes I wished I could have just gone stark, raving mad and be carried off, so someone would have to take care of *me* for a change. But I just couldn't let myself do it.'"

It *had* been a miserable time. I walked around performing duties, tears clinging to the edges of my eyes. My body carried the same ache when I rose in the morning as it did when I lay down at night. I felt like a rat in a maze. To fit in this Procrustean bed of marriage and motherhood, I'd cut off my limbs, principally my head. I couldn't think above the din, had no time to read, was bone-weary all the time. The most stimulating hour of the day was "Shari Lewis and Lamb Chop."

Still, I often performed my chores like some automaton on speed: *make the beds fill the dishwasher mop up the milk find the boots pull on the snowsuits pull off the snowsuits warm the soup change the diaper. . . . .* like I was trying to find some activity worthy of my full attention. If I could just get these details out of the way, my life could begin.

"But," I said to Chris. "You asked me *now*. Not then. *Now,* I've got all these great grown up kids, and I still have a lot of energy left."

Funny how I'd finally escaped the trap: One day in the backyard I watched my kids playing, running around. They were cute and darling, but cunning and clever. Each was such an individual. Their personalities were so sharply defined and so clearly their own. One would bop the other, and the other would bop back, and they would run and cry and laugh and dance around and scream and throw things. As I watched them, I saw for the first time what real little people I had created out of my own body. They were not controllable by me or by any other force. They would be what they would be. I could revel in them, but I couldn't let them live my life for me. It would be foolish of me to hang my identity on whirlwinds. I was merely their caretaker for awhile.

At that point I began to relax about my role and whether I was performing it adequately. It was futile to think I could live through them. If I were to have anything of my own, I would have to do it myself, quite apart from them.

Soon I found a nearby college and enrolled. I decided that I would stay in school until I knew everything about everything—or at least until I had graduated from "Lamb Chop."

What strange things crawl out when you turn over the stones of history. I hear my Mother's voice: "I don't understand these women who complain that their arms ache to hold a baby; my arms ache *from holding* babies!" It had taken me years to understand that Mother had been caught in the same talcum trap as I.

Timing is everything. I envy and actively support the choice that Chris and other young women have today. I envy their maturity and security, their ability to negotiate better with the fathers of their children. But then, on the other hand, I wouldn't have wanted to be a new mother like Chris at forty-three. *Forty-three? God!* At that point in my life I had just about dug out from under motherhood and established a career. Either way, if you want a family, it's a struggle. Even marriage is a struggle if you don't have a *self* first. Get a self! Why can't this simple information be passed along like family recipes, or downloaded like the gene for blue eyes or auburn hair?

I recall a wedding several years back during which the bride and groom carried lighted candles down separate aisles, lit one large candle, and then blew out their own. *No, no!* I'd shouted under my breath. *Don't blow out your own candles!* The symbolism beneath the lovely little ritual was appalling. One big fat candle does not a couple make. Besides, when there's only one candle, I know whose it is—and it *isn't* the bride's.

Who would have *wanted* to be married to such a cipher as I was then? I wonder, recalling the days after the wedding trip to Dallas. ("Please don't call it a *honeymoon*," Mollie had said, heading for the dictionary. "Where does that silly word come from, anyway? That is the most saccharine description of this experience I have ever heard.") And how insane it was to have a child, when I was still a child myself.

Yet, I know now that this child made me grow up in a way that nothing else—college degree, *Great Books*, husband, strawberries in Paris—could ever have done. As a child myself, I discovered that I could do what was required of me, even when I didn't want to, even when I didn't know how, even when I was terrified of making a mistake. I'd done it myself, and nobody could take that away from me. I recall a line from a book by a poet who has overcome innumerable hardships: "That's how we get wise," Nancy Mairs wrote, "by taking on in ignorance the tasks we would never later dare to do."

If I'd had a choice, would I have chosen to stay a silly, self-absorbed girl forever? Dared to make it? And knowing what I did not know at nineteen, would I have deliberately started a family at a later age? Would I have passed up the chance to do something all by myself that nobody could take away? Would I have passed up the chance to begin getting wise?

PART II

4

One does not discover
new land without
consenting to lose
sight of the shore for
a very long time.
—Andre Gide

F·L·I·G·H·T

MY YOUNGER SON PAUL dreams of ships bobbing aimlessly on endless oceans. I dream of an enormous house with many rooms, all of them filled with children calling my name. These are recurring dreams. We both record our dreams with regularity and discuss them on the phone, though we live on opposite coasts. Does Paul's dream suggest insecurity, lack of direction; is it evocative of his loss of a stable point—a home? Does my dream suggest the interiors of the many homes I have made for my family all over the country and the many needs of children I have been called on to fulfill?

Paul and I have a special bond: we ran away from home together. I knew even as we were running that everyone experiences two childhoods: our own and that of the memories of our parents. But I knew as well that nothing has a stronger psychological influence on children than the unlived lives of the parents. Jung wrote that somewhere, and I believe it. Moreover, I was aware that I had a passionate unlived life of which I didn't want my children to be victims. But they have been anyway—and of my lived life as well.

Because I'd been frightened too early by reading *Oedipus*, I used to say I'd never go to a fortune teller. The idea of learning your fate in advance was scary: you do that and then, watch out! you march right into it. What a trap. You have no more control than an insect marching resolutely into a Roach Motel. You check in, you don't check out. As I get older, I realize that fate is just how life turns out for you, and there's no way to separate that from your character; one is the by-product of the other. But you never know which is which.

I used to talk about these things with Mollie and Mother years ago when the three of us would lie across Mother's big bed upstairs in Thalia and try to sort out the mysterious ways of the universe. There was just one rule: you couldn't be afraid to ask *any* question. I asked a lot over the years:

"Why do people think they can make you do what they want by scaring you? Why don't they just ask you, please, and tell you why it should be done?"

"If there wasn't such a thing as bad, how would we know what was *good*?"

"Why can't girls go without shirts like boys?"

"How long does it take the light to get from the stars to us?"

"Where did Adam and Eve's sons find wives when there weren't any more people invented then? Did they marry apes, and that's the missing link?"

Mother had a favorite question: "If you found out tomorrow there was no God, would you change the way you behave?" Mollie said no, and I said yes.

"I behave myself because it's the right thing to do, and if you behave, you don't violate other people. I don't need God to tell me that," Mollie said firmly.

I said, "Well, in Sunday School Mrs. McDaniel said that God is watching you all the time, so you better be careful. If He weren't, I think I'd be a lot more relaxed."

"What do you mean by *relaxed*," Mother wanted to know.

"I mean if God weren't watching, I wouldn't go to Methodist Sunday School anymore. I'd go over to the Holy Rollers because they look like they have a lot more fun."

The Methodist Church in Thalia did promote a fairly tyrannical God. I recall being presented at age thirteen or so with a pledge card to sign that alcohol would not touch my lips during the coming calendar year. I signed it for three or four years, since I couldn't stand the taste of the stuff, anyway. But eventually, in a pretentious fit of rebellion, when the plate came by with the pledge cards in it, I grabbed one, crumpled it up, and threw it under the pew unsigned. I hoped old busy-body Frannie Tucker saw me. That would show her! That church was filled with too many little old ladies trying to make ice cream socials out of everything, when all we wanted to do was square dance in the basement of the church, an activity they saw as the work of the Devil.

The Methodist God may have been omniscient in His earthly forms of Mrs. McDaniel and Frannie Tucker, but He wasn't as ferocious as the Baptist God. The Baptist God wouldn't let you read some of the best books or dance anywhere! He was a lower-class God anyway. The only people who went to the Baptist church were newcomers to Thalia, who'd only been around for thirty or forty years.

When I was still in high school, I'd done a little theological research by climbing the roof of a nearby house with Duane and hanging over the side to see what *really* went on with the Holy Rollers across the street from the Baptist Church. We drank Cokes up there with peanuts pushed down into the bottle neck, and told Little Moron jokes, but all we saw was a bunch of arm-waving and shouting, as far as I could tell. Still, it beat sitting in a pew listening to the preacher drone on.

The First Methodist Church was always getting a new preacher who was on his way up to somewhere, or on his way down from somewhere, but they never seemed to get one that thought Thalia was somewhere. And with its pale Apostle's Creed and sprinkling on the heads of crying babies, it wasn't nearly as interesting as the Baptist Church. What the preachers lacked in inspiration there, they made up in the dunking. When they raised the curtain in the back of the church so you could see the dunking place and the people—these were grown-up people—in their little white robes getting pushed down there, it got more colorful. Once when I visited with a friend Patsy, there was a giant fat man that Pastor Pile couldn't quite get under the water, so he put his hand in the middle of the man's huge stomach and swooshed real hard. The man went down, but his toes stuck up. When I got home I asked Mother if he would be like Achilles and have a weak big toe for the rest of his life.

Kinder, kirk, kuchen—in whatever order. That was a woman's life in Thalia. And there was no exit. I never saw a man do one lick of housework, or a woman start a business, unless it was a beauty shop in the back of her house—real estate owned by her husband. Even

Aunt Celie, who ran the ranch because her husband was incapable of it, also had responsibility for kids, kitchen and Sunday School.

Housework. A no-brainer. I wonder why anyone thought it needed to be such a big deal, expanded into a full-time job? But, like most women of my generation, I succumbed for a number of years to the myth that *only I* could do this mystical job and do it right. And, in fact, it *was* my job to do it. I can remember the days when I'd wash eight loads, and the only thing of mine in the whole shebang was a pair of underpants. I'd noticed this as I put everything away before Greg got home. At that time, I'd thought it a badge of honor to show how easily, how effortlessly, how *gracefully* I could do all the housework. I did it so well you'd hardly notice. I'd iron Greg's shirts and have them hanging Rinso-white clean in his closet before he could even miss them. *Rinso-white! Rinso-white! Happy little washday song!*

What a crock! Why didn't I let them all know how grim it was, how mindless and even lonely; how much I hated housework? If everyone had pitched in, no one would have to think of it as "a job." It would just be routine maintenance with everyone responsible for a round of it.

Last month I was visiting Carrie, who now lives in The Woodlands near Houston and has two little kids of her own. Carrie, folding laundry on the bed, was getting ready to put it away. I stood between her and the dresser with my hands out like a traffic cop.

"No. Leave it out for Jack to see. He should be aware of all the things you do around this house—as well as make a very good living in your *professional* job, I might add. Women put themselves at a disadvantage by being so efficient and thorough that it looks like nobody has broken a sweat. Leave the stuff out. Let them see it. Don't let them think a Tooth Fairy runs this household."

Carrie looked at me as if summoning vast patience, but she walked away, leaving the neat piles of clothes on the bed.

How many washing machines, how many clotheslines, how many dryers had I had? And how many homes had I established in how many places? I'd *forgotten* more pieces of furniture than most people ever *owned* in a lifetime.

True to his word, Greg had taken a job out of Thalia shortly after Carrie was born. It wasn't Paris, but at least Chillicothe, Texas, was someplace besides Thalia. In Chillicothe, we had a house so small that only one person could get into the bedroom at a time, if the other wasn't already in bed. And the foundation of the house sloped so that when Carrie put her toys on the floor in one corner of the kitchen, they immediately slid to the far corner. Nevertheless, I painted the old linoleum navy blue and used a sponge dipped in white paint to make splashy designs on the floor. I made blue-checked curtains and painted the old table and chairs white. Then I found a second-hand black sofa and a boomerang coffee table, screwed together black industrial shelving for my books, and tried to do something about the shower that Daddy called "an adventure" the first time he came to visit. After that, there wasn't much else to do but play with Carrie and read. I was into *Aquinas I* by this time, having, I must admit, decided to put off *Euclid, Archimedes* and their buddies to a later date.

One day while I was ironing and watching TV, I saw an engrossing play by Rod Serling about a rural Southern family in the Civil War. The plot was so simple, but so moving—basically an anti-war play—that I couldn't get it out of my head. I nearly scorched Greg's shirt when it occurred to me that I might be able to get a group of students together in the high school and help them put on that play, since it had only a few characters, no location shifts, and didn't require a lot of fancy props. So I called the TV station and found out Rod Serling's address. I wrote him a letter requesting permission to stage the play in Chillicothe, Texas. Well, why not? I still had some of that old Jacy *hubris* buried somewhere, despite being a boring wife and mom who had never set foot in Greenwich Village or Paris, France. To my surprise, Serling wrote right back with permission and included a play script. I was elated. *Nobody in Chillicothe, Texas, had ever received a real live letter from Rod Serling before!*

The drama students, whom Greg helped direct, while I did the sets and makeup, were so good that they won the Texas Interscholastic League competitions all the way to state, something they'd never done before or since, and Rod himself sent us a letter of congratulations. It wasn't a *football* state championship, which would have been celebrated louder and longer, but what the hell, this was Texas.

Many years later I happened to meet Mr. Serling, and he told me something I never forgot: That piece about the Civil War was one of the last period pieces he'd done. Shortly after that, he quite deliberately moved into space, into aliens, into *The Twilight Zone* for his dramatic location and persona. The reason he shifted to these kinds of plays during the fifties, he said, is that they offered a way to write radical political and social commentary disguised in futuristic garb, which he could not get away with writing straight during the McCarthy era. I never watched old re-runs of his work in quite the same way after that.

Greg kept getting better and better jobs, so we moved from one small West Texas town to the next bigger one. I found staying home intensely dull, once I'd painted the next house pearl gray and made red and black fake Mondrian-patterned drapes and laid gray carpet myself. So I sprayed clay pots white and filled them with red geraniums to set all around, then looked to see what else I could paint or fix or make. I was becoming my mother—always looking for something to keep my imagination ginning along. "See what you can make out of nothing," Mother often said. "You'll find it's a lot more fun than just going out and buying things."

Back in Thalia, Mother and Daddy hadn't much believed in buying toys—beyond bikes, dolls, and a Lincoln Log set or two. What they believed in was resourcefulness. Because of that, we kids found an infinite number of things we could do with a ball of string and a stick. If we begged for something we didn't have, we were given an hour to come up with a reasonable facsimile. If we whined that there was nothing to do, we were told to find something quick, or it would be found for us. Since we knew that to be an oblique reference to *work*, by some miracle we plucked something to do out of thin air. "Be self-sufficient," "rely on your inner resources," and "make the most of available resources" were incantations uttered so often that our eyes rolled at the sound of the first syllable of any one of them.

One rainy day when we complained there was nothing to do in this dumb hick town, Mother suggested that we play checkers. We thought this was a swell idea but informed her that she'd overlooked the minor detail that we had no checkers. "Of course you do," said Mother. "Look in the broom closet." The broom closet held only a broom. But by the end of the day, with Mother's instructions, we had sawed disks from the broom handle, dipped them in red and black paint, and blocked out with the paint on a slab of leftover plywood the squares for a checkerboard. I don't think we ever got around to playing checkers—a pretty dumb game anyway. The real game, as Mother knew, was making something new from ordinary old materials.

I stenciled drums and dolls in a blue border around Carrie's nursery and decorated an old trunk for a toy box. Fortunately, before I could start dressing Carrie like a Barbie doll, I found a job as a reporter on the local weekly newspaper, *The Olton Enterprise.* I loved the work and soon had my own column. I could write anything I wanted. The editor's column was called *The Cracker Barrel,* so he suggested that I call mine *The Cracker Crumbs.* I was so delighted to be writing something that actual people would actually read that I didn't care what he called it. It was years before I gave a second, appalled, thought to the name he'd given my first professional writing effort.

I wrote funny things about family life, small town politics, local history and architecture—anything that struck me as interesting. Once I wrote about Miss Kykendall, my old piano teacher who called herself "an unclaimed blessing," and in whose stuffy little house even music was a thing imprisoned behind black bars on the page.

In another column, called "Take Me Out to the . . . . Oh Just Take Me Out," I wrote a TV script in which *Master* is sprawled out in the living room, while *Slave* is trying to vacuum.

Master: What in the world are you doing?
Slave: Just vacuuming, Sir.
Master: In the middle of a ball game? Are you crazy or something?
Slave: Yes Sir, I guess so, Sir. (*Exit downstage*)
Master: (*To Heiress*) Move over baby. No. Over to the left . . . no no the other way. What? Well that way is *right.* No, you moved the *right* way, but it's called *left* . . . hey hey look at 'em, look at 'em. He stole another one. That little dickens Apparichio can get away with murder. That's 51 out of 62 he's stolen. Hey. Hey did you see that!

Slave: (Enter upstage right) Huh? *(Exit downstage left)*

Master: Did you see that man run? Boy! Watch it . . look at that . . . he's loose again . . Aww, I missed it. Baby, can't you sit down so Daddy can see. The TV. Daddy's trying to see the ball game. Now move your . . watch the coffee . . Watch it! Oh, now see what you've done. Go tell Mamma to bring something to get the mess off the carpet. Run on! Right now RUN ON . . . . *(Heiress exits weeping)*

Slave: (Enter stage right with damp cloth. Goes about business on hands and knees) Isn't that a little loud, Sir?

Master: Naw, naw. I gotta hear this. Look at that! Got some coffee? More coffee.

Slave: (Exit downstage)

Master: (To Heiress) No, don't touch it . . I said *don't touch it* . . . . Oh . . . for heaven's sake. *(Loudly, to Slave)*: *Would you come get your child, she turned the set off!!!!!!!*

The play went on much longer. When I showed it to Greg, he laughed and thought it was funny. What did he know?

Back in Thalia, Mother had told me that the only way a housewife can stay sane at all is to set aside some time *every single day to do just exactly what she wants to do*—something for herself, something she enjoys. While I was writing my columns I felt—for the very first time in my life—that I should not be doing something else. Though I had kept diaries as a girl in Thalia to tell myself what I thought about things, I discovered in my twenties that writing also kept me from going a little mad. After that, I was never without a pen and notebook.

Greg belonged to a lot of organizations, and every couple of weeks I had to entertain. I got tired of cooking, so once I bought about two dozen frozen chicken pot pies, took them out of their little foil tins, and dumped them upside down into a big roaster. When the dish was about done, I added a few peas and a few herbs, and *Voila!*, served on my best wedding-gift Lennox with a sprig of parsley I'd grown in a pot, this dish was the talk of the party. I had a hard time keeping a straight face when people asked for the recipe, which I of course refused to give on the principle that I didn't divulge old family secrets. Mother loved it and vowed she'd try it.

JACY'S SECRET OLD FAMILY RECIPE

At the supermarket get about twenty frozen chicken pot pies. Watch for the ads: Sometimes you can find them ten for a dollar. (Circa 1960.) Get an old roaster—the kind that's dark blue and has speckles on it—and grease it real good. Take the frozen pies out of their foil tins and dump them upside down in the roaster. If you want to be fancy, you can layer them like a bricklayer does, sort of overlapping the edges. Cook for however long the instructions say on the directions on the back of the package. (You will probably have to reach back into the garbage can and get a package to see.) Cook it that long, but multiply that by about fifteen or twenty. (You'll have to experiment with this.)

When everything in that roaster has risen a good five inches or so, it's about done. At this point scatter on top about 1 pkg. frozen peas and about 1 pkg. frozen carrots (optional). You can cut up a little celery on it too. Cook about another minute. Let it cool just long enough so it's not soupy. Then serve it with a silver ladle (about two dips) on your very best china, and put a little dab of parsley on each plate.

This dish will serve forty at a women's luncheon. (If you want to serve this to men, allow two pot pies per serving and use different plates, like Melmac. If you have a problem, call me.)

At this time, my back began to give me trouble. I was seventy pounds thinner than I had been when Carrie was born. ("Jacy, dear, what *are* you doing to yourself?" Grandmother Mollie scolded when she came for a visit.) By this time, my cheeks sucked in all by themselves, and my clothes hung off me as if I were a wire hanger. People were giving Greg a hard time at work, as they always did anyone who had ideas, and I'd begun to feel tired.

A trip to the doctor confirmed that I was pregnant again, and the baby's weight was distributed wrong. The pain in my back increased so I had to go to the hospital for two weeks of traction. When I came home, I had to lie in bed with a twenty-five-pound weight on each foot for a good part of the day. Greg would put me in the weight contraption in the morning and settle Carrie to play around me until he came home at noon to release me from the weights. Once, when the phone rang, Carrie picked it up and told the caller: "Daddy tied Mommie to the bed and went to work." Much as it hurt to laugh, I couldn't help it, thinking the caller must wonder what kind of sick games the school principal was up to with his wife.

Spring in West Texas was a blast. Literally. Whirlwinds picked schoolchildren off the playground and tossed them in the air. Then, the big one came. A tornado! I lay in bed with weights on my feet, Carrie playing beside me. I grabbed Carrie as I heard it hit the back part of the house and rip off the attached garage and storage shed. Then I heard another ear-splitting roaarrr! and . . .

Nobody has ever been able to explain how tornadoes can ram straws through telephone poles, or demolish an entire house but leave the door frame standing. Nobody has ever been able to explain how my old friend Janine in Wichita Falls once managed with her two young sons to survive a tornado by climbing into a meat locker inside a Safeway that was itself demolished, or how a woman in Jarrell crawled into a bathtub and rode it to safety until it disappeared from under her. And nobody has been able to explain how in a flash I found myself out in the middle of the road that ran by the front of our house with a thirty-pound daughter cushioned tightly against my bosom and fifty pounds of weights still attached to my skinny ankles. No one could figure out how I came to be in that particular spot, for the front part of the house was not torn away, only the back part, and the front door was locked. Later, I came to see this as simply another of the many inexplicable acts of God that changed my life like a wrinkle in time.

Greg planned to use the insurance money to supplement the fellowship he'd received to finish his doctorate in Colorado. In the midst of trying to get the stuff straightened out about the tornado damage to the shed that had housed most of our wedding gifts, I called my mother to tell her we were moving.

Mother had an attitude: "Jacy, you are sick, you are pregnant, you are stressed, you have a child, and you have a job that you love. You do not need to be going thousands of miles away to establish a new home for Greg and Carrie, and to have a new baby. This is not sane behavior."

I cried and complained and said I didn't want to go, but I didn't know what to do, since that's what Greg had decided to do, and so on and so forth. I told Greg I didn't want to go, and that Mother didn't want us to go. Greg said that my mother and I were not running the show, that he knew what was best for his family, and to please get packed. I called Mollie, who said helpfully that a wife belonged beside her husband wherever he was. Greg promised Daddy that he wouldn't drive more than 500 miles a day dragging the U-Haul. Greg also called his own father to come and help him pack, so I wouldn't have to do anything.

Several steamy summer days later when we arrived at the basement apartment in Greeley with the U-Haul, I found that Greg and his father had packed the refrigerator leaving all the food in it, and it was . . . well, you don't want to know. When I looked into it, everything looked back. I threw up in the driveway and wished I were dead.

Clearly I had to find a doctor, so I asked around to the other graduate students' wives. As I waited in the office for Dr. Hammersmith, I read the plaques on his walls and the titles on his book jackets. After a while, the doctor strode in and slammed the door behind him.

"Well, I see you've got yourself in trouble," he said testily. "And I suppose you want me to do something about it."

I was dumbfounded. I didn't know how to reply and simply sank into a chair. Throughout the months that followed, his manner never changed, and I thought I surely must be doing something wrong. The doctor who had delivered Carrie had been an old family friend who held my hand and sponged my forehead. This doctor seemed to enjoy my increasing discomfort.

Why didn't I question the attitude of Hammersmith? Why didn't I simply walk out? That's what I'd do today. How was I so brainwashed as to accept *everything* a man, and especially a doctor, told me? At that time, the other young women I talked to spoke of their doctors as gods: *Doctor said this, Doctor said that*, they parroted. Doctors were extensions of fathers and husbands, and you did what they said. It never occurred to us that we knew our own bodies better than they did.

Flight

How had my mother been able to keep a sense of humor about all this? She had once written a verse about the birth of my brother:

CRUCIAL FUMBLE

She twists and writhes as birth pangs strike
while muffling every groan.
Her mother suffers each new pain
as though it were her own.
His ear is glued to crucial game
on pocket radio.
The nurse checks temperature and pulse
and bustles to and fro.

Her mother knits a last bootee;
she's racing to the wire.
While husband smooths his wife's damp brow,
and stoops down to inquire:
"Hon, does it hurt. Now just be brave,
I know how you must feel."
(It's half-time at the football game,
and his concern is real.)

They start again—the game and pains.
Nurse times a strong contraction.
"How far apart?" her mother asks,
and gasps at the reaction.
While Mother darts a lethal look,
Wife clutches solar plexus,
When, to his life-long shame, he shouts:
"Fourteen to nothing . . . . Texas!"

Mother could always make the most dismal situation funny, but this time she wasn't even trying: She told me she could not come to Colorado for the birth of the new baby. She had the other kids at home, finishing high school, engaged in activities that required her attention, she said. Besides, our relationship at that time was strained. Mother was upset with me for moving so far away from home with

Carrie, and another baby on the way. She was irked with Greg for insisting that we move, and with me for not bucking him.

"If you don't want to go, say so," Mother had said.

"I did," I whined into the phone. "But he won't listen."

"Make him listen. Refuse to go."

"Mother, I can't. I don't know *how*. I've never told him *No* before, and I don't know how to start. I just feel torn up, pulled between you and Daddy, and Greg. I don't want to go. I can't stay. . ."

"Jacy, grow up. Take some responsibility for your choices."

What could Mother mean by that? I didn't *have* any choices. I hadn't chosen to be in this fix to start with. I'd just done what I was supposed to do—what girls *do!* I didn't like anything in my life but Carrie, and I just wanted to take her and run away. But where would I run? How would I live?

Greg wasn't a monster, he was just overbearing and always got his way. He wanted me to remain like the child he'd married: When I asked a question, or raised an objection against him, he would say, "Look, Jacy. I've thought this through for both of us, so you don't have to." That was certainly a far cry from the times when I could ask any question I wanted to of Mother and Mollie. He thought he was saving me a bunch of thinking, but I knew I was regressing. Greg had such a strong personality, I always caved in.

Greg was annoyed with me when I did act like a child, whining and making excuses, but he didn't want me to grow up—if growing up meant I had ideas different from his own. He kept saying that he thought he'd married the *ideal girl*, but I kept disappointing him. *Disappointing him!* I wondered if he wasn't getting me mixed up with a *perfect wife* that he had hidden away somewhere. I thought *he* was supposed to turn into a handsome prince, and instead he'd just turned *me* into a *frog!* What was this disappointing *him* crap? Wasn't *my* disappointment meter running too? Or did that matter?

"I like to have a wife I can put up on a pedestal," Greg said firmly.

"Well, there's not much for me to do three feet off the ground but sit there like a stone, and I didn't sign on to be a statue. Go to the Uffizi if you want that," I retorted, proud of my clever comeback. Usually I had no comeback at all.

Then I thought I should have told him that statues on pedestals didn't fix dinner or change diapers. "Why," I should have said, "don't you just choose one or the other, a princess or a slave? You want both in one person, and I'm not either one!"

But I was tired all the time, and it took too long to argue. Instead, I wept and cursed myself for marrying a man so much older than I— and a teacher to boot. He'd always be the teacher, and I'd always be the student. He would always push me around because he knew more than I did. And besides, that's what the culture demanded. Some day I would find a way to know as much as he did. What had happened to me? This was the place in the plot where I was supposed to be a happy little wife in a happy little Donna Reed dress baking happy little apple pies to set upon the window sill. *Ideal girl, ideal life, ideal phooey!*

To get out of the airless, ugly basement and give Greg room to study, I took Carrie on long walks. We'd have picnics in the park and stroll over to the playground. At the swing set, I overheard a woman pushing a little boy in the swing say that her husband was going to Berkeley for another degree, so she had to find someone to rent their house. I opened a conversation and got the details. The little house in a suburban area was perfect. It had a fenced back yard and a patio with a grill. It was even mostly furnished. We couldn't afford it, though, so we advertised at the university for a couple of college kids to live in the finished basement to help us pay the rent. Phil and Ron signed on.

The delivery room was surreal. After all my pushing and pain, the doctor used the forceps and I felt something rip from my body— a palpable rip I could hear as well as feel. I heard the doctor speaking through a fog:

"The kid doesn't look good, get me some blood."

The nurse replied after a few moments, "Doctor, we don't have any blood." I heard myself screech something, then all went black.

Later, I would lie in the hospital bed wondering why a doctor, who knew I was conscious, would say these words within my hearing? Today, if anyone should ask what words in my entire life were most scorched into my brain, I would say: *"The kid doesn't look good, get me some blood." "Doctor, we don't have any blood."*

The baby boy, born premature and breach with the umbilical cord around his neck, went immediately into the incubator. I asked to see my baby, but the nurses would not bring him. I was sure something was terribly wrong, but when the doctor came in, he just shoved me around roughly and left without saying a word. I cried all day and lay awake all night. Greg, who had seen the baby through the nursery window, assured me that little Ben was okay, simply very small and needed to be left alone for a day or two. But I didn't believe it. Everyone was lying to me, I was sure. Why would the doctor use the forceps on a premature baby? Nothing made sense. I was out of my mind with grief, and my life was a nightmare.

"Something is wrong! Tell me what's wrong!" I wailed over and over. On the third day, when the halls were still and the milk had rushed into my breasts so I could hardly lift my arms, I rolled myself off the high bed and crept down to look in the baby window. But the curtain was drawn. I went back to bed weeping and turned on the nurse light. Nobody came.

The doctor strode in the next afternoon, and I started to tell him how worried I was, but he looked at me with contempt. "What the hell is wrong with you? You bring this on yourself, and then want sympathy from me?" He swung the chart back to the foot of the bed with a clank and left the room.

I was lonesome for Carrie. And I was annoyed with my roommate, who had just produced her fourth child and was in no hurry to go home.

"Take it easy, honey," Rhoda said. "You're going to be home with that kid long enough. You're on a vacation now. Relax." She went back to her paint-by-number picture of a cat on a purple cushion.

On the fourth day, they finally brought my baby to me. His little face was paralyzed on one side, and he weighed scarcely five pounds. Everyone assured me that he would gain the use of both sides of his face muscles, and eventually he did. But I continued to worry about him. He'd not got off to a good start, and I was pretty sure the doctor was to blame.

The new house was clean and fresh and had a good-sized nursery. It had bookshelves, and a whole rack of psychology books I had not read. Phil and Ron were okay boys, though I did have to make their breakfast every morning—not always when my own family was ready to eat—and I did their laundry and ironed their shirts. There was a lot of work with two big boys and two babies in the house, plus Greg, but I didn't have anything else to do with my time, except, of course, take care of the emergencies: Carrie swallowed a bottle of baby aspirin and had to get her stomach pumped. Phil wrapped his car around a pole one night after drinking too much, and we had to bail him out of jail. The boys liked to have parties downstairs, and when they did, we had to listen to Chubby Checkers all night. I kept wondering if I'd ever get a house with just my own little family in it.

The night of the Nixon-Kennedy Debates, we ran entirely out of baby food, milk and money. We'd been low before, but this was it. Broke. Not a cent. We took up a nice wedding-present rug from the living room floor, and drove it down to the thrift shop, where we got twenty-five whole dollars for it! Later we sold the card table and folding chairs—who had time to play bridge, anyway?—then a silver tea set. On Thanksgiving Day we couldn't find anything else to sell, so we ate oatmeal and Jell-O. My old Domestic Science recipe for Broken Glass Salad came in handy for the first time. The stuff was awful, but the kids loved it: It *wiggled!*

None of this seemed like much of a hardship. All the other graduate students were poor too. We had $200 a month to live on, out of which we paid $110 in rent. We loaned one another butter and other luxuries, and took turns babysitting. A big night out meant putting the children in the car, Ben in a crib in the back, and driving to the newly opened McDonald's place where for one dollar you could get four hamburgers. Then on to the drive-in movie—one dollar per car to see Natalie Wood in *Rebel Without a Cause*. I thought the little skirt and blouse she wore were okay, if a little bland, but I didn't have much time to update my clothes to picture show standards by then. I'd pretty much settled on black toreador pants, my husband's old white shirts, and black ballet shoes to do my housework in. This may have struck the fashion conscious as a little *retro* when we were getting on into the 60s, but then, I didn't know many very stylish graduate student wives.

And trust me, Audrey Hepburn never goes out of style.

I had only one problem with this scene: I yearned to be *the gradu-ate student*, not the graduate student's *wife*. When I was with the kids on the grounds of the university, I envied the people going in and out of the library carrying books. I didn't *want* to push strollers, I wanted to pull all-nighters cramming for exams. Several years later when my husband got a post-doc to Harvard, I refused to go. I couldn't bear being a swing-set mom at Harvard, I told him. He wouldn't go without his family, he told me, so from then on, I was to blame for his not carrying that credential on his résumé.

By the time Ben was six months old, he was a gorgeous, fat child with a thicket of black curly hair. He grew very fast and was strong and active. By the time he was a year old, he was strong enough to rock his crib so fiercely every night that the screws fell out. I would find him in the morning lying on the mattress on the floor, the crib feebly standing up around him. Then he began taking off his diaper to wipe its contents on the wall around his bed. He rocked his crib over to the closet, slipped open the doors and threw all the clothes from the hangers onto the floor. Then he rocked his crib over to the chest and opened all the drawers. Out came all his clean little-boy clothes. I was half out of my mind trying to keep up with the messes and keep some semblance of order in Carrie's life.

"Hyperactive," the doctor said. "Take him off sugar." Sugar? He didn't eat sugar; he was a baby—he ate prunes.

I got little sympathy from Greg: "What do you mean difficult?" he said. "I have *perfect* kids. You just don't know how to handle them."

In the evenings, Greg brought a group of classmates over to study at the big round table in the kitchen. After I got the kids to bed, I would pull my chair just outside the door, where no one could see me, and, pen poised, listen to the conversation, with Ben insistently rocking his bed down the hall. Here I learned words like *homeostasis* and *eschatology* and *Malthusian* and *exponential* and *causist* and *archetype* and *individuation*. Especially *individuation*.

After reading a book about this subject, I wrote a long letter to Mother:

Dear Mother,

I realize I acted like a baby when I told you that Greg was moving me up here, and I didn't want to come. I was afraid if you and Daddy thought I was coming willingly that you'd get your feelings hurt, that you'd feel rejected, and also I knew you didn't want us taking Carrie so far away from you. So I played like I was a victim in the middle. But I really wasn't. I could have really dug my heels in, and Greg would have reconsidered.

But I didn't, Mother, because half of me wanted to come. Half of me wanted to leave you and Daddy, because you live a life in a place that I don't want to be. I don't want to be in Thalia all my life. I don't want to settle for what you have, Mother. It doesn't stretch you, and it wouldn't stretch me. I want to continue to grow and test myself, like you and Mollie have taught me to do. You taught me to use my mind, you taught me to want more. Now I can't be something less or something other just because it's more convenient for everyone else. I wasn't brought up like that, Mother; you know that.

You know too I have always wanted to have adventures, not live in a little place like Thalia, and you encouraged that. You said I could be anything I really *wanted* to be. But the adventures sort of got cut off at the pass with the birth of Carrie. That is, what I had always thought of as adventures. Now, I am engaged in another kind of adventure—raising children—which is very hard. Every day I have to do things I don't have the foggiest idea how to do, in a place far from home with no one to help or encourage me. This has to be an adventure of its own kind, and someday I will have the ones I dreamed about. If I'm going to be ready to do that, I have to do this.

I was so angry at you, Mother, for not coming when Ben was born, because I was so scared. It was even worse than with Carrie, because all kinds of things went wrong. But I got through it, and I guess I'll get through a lot of other things before I can really call myself a grownup. But I'm trying, Mother, and I miss you. I want you for a friend.

Love, Jacy

I let the letter lie around the house for a few days. I was afraid I would *really* hurt my mother's feelings if I told her exactly how I felt: how she'd brought me up to be one thing and then was disappointed that I wasn't something else; how I thought she had settled for less than she might have, and how I didn't want to do that. All the influences of my life, both explicit and implicit, had instructed me not to tell people honestly what I thought, for I might hurt them, make them feel uncomfortable, make them think I wasn't a nice person.

But maybe Mother was right: Everything is mixed. You treat people in ways—even in what you think of as kind and unselfish ways—not so much to protect *them* as to protect *yourself.* Or for the mutual protection of both—to be safe yourself and make others feel safe. Is this wrong?

Maybe not. But maybe it's better *not* to be safe, but to be honest. To get it out there. Even if doing that hurts someone a little. I worried about what was right. But then I considered that keeping quiet about my feelings had clearly not helped this matter with Mother. So I finally showed the letter to Greg, who took it from me firmly and put it in his pocket. The next day, he told me he'd mailed it. I protested mildly, but, as it happened, this was the third best thing Greg had done for me. After giving me Carrie and Ben, he gave me back my mother.

The next month Mother called saying that she and Daddy would like to come for Christmas. Was it okay if they came and maybe brought Ellie as well? I was delirious. But wait. What was I going to do? We had a nice house, nicely furnished, but we had no money at all. Zero, zilch, nada. We couldn't have guests with no food and no gifts. What could I do?

I called one of Greg's graduate student friends who had a jazz band and told him that I could sing, and that I needed to earn about a hundred dollars fast. The next thing I knew, Greg was home with the kids, and I was singing "Bye, Bye Blackbird" with *The Scholars* in a campus coffee house. After five nights, I had a hundred dollars, so I did it five more nights. When Mother and Daddy came bringing my sister, we had roasted turkey and all the trimmings.

"This is almost as good as Christmas in Thalia," Daddy allowed, forking his black-eyed peas. He never suspected that I, literally, sang for his supper.

My cabaret career was brief. Greg graduated that spring, and we were off to a new adventure in the Northwest where he had a job that would kick us into the great middle class. We could buy a house, and I could live in a beautiful part of the world where I'd never been, where things could grow. At twenty-three, with a husband, two kids, a borrowed thousand bucks and a U-Haul trailer, I was off to have an adventure. Paris could wait. Paris *had* to wait.

5

We have not passed that subtle line between childhood and adulthood until we move from the passive to the active voice; that is, until we stop saying, "It got lost," and say, "I lost it."
—Sidney J. Harris

S·E·A·R·C·H

MOTHER WAS ALWAYS THERE for me after we'd overcome what she later called "Jacy's little rite-of-passage eruption." I carried the image of her grounded down there in dusty little Thalia holding a slender kite string, while I floated about the country like a kite—all puffed chest and crosspieces, tissue and skeleton, thin membrane over fragile frame. The kite string, over time, transmogrified into a telephone cord, less and less umbilical, more and more a means of two-way communication between equals, between grown-up women living very different lives. Mother had indeed become my friend as I called for company, for advice, called to share the latest things the kids said or the most recent political hassles in which Greg found himself embroiled. Greg had chosen education for a profession, but, it being the sixties, he found himself deeply into politics, which demanded different skills.

"I needed to hear those things from you, Jacy," Mother had said when she came to Colorado for Christmas that year after she'd read my letter. "I needed to see you take hold of your life, not to allow yourself to be a pawn in an emotional tug-of-war between your parents and your husband. I needed to know you *could* stand up for yourself, even if your doing so hurt me a little. Remember how your grandmother says that the best teachers eventually put themselves out of business: If the teachers are good enough, their students surpass them, don't need them anymore. That's the way it is with mothers, too."

I am on my way to West Texas to interview some old-timers for an oral history project. This trip could take a couple of weeks, since I'm flying to Houston first to visit Ben, where he's interning as a physical therapist. Then I'll drive to Thalia to see my father. Since Mother died, he has hardly gotten out of his leather chair except to do fix-up jobs around the old house that's about to fall in around his shoulders. Otherwise, he hunches in his chair, grieving, while neighbor ladies bring him peach cobbler from time to time.

At LaGuardia, I buckle myself in and immediately open my book, fastening my eyes to the page—my foolproof way of warding off unwelcome conversations with seatmates. In airplanes I let my mind go blank—completely, totally. Where others might be white-knuckle flyers, I seem to have no knuckles at all, or any bones for that matter; I'm like a limp doll. Or I'll stare impassively at a movie screen, the audio for which I have quite deliberately declined to purchase, or I'll fall into a book, its highest recommendation being its entirely unchallenging contents—a mystery with a woman sleuth, or some other cotton-candy for the mind. I love to fly; it's about the only time my head gets a break.

Now I sit stupefied, staring blankly at the pages of my new sleuth book, remembering my very first plane ride. It was from Eighty Lakes, Washington, where we'd gone to live after Greg finished school in Colorado, and I was then, as I am now, on a trip to West Texas. I was in my mid-twenties, and Mollie was dying.

I was also three months pregnant.

"Don't come, dear," Mother had said. "Your grandmother will understand. She wouldn't want you to come, in your condition, and having to leave the children." But at the last minute, I went. Mother hugged me ferociously when I arrived, pale and exhausted. What would we do without Mollie? She had been the cornerstone of Mother's life, as Mother had been of mine. She had given us both our love for words, music, magic, poetry.

At the sound of my voice, my grandmother, lying on the white sheets like a feather, fluttered her fingers. I took her hand, which felt like parchment. "Mollie?" I said, leaning to touch my lips to her translucent cheek. "Pippa passes, dear," she whispered. "God's in his heaven, all's right with the world."

"Well, here's where I disagree with you, Mother, but more power to you," my mother said, teasing, even as she let her mother go.

Mollie's lips curved upward for a moment, and then she was gone—the sweet, breathy voice, the searching intellect behind the wise little furrow between her eyes. We buried her in her new padded bra, and a pastel blue dress of the softest voile.

I wonder vaguely whether other deep and abiding relationships are built so much on words. It seemed that my life in Thalia had been enveloped by the sound of my mother's and grandmother's voices, like the thrum of cicadas on a summer evening, or the white noise of the refrigerator humming constantly amid the din of more insistent noises. Even when I wasn't listening, their voices encircled my days and wound around me lightly like a dreadnought in the night.

As I maneuver my rented car along the freeways for the long trip north from Houston to Thalia, I glance at the suburbs behind the high fences that line the highway and think of the Washington suburbs where my family had lived a good part of ten years. Eighty Lakes was beautiful, lush and green, and so named because, as the Chamber of Commerce legends had it, there was a lake within five miles of every home there. Magnolia Terrace was a cut above the suburb we'd left in Colorado. Our daylight basement with a fenced yard and a two-car garage was the first house we owned. It set us back twenty-five thousand dollars! What would that buy today? A new car, maybe; send a kid to college for a year. I remember asking my father's advice about the house, and he was aghast. He'd never owed anyone twenty-five thousand dollars in his entire life, and he couldn't believe his daughter was about to bite off that kind of debt. Greg told him he had a "depression mentality"—nobody actually paid off a house anymore anyway—so Daddy butted out.

Brand new, the house sat on a dirt lot not thirty feet from equally new and grassless (graceless?) houses on both sides. I went into my clean up, paint up, fix up mode, and soon the tall white house had a yard and rock garden. And, I recall, I had foot fungus from standing in fertilizer. The house also began to sprout shutters and petunias in the window boxes. Flowers wouldn't grow in Thalia when I was a child, and I'd been busy growing children in Colorado. So in Eighty Lakes, I saw to it that my garden exploded with orgasms of impatiens.

I enjoyed setting a house in order, but I didn't particularly enjoy doing it over and over again, which eventually seemed the pattern of my days. I soon felt as if my head were beginning to fill with Styrofoam. A yearning tugged at me for something I couldn't name. My neighbors were pleasant, but their conversations were bookended by children and housework. After you'd thrown in casseroles, pets, yards, and croup, and then started all over again, your mind went a bit wooly.

At neighborhood or office parties I went to with Greg, I frequently sidled over to where the men were talking to hear what they were saying, which was usually a good deal more interesting than women-talk—when they weren't discussing football, that is. I thought I'd left that unspeakable subject behind in Thalia, but like an old smell that clings to the inner sole of your sneakers, it followed me even to the Great Northwest. Back in Thalia, I sat through hundreds of football games and watched Sonny and Duane lumber into boys from Crowell or Paducah every Friday night. Once I actually tried very hard to care about who got what into which end zone, or over which goal post.

I knew the rules of the game, of course—who wouldn't with all those brothers and fathers around?—but when I tried to concentrate on it, my mind would slip off and start wondering what would happen if somebody like Heathcliff came along to Thalia, or if I would act like Trilby if Svengali was my teacher? I wondered what it would be like to dress up in men's clothes like Shakespeare's Rosalind—a man actor dressed as a woman character dressed as a man character . . . . funny. Shakespeare must have had a ball dreaming that one up.

So my football spasm passed as quickly as it had come and never returned.

I didn't understand the suburbs any more than I understood the national enthusiasm for football. One morning the doorbell rang, and I greeted at the door one of my neighbors, a man who lived down the street. He was dressed in suit and tie, ready for work—I in shorts and T-shirt, ready for work—and he seemed to have nothing to say. He just stood there, so I invited him in for coffee. He sat and drank his coffee while the kids and dogs ran around his legs, and I tried to keep them from crawling all over him. He seemed to have no agenda. After we had finished our coffee, he got up, shook my hand, thanked me and left.

Well, I thought, raising my eyebrows a bit, I guess if neighbor women can come for coffee, neighbor men can too. Then I promptly forgot it. A few days later, I ran into the man at a neighborhood market.

"I've been meaning to apologize for the other day," the man said, looking embarrassed.

"Why? What for?" I was genuinely puzzled.

"Well, the guy at the service station bet me twenty dollars I wouldn't make a pass at you. So I came to your house to make a pass at you."

I blinked. "But you didn't. You were a perfect gentleman."

"Well, I'm sorry. I apologize." He turned on his heel and walked off. I stood in the aisle holding a head of lettuce wondering what to make of it all. He was apologizing because he didn't make a pass? Did he win the twenty bucks or not? Some things are just too mystifying to contemplate in the supermarket with a head of lettuce in your hand and children pulling Fruit Loops off the shelves.

I narrowly escape being sideswiped by a blue Buick headed for somewhere lickety-split, then flip on the radio. Yeah, it's clear I'm back in Texas. Hank Williams sets me off on a reverie: "I'm sending you a big bouquet of roses," "Hey Good Lookin," "Why don't you love me like you used to do?"

A fellow in a black pickup with a rifle fixed in the rear window and beer can in his hand honks at me to speed up, get out of his way. He mouths something like "bitch" and passes in a roar. "Got a feeling called the blu-u-uuu-uze," I am singing now, finishing that one and launching into "Didn't know God made honky-tonk angels."

As I wind up "Oh wheel of fortune, oh let it be nowwwww," I think of the house I'm heading toward in Thalia. Daddy had bought it from Mollie for two thousand dollars and never had a mortgage. Daddy was a good planner. I was grown before I realized how little money we'd actually had; I had always felt rich. When I asked for something I was obviously not going to get, Mother never couched her refusal in dollar terms. I never heard anyone tell me that we could not afford something. In fact, nobody talked about money much at all. That was considered bad form. It was always, "Do you really need that, Jacy?" and I usually had to admit that, no, I didn't. It was a reasonable question, and I seldom argued with it.

I'd been less judicious with my own children, though plastic toys offended me, and I'd balked at buying them no matter how the kids begged and pointed them out on the TV. "But everybody has one," they'd whine. "Well, *everybody's* wasting their money. Go play in the sandbox."

I monitored their TV and hardly ever watched it myself, even when Greg was gone. When I finally got the kids to bed in the evenings, I would sit down at the typewriter and write stories. Once I actually won a *Redbook* magazine contest.

In the spring of 1965, a young woman, Anne Taylor of Orange, Texas, had written an article, "I Don't Know Where to Look for Me," in *Redbook's* "Young Mother's" series. The piece was an emotional description of the confusion she felt about her role as mother and wife, the "nervous days" when she felt inadequate, empty and restless. As young mothers, "should we want less?" she asked. "It's just that I have a feeling that something is wrong, a feeling that maybe I am not doing all that I should, not trying hard enough. What makes me feel this way?"

The piece moved me because a disappointed young Texas woman like myself was reaching out for help. I felt empty and restless too, like I'd been sold a misrepresented bill of goods, and I was stuck with them. Apparently I was not alone, for seven thousand young women wrote in response to the article.

My "Letter to Anne" was published in August of 1966, and *Redbook* sent me two hundred dollars. My first published piece—at fifty whole cents a word!

"What makes you feel this way?" I wrote angrily. "Namely, deception. A national myth that is false, hypnotic and devastating: The American Dream—a dream of misplaced values—and an out-and-out lie. This dream of youth, money, success, love, beautiful women, virile men and everything ending happily-ever-after has been intensified and exaggerated by television, movies, literature and advertisers. Our problem as young women is to face this sham, come to grips with it, and then ignore it. We do not, finally, after a thrilling chase, catch a brilliant, rich, adoring husband and painlessly produce sons in spotless sailor suits and daughters with long, glossy curls hanging over ruffly collars. We have tired, worried spouses, grimy little boys in muddy boots and daughters in teeth bands. We are nothing like the fey, sprightly housewives constantly depicted. We have weary bones and red knuckles. We have let people tell us what we ought to want, then let them glamourize the life they have sold us. We've been fools! That's why we feel this way."

My letter offered Anne ways to pull out of her depression: "Look within yourself. What do you personally need and want from life? Answer that, and then ask yourself the best way to go about getting it. You don't have to want what anybody tells you that you *ought* to want. Take chances, and when you're defeated, laugh."

I wrote my heart out. If ever there were a subject on which I was an authority, it was how to keep from going mad when one is young, housebound, and pressed into an ill-fitting role that doesn't seem to allow for much creativity. I wrote how to set short-term goals: paint the woodwork, make a birthday cake in the shape of a space cap- sule. How to set medium-term goals: recover an old chair from a thrift shop. How to set long-term goals: make five new school dresses for your daughter—one for each day of the week; learn to strip and refinish floors. (I had better sense than to mention my real long-term goal, which was just to finish—forget *understand*—*Appollonius of Perga*, volume 11 of Mother's *Great Books*—which I had been so chicken as to skip over after taking a gander at all those diagrams, and propositons and conics.)

A few people in Eighty Lakes saw my article and called me; for a couple of minutes I felt like a celebrity. That's *really* what I want to do, I told myself. Sit here at my typewriter forever, thinking up things to tell people. I would never run out of things to say.

I had set little exercises for myself: write about a rat, write about a chair leg, write about a sock. I'd sit and write paragraph after para- graph about these and other ordinary subjects. This was my own brand of sit-ups for the brain that Mollie had prescribed years ago in Thalia to ward off terminal neuroatrophy. But it was hard to find magazines interested in what an antsy twenty-something housewife in Eighty Lakes, Washington, thought about anything. I kept myself occupied with writing and mailing things out, and routinely opened my mail to rejection slips.

When Carrie was seven, I opened my mailbox with my usual resignation, and surprise! An acceptance letter! The story, called "A Time for Tears," described the emotions of a mother sending her son off for his first day of school. It had what I thought was a clever "O. Henry" ending. And nobody changed a word of it! Carrie loved to hear the story because she knew it was about *her* first day at Eighty Lakes Elementary, only Mom turned her into a boy to make the story work. She knew that's what you had to do with stories: change things to make them work. Even *true* stories.

Actually, the texture of my life began to change in Eighty Lakes in 1963. I'd exhausted the courses at the Y—home decorating, *decoupage*, and "your perennial garden," and I'd already read everything the book clubs were reading. I looked for other possibilities, finally spotting a few lines in the newspaper announcing that a professor of a local college would address a group of women about a controversial new book that claimed that women were "unfulfilled in their roles as housewives and mothers and beginning to look for other outlets for their talents." Whoopee! I called and reserved a seat. Then I bought a copy of the book.

Greg was gone to San Francisco for a conference. He called with excitement in his voice. The conference was great! His keynote speech had gone over swell! He'd met some terrific people from Minnesota! He was having a wonderful time at a cocktail party at the Top of the Mark! I told him that I was exceedingly glad he was at the Top of the Mark because I was at the Bottom of the Barrel. I told him that Ben had just set a fire in the closet again. I told him the toilet had run over, and the plumber wasn't answering his phone. I told him that I'd just about finished a new book about how housewives suffered from "the problem that had no name." Clearly, I pointed out, a book about myself.

Greg was not used to such impertinence from his wife. And a few days later, when he came home on a Sunday afternoon, he found a babysitter with Carrie and Ben. This was odd. He paced around the house, read his mail, had a Scotch and water. Where was I? The sitter, who'd been late and hadn't taken good notes, was no help.

At eight o'clock I arrived home, exhilarated. The lecture was riveting. I was sure the professor was talking directly to me. Afterward, I'd spoken with him, and he urged me to register for evening classes at the college. Then I'd talked to two women who invited me out for coffee. Alex and Joan. I couldn't believe it. They were so smart; they had read so much. Like me, they'd just read the book the professor had discussed: *The Feminine Mystique*. For three hours, as night fell, we sat in a diner and talked excitedly about the ideas in the book. As we prepared to part, Alex suggested I join her at the college, where she'd taken a literature class the semester before. It had given her a whole new life, she said, promising to call with particulars.

I had met some women like myself for the very first time in my life! I had not known such women existed.

Back home, it didn't matter what Greg said about being worried. How many times had he been out without me? It's not like I was at the Top of the Mark for pete's sake. I was with some women having coffee. Enjoying myself *with women* for the first time since Mother and Mollie and I had lain across Mother's big bed upstairs and talked about ideas.

I trooped out to the college with a toddler in tow, feeling awkward and silly. First of all, I was pregnant again, and second, no one—*no one*—brought children to a college campus in those days. I felt out of place and somehow discounted, like I had those years in Colorado when the *real people* were going in and out of the library, and the mother people were pushing kids in strollers. I swallowed hard and enrolled in one course. I'd have time to complete the semester before the baby arrived; I had a belly, but at least maternity fashions were no longer limited to baggy skirts with giant holes. Shifts were in, and long, straight jumpers, so you could hardly tell a woman was pregnant: Lucy Ricardo's bosses would have loved it.

About the course, Greg said, "Just remember the children are the most important thing in your life"—a phrase that was to become his mantra throughout our marriage.

Before long the neighbor women with their talk of measles, leaf mold, and kitty litter were replaced by Phaedra, Candide, Faust, Tartuffe, Madame Bovary, Solveig, Hedda Gabler, Anna Karenina and more, more, *more,* and their dramatic outpourings. It came to be that Tuesday nights with Tristan and Isolde made it possible for me to live the rest of the week in the suburbs with Donna Reed and Harriet Nelson.

Alex and Joan and I talked on the phone almost daily. All of us had children and husbands, and none of us could wait for Tuesday nights and our coffee appointments before or after our classes. I thought of us as "Recovering Housewives"—we read our assigned passages, met frequently to discuss them, and often testified about our good luck in finding one another just before each of us went around the bend. We were our own support group. Our bodies and minds grew healthier. Furthermore, we were on the constant lookout for other women-on-the-brink we might rescue with our succor and counsel. At least we were in Step One of what might or might not be a Twelve Step Program. We had rescued ourselves, come to our senses, just in time.

We were also ravenous to learn. So much so that we wrote down even incidental citations a professor made in his lecture and checked the books out of the library. The three of us were so prepared as students that we often caught a young professor by surprise; he had to read several chapters ahead to keep up with us. I carried a suitcase full of books in my car. Mother, delighted in my being able to study once again, sent me my first "briefcase," a green paisley number that I carried until the handles fell off.

We went to Bergman and Truffaut films, listened to "Lucy in the Sky with Diamonds," and "Hard Day's Night." We read Bellow, Updike, Roth, Golding, Ortega, Albee, Barth and Chairman Mao. We discussed the space race and followed the horrifying things going on in Vietnam. We saw *Dr. Strangelove* four times.

Once when we were walking down the hall three abreast, a professor called: "Watch out for the Formidable Phalanx."

We were, in many ways, like girls again—or like the girls we might have been had we been *boys* in the fifties; or at least had we been girls who had not taken on responsibilities so early. Alex had married at sixteen, Joan at nineteen. Joan, the most advanced of us, introduced us to pantyhose. Pantyhose! I was sure I could never struggle into such eeny little things. But soon we all threw away our Playtex panty girdles with their little dangling hooks that kept our stockings up. And once when Joan pulled her notebook out of her purse to show the professor something, her little plastic circle of birth control pills fell out at his feet. She was mortified, but said later it was "symbolic." Without them, she wouldn't be able to be here enjoying a full intellectual life for the first time. The "traditional" undergraduates seemed to admire us—returning women students were unheard of on this campus in 1963—and sought us out for study groups, even though we ruined the curve. Who was brighter than we were? Hey nobody!

The baby was due in May. I was sitting on the floor of a friend's house cutting out the pattern for a maternity dress, when a knock came on the door. Loud. Insistent. Louder still. Puzzled, my friend Nancy got up, looked out the window and saw a television repairman's truck in the drive. The man was beating the door, beating and yelling, so Nancy opened it a crack. "The president's been shot; he may be dying; he may be dead!" The man pushed in the door, rushed past her to the TV set and turned it on. We watched, riveted to the scene in Dallas that ended an age of innocence for me, as for the rest of the country. The dying man was the first president that I'd been old enough to vote for. He had impressed me during that debate with Nixon, when Greg and I sat watching without any money or milk for our children. Jackie Kennedy had children about the same age as mine; though she had buried her third baby, and my third was about to be born. After all these years of picture shows as model, shaper, and style setter, in her I had finally found someone worthy of imitating: *a real live First Lady with some class.*

After the death of Kennedy, there was, as the poet said, no other. My concerns took on a new, more immediate, more serious dimension. The world was a scary place. How could I simply hide from it? How could I ignore the social turmoil of the only life I would ever know? Little by little my articles began to be published here and there, and my work was being taken seriously in classes where professors read my papers aloud, passed them around to their colleagues. *I wasn't dumb! My head was not filled with popcorn!* I had begun to feel like a *real* writer, no longer a housewife who scribbled things and hid them in her drawer for fear someone would discover what she *really* thought and felt. I reveled in criticism as well as in encouragement. I knew, as I had known in Thalia, that something there was in me that did not belong in the suburbs. Another, more engaging, life was tugging at me, though I didn't know what that might be.

What kind of life could you let tug at you when you had two—soon to be three—little children needing three meals a day?

I had come alive, hit my stride. I was reading *The Brothers Karamazov* when the first pain came. I read it in the waiting room, the prep room, the labor room. I would have read it in the delivery room, except the doctor had introduced me to a new machine, called *The Bubble*. When a woman was near delivery, the big plastic dome was placed on her mid-section and pressure was exerted to help her expel the baby without a lengthy labor. The doctor was convincing; so with my history of long and painful labor, Greg and I decided to go with it. After a few pangs, I was put into what looked like a big see-through turkey roaster, and after a little pressure, Paul emerged pink and healthy. I couldn't believe it. He was there. He was mine. It hadn't hurt.

I was positive Paul would be the last, so took Joan's advice and accordingly had the newly available birth control pills prescribed before I left the hospital. But to this day, I have never heard of another birth produced with the help of *The Bubble*. I have asked a number of doctors about the machine, but no one knows what I am talking about.

Near the Dallas exit I pull in at a barbecue shack. As I munch my sandwich and watch the bowlegged cowboys and women in Gap jeans skirts come in and out, I recall the last time I lived here. Politics were visual and vigorous. Sissy Farenthold was running for governor, and I would put up her sign in my North Dallas yard every morning before I went to work. When I came home, it was pulled down and thrown on the grass. Every day. And in the front yard across the street was a statue of a black stable boy holding a brass ring, which I detested. One day I saw that someone had doused it with white paint. From then on, a white stable boy stood holding a white noose in the lily-white neighborhood. I wasn't sure which symbol was more offensive. Those were difficult days in Dallas for the kids and me, and especially for Greg—who was under a court order to integrate the public schools, when few people wanted to see that happen.

Back on the road to Thalia, I hear Waylon wailing from my radio. I turn down the sound and my mind wanders again to my life in Eighty Lakes. The long talks with Alex and Joan, the rapacious reading, my fascination with Eastern philosophy. When I finally got some guided reading in college, I yearned to understand things I couldn't define, things Mother had made me aware of. I read more Aquinas, Pascal, Martin Luther, Buber, Bultmann, Tillich, Neibuhr, Teilhard, C. S. Lewis, Malcolm Boyd, Bishop Robinson. I had graduated from the naive questions once aimed at Mother and Mollie to questions whose answers raised even more questions.

I took my children to Sunday School to make them a part of a cultural tradition, and to give them the rudiments of Biblical literature. Then, I figured, they could decide how to use all that as they got older—accept it, reject it, explore it, try it on, make it an integral thread of the fabric of their lives, compare it to other spiritual quests and learn from them all. I thought knowing something about myths—the earliest ways people tried to explain their world—was part of being a cultured person. But for me organized religion—authority, tradition, and ritual—got in the way of mystery, grace, and a personal faith. Like Mother, I couldn't accept the stuff they were giving out in church, no matter how hard I tried to suspend disbelief.

One Sunday morning I doggedly moved through the routine. While Greg sat and read the newspaper and drank his coffee, I got the children out of bed, fed, bathed and dressed; polished little shoes, brushed hair and tied sashes, found vests and booties. I cleared the breakfast table and put the dishes in the dishwasher, made the beds, put roast and potatoes in the oven and made the salad for lunch. Then, while keeping an eye on the kids so they wouldn't destroy themselves or the house, I dressed myself in my best black-and-white checked suit, red hat and white gloves. As I herded the family toward the car, something inside me went on strike, and I turned around and headed for the living room, where I stood in the middle of the floor.

Greg and the kids sat in the car, honking and yelling for me to come on. Finally, I went to the door. "Greg, I'm not going. Please take the kids on without me." He was astonished.

"What do you mean you're not going? Are you sick?" he called.

"I mean I'm not going. And no, I'm not sick. Sunday is supposed to be a day of rest and rejuvenation and getting in touch with the spirit. It's not nine o'clock yet, and my spirit is already exhausted. Getting this family ready for church has put me in an unchristian mood. I'm staying home. Goodbye." I slammed the door.

After a few minutes I heard the car start up and move off down the street. I turned around, breathed deeply, threw off my Sunday clothes, and put on my shorts. Two whole blessed hours stretched before me. I made a cup of tea and wandered into the study to find something to read. My eye lit on a new text I'd just bought for a class I'd be taking next semester, "World Religions." I picked up the book, and it fell open to these lines: *The people went to Buddha and asked: "Are you a god?" "No," he said. "An angel?" "No." "A saint?" "No." "Then what are you?" Buddha answered: "I am awake."*

Aha! What a startling way of looking at religion. The religion I knew put people to sleep in the pew. A religion that was awake! I sat down and spent two hours reading the Buddhism and Taoism chapters of Huston Smith's *The Religions of Man.*

Those two hours when I was not yet thirty years old changed my life. They gave me, I often think, the other half of myself, the part that an authoritative, ritualistic Christianity had left out. It gave me the grace simply to *be,* to stop striving, stop desiring things, to let go of ego, of envy even. I came upon this philosophy exactly when I was ripe for it. My frantic flailing for perfection in everything I did, whether with children, home or school work, and the depression from inevitably failing, diminished. My blood pressure went down. My entire demeanor changed. Even my kids grew calmer. Thank God for Buddha!

I took the course and found there a philosophy that absorbed me—and one that still does. Though I continued taking my children to Sunday School, and, later, to church, the ritual held little meaning for me. I *knew* what spiritual growth meant for me. It was personal; it was private. It didn't take a cathedral or a minister. And it helped me solve a lot of problems *just by sitting still.*

I am headed into the homestretch. No good trying to discuss this with Daddy when I get to Thalia, I think, passing Decatur—*Eighter from Decatur, the county seat of Wise*—I repeat a line from my childhood that I do not now, nor did I then, understand. What's an eighter? I think vaguely that it has to do with throwing dice, gambling . . . why?

Daddy thinks I'm crazy enough as it is. He'd asked me, when I was moving to New York later in my life: "What in the world do you want to go up there for? It's too far away from Texas to ever amount to anything." My first sin in his eyes was leaving Texas. God knows what he'd think about his little Methodist daughter and Buddha.

There wasn't much to talk about, anyway. Saying you were "a Buddhist" was silly and pretentious. It missed the spirit of the thing. Mother understood that. She knew about being awake. She'd read the books I sent her from Eighty Lakes—all my "World Religion" texts—and received them in the way I knew she would. When I visited her and we set the children to napping or playing, we'd sit down and have a Tea Ceremony. We had no kimonos, but her long dressing gowns did the job. The idea of our dressing, and sitting there contemplatively, and doing this so seriously right there in Thalia, Texas, amused us. We made up *koans*, and one day I wrote a haiku for her:

Look at that puddle
in the gutter
a rainbow

She wrote one in return:

The face of the full moon
crumples in the lake
the boat passes on

The only neighbor I had in Eighty Lakes who liked to read was Carol, who had three young children about the ages of mine. Before I returned to school, we often had coffee together, talked about what we were reading, and exchanged books. Later, I didn't have any time to do that, but once I went to see her to invite her to visit a class.

"Carol, you'll love this. It's made me feel alive again. Come to class and meet some of my friends, women like us, who like to read and think. Just take one course and see. You'll want to take another and another. You'll never want to stop."

A few days later, Carol called to say that she'd discussed it with her husband, and Cliff had said, "What do you want to do that for? You'll be forty years old before you finish a degree. It's a waste of time."

I told her that she was going to be forty years old some day anyway; she might as well be forty years old with a college degree. Besides, that wasn't the point. The process was the goal. But the argument didn't wash with Cliff, and Carol stayed home with the kids. I saw her less and less. A few years later, after I'd finished my undergraduate degree and was on to other things, I heard from Carol. Cliff had died from a massive heart attack at age thirty-six, and she was left with three children and no way of earning a living. I was so mad at Cliff I'd have killed him if he weren't already dead. *The patronizing arrogance of it; the horror!* Why did women succumb?

Late in the 1960s, campuses from Berkeley to Columbia were in turmoil. Along with Kennedy, Martin Luther King, Malcolm X and Robert Kennedy were dead, brought down by insanity run amok. Watts, Chicago and Cleveland were on fire. Klan attacks were rampant in the South. Vietnam protests raged. Greg and I followed the civil rights marches on the news and looked around our white suburban enclave with new eyes. What were we doing here when the action was elsewhere? Who was going to take on their struggles? Who was going to fight for the right things? Our country was all torn up, and LBJ was standing for the *wrong* things internationally. How could a *Texan* get us tangled up in Vietnam? We attended Dr. King's memorial, two of a handful of white people in a black church.

Mainly, in the placid little college in placid Eighty Lakes, students went about their placid business. One professor, however, was having a life crisis. He'd read Denis DeRougemont and Alan Watts and Norman O. Brown. He'd tested the waters at Esalen during break and, as if they had been those of Lourdes, had come back to campus a changed man. *Nature, Man and Woman* became his *Bible.* Professor—"call me Brad"—Kent threw his desk out of his office, carpeted it in a thick oriental rug, and tossed large, overstuffed cushions all around the floor. He wore blue jeans and hippie shirts and sat on his floor while reading and grading papers. Sometimes he moved his smaller classes into his office, where my classmates and I sat on the floor and discussed D. H. Lawrence and his "spiritual brides."

Brad Kent loved smart women. Brad Kent loved good-looking women. Brad Kent was in hog-heaven. He concocted very sexy assignments. You had to read *Women in Love,* for example, and argue in a paper whether you would or would not have a homosexual relationship. You read *Madame Bovary*, and *Anna Karenina*, and *Lady Chatterly's Lover*, and had to decide on the basis of these books whether you would or would not commit adultery. Alex, Joan and I thought there was something specious about the spin that Brad gave literature, but we wrote our papers, concluding that we didn't believe we would have a homosexual relationship or commit adultery. Brad didn't like these conclusions when we sat on the cushions in his office and read them aloud. He would frown and make faces, or look at us unblinkingly with cold blue eyes.

One day after class as I was discussing an assignment with him, Brad grabbed me and kissed me. He tried to pull me down on his floor cushions. When I pushed him away, he offered me wine. Before I could get myself out the door, he pulled open his wall shelf, and out onto the carpet tumbled a tall goblet with a cranberry stem. I stared at it as I grabbed my books and hustled myself into the hall. His attentions were unsettling and made me feel slimy. I was afraid he'd give me less than my usual A if I kept rebuffing him or didn't write in my papers the conclusions he wanted. I made it a rule never to go into his office unless surrounded by a group. Once he caught me as I was leaving, blocked the door, and whispered: "I have rented a room for us, Room 226 Starlite Motel. I want you there tomorrow at 6 o'clock. This is just between you and me. I love you." He stuck his tongue in my mouth.

I gulped and left. Baffled I drove around aimlessly awhile, then pulled into Alex's driveway.

Sitting at her big round kitchen table, where we often studied, I told her about Brad's behavior. Alex looked stunned. "He's been doing that to me, too," she said slowly. "He's been telling me he's in love with me, wants to leave his wife and run away with me. He'll help me get into graduate school; he'll help me get a Fulbright, etc., etc. He's even begun calling me at home, and it's been making me a nervous wreck."

Alex rose and went over and opened the liquor cabinet by her fireplace. "Let's have something to drink," she said briskly, setting out two tall wine goblets with cranberry stems.

"Alex," I said slowly. "Your wine glasses . . . he has one."

Alex turned her back to me, placed her palms flat on the cabinet top, leaned on her arms. The room was stifling. I could hear the clothes dryer in the laundry room spinning. A dog barked.

"Alex . . . ."

"No, Jacy," she said quietly, her voice choking. "He has two."

Abruptly, she turned and looked directly at me. "Yes," she said. "I don't know what to do about it. I've been seeing him for three months. At first it was exciting, fun, an adventure, different . . ." she made a sweep with her arm indicating her suburban home with a husband due wanting dinner as usual in an hour. "You know what it's like here. . . . I've been married fourteen years, and I'm not even thirty. *The closest thing to passion in my life is reading Milton, for godsake!*"

We laughed. I got up and went toward her. "I know. I'm sorry I said anything. Do you love him?"

"God, no, I don't think so. He's exciting . . . but he scares me. It keeps me on edge all the time. I want to be free of it, but I'm worried about how it will affect my grades. I don't know how to get disentangled. I've told him I want to stop, but there's this pull. I can't stand it anymore."

I told Alex about the motel date he'd cooked up. Her mouth dropped. "I'm supposed to meet him there *tonight!*"

"Tell you what . . . ." I said.

And so it was that when Professor Brad Kent came to Room 226 at the Starlite Motel that evening at 6 o'clock, he found the door open, thanks to a couple of fast-talkers at the key desk, and two lovely women sitting on opposite sides of the room, waiting for him. He lurched forward toward Alex, then saw me and stumbled back.

"Look, Brad," Alex said, eyeing him coldly. "We've got your number."

"Yeah," I said. This is where I was supposed to add, "the jig's up." But I restrained myself. "We're in college to learn, but not some of the stuff you're trying to teach us."

When he finally got his mouth to work, Brad uttered apologies, saying he was having trouble at home, wasn't himself lately, didn't know what was wrong, was taking pills, etc. We extracted a promise that he wouldn't bother us again, and that this incident would not affect our grades. "We both have A's in every class we've taken here, Brad," said Alex. "We don't accept less. If we get it, we're going to tell some people why."

In the parking lot later, Alex turned to me: "I feel like we're in a very bad movie," she said.

We never told a soul. But before long Professor Brad Kent announced his resignation "to pursue other interests." He was gone by the end of the year taking his cushions with him. I never knew whether there were other women, too, and whether someone finally blew the whistle, but there was gossip that he had targeted a woman in each class he taught. I had no word then for what had happened to us; it was long before I'd heard of sexual harassment. And I was never sure we'd handled the situation properly. But we did put a stop to it.

Coffee Houses became popular, even in Eighty Lakes, and we often went there after night classes to drink coffee, listen to poetry, and discuss our favorite *existentialist du jour*—Nietzsche, Sartre, the absurdist playwrights. I got caught up in a book about how people could motivate themselves when all their familiar goals in life were snatched away. What is the last of human freedoms? was the question posed by the existentialist philosopher Victor Frankl, who had been stripped of everything—family, clothes, belongings, dignity, even his hair in a Nazi prison camp. He survived the Nazi camp and answered his own question, building a philosophy of *logotherapy* around it: *The ultimate freedom is the ability to choose your attitude toward it when you are placed in a particular set of circumstances. How you accept your fate is a choice.*

Existential thinking appealed to me. I had always been fascinated by the relationship between fate and character, brought on by reading Greek drama when I was young. And, odd as it seems, Frankl's idea even echoed my grandmother's homelier advice: "You can learn to be content in whatever situation you find yourself." How did a homespun, Texas pioneer woman come to the same conclusion as a Viennese Jewish Nazi prisoner? It was *this* kind of mystery that I loved in philosophy. Not the churchified religion of my youth.

I was finally creating a life for myself. It wasn't Paris, but it was a start.

The four years I spent in intense study in the little college in Eighty Lakes gave me a soul where a hollow place had been. As I approach Windthorst, on my drive to Thalia, near the death place of my grandfather, I wonder briefly why my mother never took me to the site of the well where he died. It must have been such a trauma that she not only didn't talk about it or write about it, but she couldn't bear to think of it. She told me once that it was after she had run for help to save her father and brother that she lost her faith in God. "I prayed and cried and prayed as hard as a little girl could. I told God that I would always, always be good after that, if he would save my Daddy and Hud. But He didn't, and after that I didn't have much use for Him."

I pass the big Catholic church on the hill, with the grotto that has fascinated me since I was a child, a little nativity scene set back in the side of the hill. This is a village . . . no, in Texas you said "small town"—of such devout Catholicism that every other yard I pass displays a statue of the Virgin Mary.

I feel I am regressing into childhood again. Well, why not: here we are in Thalia. I see the familiar water tower rise in the distance. It's funny, I think, but each time when I see it, it's like I'm seeing my own bones up there holding up that water tank. Like, sometimes in New York, when I unexpectedly turn a corner and see a Texas license plate, it's almost as if I see my own face in that map. Odd. Very odd. No wonder Daddy thinks I'm crazy. No, clearly I hadn't better bring up Buddha.

6

H·E·A·R·T

Love makes people believe
in immortality because
there seems not to be room
or time enough in life for
so great a tenderness, and
it is inconceivable that the
most masterful of our
emotions should have no
more than spare moments
of a few brief years.
—Robert Louis Stevenson

I ALWAYS FIND IT HARD to go into the house in Thalia since Mother's death. This is the third time I've walked up to the back door startled to see the door knocker and sign still there. It's not your ordinary garden-variety door knocker. This is a little mallet made of raw wood with a rough twig for a handle that Mother had bought somewhere in Ireland a few years ago. In their later years, she and Daddy had grown a little hard of hearing, and they usually had the air conditioner blasting away, anyway, so they couldn't hear anyone who came to the back door. So Mother had hung the mallet from the door handle and written in her round, clear hand: "Please knock HARD," and underlined the hard three times. The note is curled around the edges and the ink a bit smudged, but the message is still clear.

I don't bother to knock. I call as I round the corner of the kitchen so I won't startle my father, who, I am sure, will be sitting in his chair reading or watching a soap opera. Ever since my son Paul played a regular role on "One Life to Live," his grandfather has been hooked on it. Paul long ago outgrew soaps, but his grandfather still never misses an episode.

"Hey, Daddy!" I call loudly, hanging my handbag on the row of pegs in the hall. I hear a *thummppp*, which means my father has released the leg extension of the reclining chair and is getting up.

Daddy is a trim, muscular man with large forearms and hands. His face is pink and as smooth as someone thirty years younger. His hair is white, and he has intelligent brown eyes that have mellowed over the years. Two operations for cataracts have not dimmed them. He hugs me hard and says,

"Well, it's always an adventure to see what color your hair is now. What d'you call this?"

I twirl around like a girl. "Uh, Redken *auburne avec* highlights *Roberto*," I say grinning.

"Well, back in my day, we just used to say brown, and yellar, and red and things like that," Daddy says. "How long'd it take you to get here?"

"Oh, about six hours, I guess. But I had Willie and Waylon on the radio and lots to think about, so it wasn't bad."

"Well, Miz Lassiter heard you's coming, so she sent over a peach cobbler," Daddy said, peach cobbler being the staff of life in Thalia. I smile to hear the way my father pronounces Mrs. I had been among those radicals in the seventies fighting for the name *Ms.* to dignify women as individuals, and not as "unclaimed blessings" like my old piano teacher, *Miss* Kykendall, or like *Mrs.* Married-Woman-Who-Lets-Someone-Else-Think-For-Her. But in Texas, they'd *always* said *Miz*.

"Which way'd you come?" Daddy adds.

"Oh, Bryan, Waco, Bridgeport, Bowie." At my father's family re-unions, which occur about once a year and last for two days, the first day is spent with the brothers and sisters asking each other how they'd come and how long it took, and the second day asking each other how they were going back, and how long they thought it'd take. His was a family so modest that they thought nothing ever happened to them and so taciturn that they wouldn't tell you if it had.

Daddy, at eighty-eight, is the third oldest of nine brothers and sisters, all still living except the first, who died in infancy. The first three were born in a dugout in Canyon, while Granddaddy built a house. He had a thriving dairy farm, which all the kids worked until they left home. Daddy was proud that every kid in his family had graduated from college. "It was the only way to get off the farm," he'd said.

I glance over at Mother's empty rocker, made by an uncle gifted in woodworking. How many babies had Mother rocked there? Nearly a dozen grandchildren and great-grands. It was amazing how, when the babies were colicky, or cranky, or teething, or just holding their breaths out of sheer orneriness, and their mothers were exhausted, Mother would take the baby in her lap in that rocker, hold its little hands and feet so it couldn't kick and get itself even more worked up, and sing the *"Woo Song"* very softly near the baby's ear—*Woo-oo, sleep, baby, sleep.* And miraculously, the baby would calm down. The *Woo Song* was a western lullaby that Mother had made up for her own children to the tune of *The Cattle Call,* to calm their fears in the night.

"Well, when you gonna move back home where you belong, Jacy?" Daddy asks, as he does each time I come to see him. I think I'll put a stop to it once and for all.

"Daddy, I lived in Texas for the first twenty years of my life, but I've lived thirty-some-odd years not in Texas. Now what makes you think I belong here?"

"Well, you lived here longer than that. You came back in about 1970 and lived in Wichita Falls and Dallas for about five years before you went way back up North again."

"You're right, I did. Okay, that's about half-in-half then, but I don't know how Ohio got to be North."

"Well it is to me."

Conversations with my father always take circular routes and go over the same ground again and again, plowing little grooves in the records of our minds. We agree on hardly anything except politics, which is a big thing to agree on, so mostly my visits skirt personal talk, as Daddy and I chew over what heinous activities those narrow-minded, addle-brained, sleazy, selfish big-business-bloated Republicans are up to now. I head such a conversation off for the moment by telling him I've brought him some barbecue from the place he likes near the Dallas cut-off. We go out to get it.

Daddy inspects my rented car. "Why'd you get one of these furrin-made things? Don't you know they'll fall apart on you on the road? Likely to get killed."

We've had this conversation innumerable times, and this time I don't bite. Instead, I walk around the side of the house, inspecting the lawn.

"Are you still mowing all this yourself?"

"Sure am. Good exercise."

I shake my head. Last time I was home, a neighbor lady came over leaning on her cane. "Jacy, I hope you'll tell your daddy to stay off the roof of that house. He gives me the heebie-jeebies dancing around up there."

I wander over to the corner of the lot. The trees are growing back, I see. A few years ago some drunk rounded the corner too fast and plowed up a couple of giant mesquites that had been there as long as I could remember. The car crumpled like a foil gum wrapper, but the old coot, anaesthetized by alcohol, wobbled out waving his broken-off steering wheel, swearing at the forest standing in his way. Daddy took him in the house and called Sheriff Johnny Blue to come do something with him.

Later, when my brothers came to inspect the damage, one told him, "Dad, you've got a good suit on your hands here. You could collect a couple of thousand dollars for those trees. That's real damage to your property."

"Heck, no. Those trees are just a nuisance. I was tired of looking at 'em anyway."

"But Dad, you've got insurance. You can collect."

"Naw, I'm not collecting on any worthless trees. That's just what drives peoples' insurance rates up. Things like that."

Daddy was immovable in this, as in most things. Now if it had been the twenty-foot evergreen over here, Daddy would have killed the old codger. He loved to tell people that "my wife planted that tree when it was just a little sprig not three inches high and put a jelly jar over it all winter. Look at it now!"

Well, my son Ben comes by it rightly—his attitude about money. I've just come from a conversation with him in Houston. "Ma, I don't think I have the proper respect for money," he told me at dinner the night before. "Everybody I'm interning with wants to go into private practice and make a lot of bucks. I know it sounds corny, but what I want to do is help little kids when I finish up here. Maybe inner city kids; kids in real trouble. They need more help than any-body."

Ben is extremely bright, and he has a large soul.

"I'm going in and have some of this barbeque," Dad calls as he heads for the back door. I unload my car and haul my stuff up the cramped stairway, dumping it in my old bedroom. The bed has the same pink bedspread it's had for twenty-five years. It also has on the wall four portraits of lovely young women in bridal gowns. The women range in age from nineteen to twenty-four or so, and all are long divorced: Ellie, Jacy, Rena, and Anne, the last two the first wives of my brothers. I almost recognize myself: plump and dewy and bewil-dered. Rena and I have remarried. I, about a dozen years ago to Marlboro, a journalist from Ohio I met in New York. Ellie has a long-time man friend. And Anne, perky sweetheart Anne, died in a hor-rible fire in Wichita Falls, along with her mother, that no one has been able to explain.

Daddy has always been puzzled, and a little sad, that not one of his children had stayed married—though most of us hung in there a long time, until our kids were grown, at least. He'd once said, "I guess I'm just a failure as a father, because all my kids are divorced." Mother had looked at him with her take-your-guilt-somewhere-else-you'll-get no-sympathy-from-me look, and remarked, "I think we just raised a herd of independent minds, and I won't apologize for that."

Downstairs, Daddy is eating his barbeque off a TV tray with the sound up loud enough to rattle Mother's paintings of bluebonnets off the wall. I take the opportunity to survey the house. I always do this when I come home; I am drawn to Mother's things—the paint-ings she did of all her granddaughters, still hanging on the living room wall, the paper thin tea set from Ireland with its little green shamrocks, the furniture she refinished herself. Once some Girl Scouts came to the door selling cookies, and when Mother invited them in, one said,

"Ohhh, look at all the beautiful antiques."

Mother looked at her. "These aren't antiques; they're just the furniture we bought when we got married," she said.

After the girls left, she stood in the door with her lips pursed.

"Well, I never quite thought of my things like that," she'd said. "But I guess they're not the only antiques around here."

My father and I go to the Dairy Queen for supper, which we always do at least once when I come home to visit. People come by to say hi, and Duane rides his bicycle up and parks it in front. He comes in and hugs me.

"You're sure lookin' good," he says.

"Funny hair," says Daddy.

Duane and I talk about *Texasville*, the picture show that was filmed in Thalia a few years before in which Duane's grandson had a bit part. "I remember us in here in the Dairy Queen, right here in this very spot. Cybill Shepherd stood just where you're standing now, Jacy. She played you pretty well."

"I was in that picture show," says Daddy, sitting in his cowboy hat eating red beans. He points with a fork: "I was sitting right there in my cowboy hat eating red beans."

Duane and I laugh about how we'd hung out together at the American Legion Hall during those days of the filming, and one night piled in a car with Ellie as designated driver and trolled to every honky-tonk within a fifty-mile radius—even over the state line into Oklahoma, acting like kids. Then Ellie and I crept home at dawn like teenagers and slept on the sofa downstairs rather than wake up Daddy.

"*What?* You did *what?*" Daddy shouts. "*What* honky-tonk? Slept on *what* sofa?"

"Oh, Daddy it was a long time ago. We're just talking."

Duane hugs me again and ambles off to play with his grandkids. "Take it easy, sweetheart. You know I think of you ever' day of my life."

"Well, you oughta tell her not to drive those flimsy cars, then," Daddy offers.

We return to the house, and Daddy goes to take a nap. Sitting in the white rocker on the porch, I think of the days I sat here as Mother lay just inside the screen door a few steps away gasping for breath. It was 106 degrees, but people came and sat anyway; mostly bringing food. Helen came talking about a silver dollar some guy threw across the city lake for Mother to swim for when she was young and pretty wild. One of my brother's classmates, Jane, came and told how she had got pregnant in high school after her mother died. When her dad threw her out of the house, Mother had gone with her to talk to her father and calm him down, and this had changed everything. Jane owed the life of her baby and her own sanity to Mother, she said. Another young woman, Kate, came and told how her mother and dad wouldn't come to her wedding because they'd found out she was pregnant, so Mother drove all the way to Odessa to stand up with her while she married Wally.

Janine and her mother came from Wichita Falls and talked about the old days when we were all close friends before our lives took such different paths. Janine said, "Remember all those Nancy Drew books I gave you for birthday and Christmas, Jacy?"

"Sure," I said, "They're still back in Mother's storage closet. You want them?"

"No, that's what I was going to tell you. Every time I bought a book for you, I secretly read it first so I'd be a book ahead."

I laughed. "Guess what. I did the same with you."

My old friend Jim, a professor in Wichita Falls, and one of the few men I know with whom conversation is totally rewarding, came and sat with me. Jim was one of those people you might not see for five years and then pick up immediately where you left off. He had a mind like mine—one that can't help asking unanswerable questions. He also knew that laughing and joking and performing polite little rituals allowed me to deal with the vacancy sign hanging inside me as the center disappeared from my middle.

Jake, once the little black boy who couldn't go to school in Thalia, and now a professor, brought his granddaughter Betsy to pay respects to the woman who had made his Christmas holidays in Thalia bearable long years ago.

One of my brothers came in with one of his ex-wives, whom he hadn't seen in seven or eight years. They held hands and spent a lot of time down at the Branding Iron Hotel. Sex and death is all the same. Love among the tombstones. In the midst of death we are in life. Both ends meet. Who said that? Leopold Bloom, maybe.

I go inside to pour my father a glass of red wine. He drinks one a day these days "for thy stomach's sake," he says. "For thyself's sake too," I add, "especially when your older daughter's at home."

Daddy laughs. "Oh, you're a fine girl, Jacy, just always been a little out of control."

"What do you mean out of control? I was a perfect lady, which I sincerely regret with every fiber of my being."

"Well, I just mean, you had a real funny head on you. I never knew what you were thinking, and you asked the damndest questions. Besides you were right purty, and I was afraid you'd attract the wrong kind of boys. I just didn't know what to do with you."

"Do you remember the three boys from Olney who came here to see Ellie and me? You called them Goofus, Poofus, and Roofus, and told them all to shine their shoes next time."

"I do, and I also remember one of them, maybe Poofus, was trying to do a ridiculous trick in the living room, balancing an egg on the end of broom handle, and he broke your mother's chandelier."

"The one that looked like an upside down birthday cake."

"And that limp-wristed one you brought in here that did the tango or some such with you and Old Man Robinson's daughter on the front porch? What was that all about?"

"He was a *talent scout* from Dallas," I explain haughtily. "That was an *audition*. He was going to put me in the movies."

"Well, I don't think he did."

"How *could* he? You came down in those *awful* plaid pajamas yelling, '*Cut out that racket down there!*' And he packed up his Stardom Kit and roared off."

"His Stardom Kit?"

"Sure, that trunk with the capes and wigs and stuff. You were determined to ruin my picture show career. I could have been a star, you know."

"You could have been a lot of things. But I sure didn't know what to make of you."

"Well, it helped to have Mother as a buffer. I didn't know what to make of you either. I thought you were real strict and didn't like me very much."

"Oh, now Jacy, you know I always loved you. You were just, well, different . . . still are . . ." His voice trails off, and he sips his burgundy.

We sit in silence for several minutes, a silence for me not uncomfortable, just familiar. My father had never talked much, words being to him wholly unnecessary in the fatiguing act of living. Even phone calls—all of them, as far as he was concerned—were obscene.

So different from Mother. A room with Mother in it was a space in which nouns and verbs, participles and gerunds tripped all over themselves playing, fussing, explaining, joking, leaning into and bouncing off each other, creating new sounds, new ideas: *Synesthesia*, she would say, *listen to the warm*. Or *Catachresis*: you said *inferring* when you mean *implying. Ho, ho, gotcha!* Or *gloaming, crepuscular, twilight*, she'd clap her hands like a child: *What lovely words for a lovely time of day!* Mother and I had word battles in the manner that my brothers had food fights, tossing them back and forth, messing up the room with sound: *Salt cellar*! No, *calla lily*. No, *cellar door*. The battle of beautiful words. And weird words: *Dismal, dicker, diddle, diarrhea.* Ugly words: *Slump, crump, sucker, scrod!*

Daddy drained his glass, sat it down, and brought up his chair with a *thummpppp*, interrupting my mother-fugue. A signal: I go into the kitchen to get him a refill, and pour a glass for myself. I flail about for another subject, asking him about "old times" in West Texas, where he went to school in a one-roomer at Ralph Switch. I love to hear about my father's boyhood days, and he likes to talk about them. I'd given him a book a year or so before in which to record his memories, and he'd written in it religiously, small anecdotes with a surprisingly forceful narrative thrust in his fine, strong hand.

"Daddy, I was thinking the other day when it was so hot, when you lived up in the Panhandle, and you slaughtered meat to eat, how did you keep it without refrigeration?"

"Well, my dad would take a calf, for example, and slit it longways, taking out all the insides. Mother would cook the liver and some of the organs, and she even canned tongue—you haven't lived 'til you've had a tongue sandwich."

I make a face.

"Then Dad would hang the two big slabs of meat on a pulley that he'd strung from the top platform of the windmill. When we wanted meat for dinner, he'd pull the thing down, cut off a slab, and send it back up. In the winter it froze up there."

"How did you keep it clean? You had a lot of sandstorms."

"Yeah, well, he'd wrap the thing in ducking, is all."

"And you had to milk fifty cows every day before you went to school?" I'd heard this one a thousand times before, when I was a kid trying every ploy to shirk my chores.

"Oh, yeah. I was a great milker. See these big hands?" he holds them up. "That's where I got 'em." He laughs. "When we weaned the little calves, we stuck our hands in a bucket of milk and then let the little buggers suck on our fingers. My fingers were so big they thought they were teats." Daddy laughs and examines his hands again. "You got big hands like I do."

"Yeah, I know. On a boy they look good. I remember you told me one time about a great flu epidemic."

"Aw yeah." He takes out his handkerchief and blows his nose. "That was a sorry time. Sorry. Everyone in the family was sick, real sick—Mama couldn't even turn her head, and Dad, who was strong as a bull, got it too and was flat of his back. All the kids got it, but me."

"How come you didn't get it?"

"Well, I don't know. No telling. Mama said God had to keep someone alive to take care of things around there, and I guess I was it. So I took care of that whole family, day and night, and the place and animals too, for two weeks or more. Cold, I'm telling you, it was cold. And everybody sick and throwing up or burning with fever."

"How old were you?"

"Aw, 'bout eight, eight or nine."

"And everyone finally got well?"

"Well, after what seemed to me a long, long time, they did."

"That must have been hard on a little guy like you."

"Well, I've never forgotten it, for sure. You do what you have to do." He blows his nose again.

"What was the best prank you ever pulled as a kid?"

"Well, I guess it was the red pepper we put in Aunt Polly's snuff," Daddy's face turns red, and he laughs until tears leak from the corners of his eyes. He gets out his handkerchief again and wipes his face.

Daddy and I talk until he decides to go to bed. Then I wander over to the bookcase and pull out the book in which Daddy has recorded boyhood memories. Odd, I think as I read, for all his taciturnity, he was an extraordinary observer of concrete details—and the ones he has recorded here are more than half a century old. Amazing.

A VISITOR

Under the shade of a peach tree, I look up from my make-believe corral and my odd-size bottle horses. One of them smells strangely of vanilla extract. Above the knee-high grama grass waving in the spring breeze, I see a flash of sunlight and a speck on the horizon. I know immediately that the speck bobbing up and down is Granny coming to visit us. My sister, Mae, abandons her playhouse dishes made of broken colored glass, and we start running hand in hand across the prairie to meet Granny. We follow three distinct tracks. Two have been cut by wheels and the one in the center was stomped out by the buggy horse. As we patter along the dusty trails, our hearts beat faster and our pace slows down.

We pause occasionally to snatch the head of a yellow buttercup or gather bunches of purple and green buffalo beans. When we meet Granny we present her with the whole wilted mess.

She has on her gray-and-white checked cardboard split-bonnet and her gray knit shawl. She wears a print dress that swishes above the grass, almost hiding her black, high-topped, lace-up shoes. She is so small that she does not have to stoop very much to hug us.

In the bright half-gallon bucket that we first saw flashing in the sunlight, are fresh tea-cakes and hard red-and-white peppermint candies. We are not surprised, because we knew they would be there. She asks what Dad and Mama are doing and how the garden is coming, and we skip around and ahead of her the quarter mile back to the house.

We can hardly wait to surprise Mama with the company we bring her.

A loose sheet of paper, dated 1977, falls out of the book. Daddy had apparently been toting up mileage.

TRAVEL

In 1912 it took me an hour to walk to the field and back to take my father a drink of cool water.

In 1914 it took my family all Saturday afternoon to drive a buggy team seven miles to town for groceries.

In 1917 it took twenty minutes to make the trip into town in a Model T.

In 1929 it took fifteen minutes to go the same distance in a Model A, and in a hurry.

In 1934 it took me five hours to drive a Plymouth from Canyon to Thalia to see my girl.

In 1946 it took three and a half hours to cover the same road in an Oldsmobile, ahead of a snow storm to see about my cows.

In 1965 it took us eight hours to drive from California to Washington in a Pontiac to see a new grandson.

In 1970 it took us nine hours to fly in a 707 from Dallas to Shannon to see the world.

In 1974 it took us five hours to fly in a 747 from London home again.

In 1977 it takes me one hour to get out of my rocking chair, walk five blocks for the mail, and straggle back to my chair again.

My god, it's nearly twenty years later, I think. How would he complete this image if he added another line? I return the book to the shelf, surprised at my father's crisp, colorful language. His view of my great-grandmother in her cardboard split-bonnet, being greeted by children with yellow buttercups and bunches of purple and green buffalo beans is vigorous, alive and charming.

Why is it Daddy never talked this way, if he could see and think this way? Why is it that he hardly ever talked at all? Could it possibly be that Mother had too often spoken for him? Was that an idea worth considering? I remember her telling me once that *her* Mother talked for her, as if the "cat had got my tongue," and I recall that on occasion when I was slow to respond in public, my mother talked for me. I also recall that in my first marriage my husband so assumed the oversight of the family finances that for years I thought I was a dummy in the math department. Clearly, I'm not. How we cripple one another without even being aware of it.

Next to my father's book is a notebook my grandmother Mollie gave me in the early 1960s, with a note in the front.

My Dearest Granddaughter,

How is it that you are always thinking up things to do—like get old people to write down their stories—when you have two babies and a husband who moves you around the country at the drop of a hat? I suppose you think up projects to keep your mind occupied. (Remember the old "brain sit-ups?") I recall that when my babies were small, if I had not known how to sew and create pretty things for them, I would probably have gone out of my mind from boredom. In any case, you asked me to write for you my most unusual experiences from childhood, so here is what I came up with. I expect I will see these in one of your little books some day. You've been making little books since you were about six years old. I can't imagine what you'll find interesting in these memories of an old fogie, but here they are.

Love, Mollie

A GRAVE INCIDENT

When we were children, our mother never allowed us to go to funerals. Our little friends described the corpse, the wild weeping of the mourners, the elegant casket, until we couldn't wait to go. One day, when I was about eight years old, school was dismissed for a funeral. My little sister, Lucy Jane, now Celie, and I went with the other children to the church, though we did not know the dead person.

We were not allowed in the church, so we went to the churchyard cemetery and waited for the people to come out.

I was determined to see the corpse and the casket. The people poured out of the church and prevented me from getting a good view, and there seemed more room on the other side, so I tiptoed around there, my eyes glued all the time to the moving casket.

Well, the empty spot I had scouted out was the open grave, and I wound up—or rather down—in the bottom of it, just as the pallbearers were about to unload their goods. I looked up and saw the bottom of the casket coming at me and I squealed in terror. A shocked-faced man pulled me out of the grave. Celie, of course, told on me, and my father didn't know whether to smile or be angry, so he just announced to the family: "This child is always getting into something!"

THE INDIAN SCALP

On the reservation in Oklahoma, where we lived, there was a young Indian girl, who helped with the children. She became very attached to the two boys, my brothers, who were four and six years old. One spring day, she took the boys across the river to look for wild poke greens—which my mother considered a great delicacy. A spring rain had caused a raging flood in the river. The girl grasped a boy under each arm and plunged into the swift stream, her one idea was getting them safely back to their mother. As she gained the shore, the arms of my father reached out to receive the little boys, but a whirling log struck the Indian girl's head, and she started to sink. My mother waded out, and, grasping her by the hair, brought her to the bank.

Years later the girl died, and my mother, helping to "lay her out," clipped a lock of her long black hair for a keepsake; after all, she had rescued her sons. My brothers, ungrateful wretches, called the lock of hair my mother's Indian scalp.

The next day, Daddy and I stand under the mesquite in the backyard and say goodbye. "What route are you taking?" Daddy asks.

"Oh, Quanah, Childress, Clarendon."

He nods. "You be careful now. Especially in that jerry-built car you got there."

I kiss him and head for the interviews in Amarillo. Just what I need, I think. Somebody else's oral history.

7

We must first come into possession of our names. For it is through our names that we first place ourselves in the world.
—Ralph Ellison

R·E·P·L·I·C·A

AT THE AIRPORT, I buy a copy of *O is for Odious* and buckle myself in for the trip back to LaGuardia. "Where you headed for, girl?" asks my seatmate, a man looking to be in his late sixties with a silver and turquoise bolo tie curving itself over a belly that sits under his pearl-buttoned shirt like a beach ball.

Girl? I blink. *Girl?* To some men of his time and culture women always remain girls.

"I'm going to New York," I say, watching him pour a shot of scotch into a plastic glass from a silver flask. Scotch in the morning? And who carries flasks anymore? Somehow I associate flasks with Jay Gatsby and raccoon coats—Long Island, not Texas.

"This here's my morning juice, heh, heh. Thought I'd tie one on before a Blue Norther hits. Want some?"

"No thanks." I open my book dismissively.

"New York, huh? That's one place I never had no hankerin' to go." He jerks a meaty thumb at my paperback. "Whatcha got there?"

"Just a book to kill time while I travel," I say coolly, but he isn't to be put off.

"I'm Amos Adams." He sticks out a rough hand, which I take briefly. "I'm going up to Kansas City to see my granddaughter, Lilly. She's fixin' to get married, and my wife Edith's already up there tellin' her what to wear and how to act and so on. She'll be settin' everyone straight all right. I told 'em I'd be bargin' in there sometime today to cheer 'em all up, and Edith said, 'Cheer *down*, you mean.' *Har har.* She's one funny woman, Edith, give 'er half a chance."

"Well, I'm sure she'll have a lovely wedding, and I hope you have a great trip," I say, pulling my book closer to my face.

"Aw, it'll be nice all right. Edith always does things up real brown. And Lilly's such a beautiful girl. Can't imagine why she wants to marry that son-of-a-gun, though, a photographer of some kind." Amos leans his shoulder into mine. "Now what kind of job is that? You ever know a photographer worth a hill of beans?"

I turn toward him for a moment, speechless.

"How can somebody take pitchers all day and call it a job, I ask you? Now Edith, she takes pitchers on vacations—Hoover Dam, Coolidge Dam, a whole *damn* bunch of dams—that's hardly a full day's work, if you ask me. We got a bushel basket of pitchers lyin' around that house, and Edith never made one penny offa them. Good thang Lilly's got her a lil' ol job runnin' a lil' ol' company of some kind in KC, or these here newlyweds are likely to be eatin' roadkill chili, know what I mean? Cain't live on love and sea breezes, I always say, specially in KC, *heh heh.* The sea breezes, I mean. Does your husband have a job?"

"Yes, my husband has a job. He's a neuro-surgeon, and on the weekends, he's a ballet dancer, but right now he's at home taking care of our eight small children, while I galavant all over the country talking to strange men." Some people say I can have a nasty streak when pushed too far, but of course I don't believe them. Today I am just weary of talking to people. I've been doing that for four days, practically non-stop—listening to people ramble on about their lives. Most of the time I enjoy it, but right now I want to read my no-brainer book, not talk to a drunk.

Amos blinks his turtle eyes, stopped only for a moment: "Oh, well then . . . you must have . . . a . . one of them unusual marriages. Now as to working, what do you do, may I ask?"

I close my book firmly and ceremoniously place it in my lap, defeated. "I am a teacher."

"Oh, yeah? What do you teach?"

"I teach English to university students."

"Oh," Amos slaps his head. "That is the *dag-nab-dest* subject. The *worst.* That was my worst subject all the way through school.

Boy, did I hate that English. And I couldn't unnerstand that Shakespeare. I'd read and read that stuff till I like to lathered 'tween the legs, but I couldn't make heads or tails out of it. Didn't seem to me like he talked right. And them poems about birds. And vases. That one about a vase with a heifer on it. The *'heifer lowin' at the skies, and all her silken flanks with garlands dressed.'* I remember them lines like it was yesterday. *'Happy, happy boughs,'* and all that, and I remember the *'unravished bride.'* Course I didn't unnerstand none of it, but I remember it. I had to write a term theme about it once because my teacher, my lil' ole' school teacher a long time ago, she said to me, 'Now Buster' . . . that's what they called me then, not Amos . . . 'Now Buster, you should unnerstand about *heifers* and this *bu-colic* setting—that's the word she used—*bu-colic* and made me look it up, I'll never forget, it means countrified—so, she said, 'you write about this poem with the heifer in it.'"

As he speaks, my eyes glaze over and my chin slips slowly into my turtleneck. I don't deserve two hours of this.

"So I did. Man, I'm tellin' you, that was the *hardest* damn writin' I ever done to this day, but I thank god it got me out of high school. Them poems never did make sense to me, and god knows I didn't have no use for 'em after entering the world of big machinery, where I've made a good livin' for forty years or so. Combines, tractors, John Deere you know?"

Amos pauses and looks off into the distance for a moment. "Yep, made a durn good livin' and bought sixty acres to build a four-bed-room ranch with a crafts room just for Edith and her plaster paris stuff, and I *still* don't know what I had to write about heifers on a vase for. The school system you know, it was all screwed up then. Still is. Worse even. Cain't say 'The Lord's Prayer,' but got to read a thousand poems by a thousand fags. But," he looked more cheerful, "you know, that there Miz Gowdy, she was one right fair lady in spite of Shakespeare. I wish all kids could have a teacher like her."

My head snaps up: "Ms. Gowdy?"

"Yup, Miz Mollie Harper Gowdy, a widder lady in Muleshoe, a pert lil' lady that really cared about her groomin'. Taught me how to speak real good. She had somethin' right magical about her, so you forgot how silly the stuff was she made you do."

Replica

"That was my grandmother, Mr. Adams."

"You don't say! Miz Gowdy was your grandmother?" Amos is caught off guard, an ambush that renders him speechless for nearly five seconds. Then he exclaims, popping his hands together: "Now, isn't it a small world after all, like my grandkids say after they've been down to Disney World." Amos claps me on the shoulder. "Your grandmother! Well, whaddaya thank of that? Miz Gowdy . . ." He pauses, then pushes the flask toward me. "Here, now, you've gotta have a drank with me on that one. Give you a lil' buzz for the trip."

"No thanks, Mr. Adams." But the oral historian in me is captured once again, in spite of myself. "What grade were you in then?"

"Aw, about the 'leventh, I'd say. I had Miz Gowdy for two-three years."

I flash briefly on my one visit to a classroom where Mollie was teaching in West Texas. Mollie stood elegantly before the class in her periwinkle blue Shelton Stroller with shoes dyed to match, reading from *Richard III*. "No, to Whitefriars; there attend my coming . . ."

The boys snickered.

"Was ever woman in this humor wooed? Was ever woman in this humor won? I'll have her, but I will not keep her long. What!"

The boys snickered again.

Mollie glared them down, then turned to the blackboard with a flourish. "Now, students, we shall diagram the next sentence. Speak with me please, now, slowly: *I that killed her husband and his father/ To take her in her heart's extremest hate/ With curses in her mouth, tears in her eyes/ The bleeding witness of my hatred by/ Having God, her conscience, and these bars against me/ And I no friends to back my suit at all/ But the plain devil and dissembling look/ And yet to win her, all the world to nothing!*

"Now, students, what part of speech is the word *bars* here? Where shall I put it on this diagram?"

The Muleshoe High School football team was about to mutiny as I, age twelve, copper hair brushed to a shine, appeared at the classroom door in my white pinafore that Mollie had embroidered with blue flowers over the shoulders.

"*All . . . the . . . world . . . to . . . noth . . . .*" The repetition came to a stuttering halt as one after another of the students spied me standing uncomfortably in the door. Jaws dropped. I looked. Heat and silence pushed the grimy windows and the blackboard walls to a fish-eye curve.

Mollie turned. "Bars," she said. "Bars. Now where shall I put this on the . . . ." Her voice trailed off as she turned toward the door and saw her granddaughter she had invited to the class.

"*Oh, Sugar lum lasses, do come in!*" she called brightly, as she pattered toward the door. "Class, this is my dear, *dear* granddaughter, Jacy. Isn't she beautiful? Please say hello to her. *Say hello, Jacy, dear.*"

Standing as if aged six and nude, I wished with all my heart that I lived in San Francisco, where the earth opened up and swallowed one whole, leaving nothing but smoke and dust in one's stead. I could not move. I could not turn my head. My grandmother's soft hands began tugging me into the room where the students had broken into titters, whispering *Sugar lum lasses, sugar lum lasses*, under their breaths so rhythmically that it sounded to me as if an entire timpani section were chattering and wire-brushing at me. I turned and fled down the hall in my shiny black Mary Janes, not looking behind as Mollie called to me, "Dear, dear, please come meet the students."

For at least forty years I have considered that high in the top two of life's most humiliating moments. Everything is magnified at age twelve, especially everything having to do with the way your family turns you back into a child in front of people, when all you want to do is grow up. But today I look directly at Amos and brave it: "Mr. Adams, this is a long shot, but I must ask you: Did you ever hear of a little girl in a white pinafore called . . . ." I gulp and think that if I had ever been to a psychiatrist, she would have told me that if I did not at some time in my life speak these words, they would be forever stuck within me growing green with mold like cheese, gumming up my works, and keeping me forever from being a whole self-actualized human being . . . . "called, called (swallow, gulp) '*sugar lum lasses?*'"

Amos looks at me, squints one eye, turns away, looks at me again, and then looks off. After a moment, he hits his knee with the palm of his hand. "*Shee-ut!*" he says. Then he hits his knee again. He turns abruptly toward me. "Sugar lum, huh? So *you're* it? *The sugar lum girl!*" He lets out a low whistle.

"We talked about you for a long time—that red hair, that white dress. Nobody believed you really existed." He pauses. "Like a fairy or something. No, a fantasyland person like Alice in Wonderland standing in the doorway. *Shee-ut!* Wait'll I tell Coondog Coffelt. He won't believe this, sure enough."

I sit quietly for a moment, and then turn to Amos. "Mr. Adams, if you'd been twelve years old right then, how would you have felt?"

Amos puts his hands on one ankle and pulls a leg up deliberately, crossing it over the opposite knee in the narrow space between him and the seat in front. "Well, miss, I don't ordinarily counsel violence, but if I'd been twelve years old and in your particular position at that there point in time, I'd a liked to wrang that nice lady's neck." He paused for a moment and collected himself. "Sorry, I mean, considering she was your grandma 'n all."

I laugh. "Shake, Mr. Adams," I stick out my hand. Amos takes it, turns it over in his for a moment, then looks back at me as sweetly as a half-drunk old coot can. "Call me Buster," he says.

"Thanks for reminding me of my grandmother, Buster, even if that *was* one of the most painful moments of my life. I enjoyed talking to you." I reach down for my big shoulder bag and withdraw a notebook. "Now, I guess I should get some work done."

Amos nods and stares off into the distance, as if back in Muleshoe High with Miz Gowdy, and Keats, and Shakespeare, and a white apparition standing in the door. Then he turns back to me.

"S'cuse me, Miss, but I need to know one thang before you get to work. Is your husband really a belly dancer?"

I do a quick-think and stifle a laugh. "No, Buster. I said, *ballet.* He really enjoys the ballet at Lincoln Center in New York. Sometimes they do *Romeo and Juliet.*"

"Oh, *Shakespeare*," he says, brightening. "I know *that* one. It's about love, but everybody dies."

I nod, then stare out the plane window as we enter a mound of clouds that reminds me of the dreamwhip on top of the lime Jell-O, marshmallow, cherry cream surprise I'd been offered for lunch in Amarillo. *Mollie taught Buster?* Did she really call him that? And did she call Coondog, *Coondog?* I can't hear those names coming out of Mollie's mouth. Surely she would have made a point of using proper names in class, but maybe Buster's memories are fresher than my own. I look down at my book and flip its pages with my thumb, like I used to flip the *Little Big Books,* watching the tiny cartoons up in the corner of the Lone Ranger hopping on his horse and riding away into the distance, as I flipped faster. *Hi! Ho! Silver!* Fifty years ago in Muleshoe, Texas, Buster and Coondog might have been Mollie's star students, who knows?

I emerge from my book and look over at my seatmate. Amos has fallen asleep and is snoring mightily beside me, his mouth open. I look away. Something about the way he gasps for air reminds me of the noises my mother made the last days of her life, and I wonder if going home to that house will ever get any easier.

At home this last time, after Daddy had gone to bed one night, I pulled out a big manila envelope I'd brought with me filled with letters from Mother through those years when I had lived miles away. I'd read a few of them. Now, I pull out the envelope and extract a letter at random.

Well, it's finally rained, and everything is green, and everybody's smiling again. People's faces were beginning to look like their dried up stock tanks. As for the new Post Office, we do not like it. It is all goofed up for parking, and then they decided to pave the street *after* the post office moved in. Dumb. And after having the same box and number for fifty years, our new box is around the corner and down against the floor on which we must prostrate ourselves and feel blindly into the cubby hole and drag out three ads from TG&Y, a Bank America card bill, and a franked copy of something John Tower read into the Congressional Record.

Your hometown, my dear, has finally succumbed to the demon rum. The county went wet for the first time in forty years, and now we can't get to the drugstore and back without getting drunk coming and going. There's a new "jiffy liquor store" where the old flower shop was. As you know, we're in dire need of jiffy liquor more than flowers around here. Also we have "Ye Olde Wine Cellar" decorated with bilious purple fruits of the vine. And somebody has put in "G's Place" where the old car wash was. The Wildcatter is rolling out the barrel like everyone else, so we'll probably be wallowing in the gutter next time you come home. A far cry from the days when we "just mustn't talk about it, and play like it didn't happen" when the sheriff dumped Old Upright J. W. Davis's booze in front of our house every Saturday night.

Daddy finally got so indignant about that old prickly pear in the White House he wrote to everybody even remotely connected with the sorry business and told them to get that crook out of there *now*. Three days later he was out. So now Dad's faith in the *vox populi* has been restored. The only thing that still galls him is the pension, expense account and security officers for life. Maybe Jaworski can do something about that. Anyway, it really is a relief after the long hot summer to have even some meager moisture and a middlin' president.

Your friend Ray Farabee won his bid for the State Senate. Maybe politics will be looking up. Sissy Farenthold did not make even as good a showing as last time, but then she never offered anything positive except that she was a woman, which was enough for me. But your dad was for Briscoe—beats me why.

We got our new passport the other day, and I was horrified to find how far baby has come in four years. Do you know *our* passport is in the name of *your father, his birthday, his coloring, etc.*, and then it says *"and wife, Margaret."* I didn't even protest four years ago, and in fact didn't notice. Dad thought it was hilarious and said, "Well, it did say *wife*, not concubine."

My dear, early in the spring I was digging in the bed when my spade sliced right through the center of a hyacinth bulb. And guess what? Right in the middle was a completely formed flower stem, and miniature bells and all. I was both sad and glad at the discovery, torn between not believing in predestination dogma, and grateful to heritage. I *still* think a body can be anything she wants to be bad enough—except maybe a silk purse.

Amos Adams has begun to stir and reach for his flask again. With a grunt and a "how you doin', hon?" he ambles off to the men's room. I put my letters and notebooks away and recall Mother's funeral. To get out of the house, my husband Marlboro and I had gone to stay with my old friend Larry, who several years before had returned to Thalia and bought Old Man Taylor's dilapidated mansion—the biggest house in town. As kids, Larry and my brothers used to sneak around the tall brick house at night, peering into the basement windows (which housed, they swore, a Cadillac, though no one could guess how it got there), swiping discarded books from Old Man Taylor's trash can and making up wild stories about the inhabitants of the house. Their tales reminded me of Scout and Boo Radley and company in *To Kill a Mockingbird*.

When Larry came back to Thalia, having earned a pot of money as the preeminent writer of Western fiction, he bought the old place and refurbished it down to its last burnished copper drainpipe. It has about six thousand square feet, about half of them filled with books. Here Marlboro and I stayed in an upstairs bedroom.

"What're we going to do, Larry?" I asked one night as we sat on his roof garden, sipping a rare Cabernet. "What are we going to do with the old house? Can Daddy live in it alone—you know he won't move. Should I give up my work, my life, and come back here to stay with him? *You* came back—at least part of the year you're here. People were so good to us as Mother was dying. Maybe I could convince Marlboro that we could live here and write just as well as we could live on the Mill Pond and write. What do you think?"

"What I think," he said deliberately, "is that you shouldn't be making those kinds of decisions in the emotional state you're in. And furthermore, I want to tell you that if you lived here you would go crazy within two weeks because there is nothing around here to eat."

I laughed.

"I mean it. Nothing. You'll go through the three restaurants with edible food in Wichita in the first week. Then you'll repeat that. Then you'll run out of things to eat. When I'm here, I have to drive to Dallas every three days to find something to eat."

Clearly, Thalia hasn't changed.

8

You don't look at the
past just once, you look
at it with the knowledge
of the present, which
was the future.
—Alice McDermott

R·I·G·H·T

AT LAGUARDIA I head for the escalator that takes me down to the baggage area. At the bottom of the stairs, among all the chauffeurs and hired limo drivers holding signs saying "George Brown," and "Peter Chambers," stands tall, gorgeous Marlboro holding a placard in front of him: "Runaway Wife."

I roll my eyes as the stairs bring me down to meet him. People around us titter as I put my arms around him.

"Just for that you get to carry all the baggage."

"What baggage?" he says. "You didn't leave here with any baggage."

"That's what *you* think," I grin at him. "And I brought even more back too—notes and more notes, tapes, photos, stuff. The lifetime baggage of half a dozen people representing various forms of the dysfunctional family in the Texas Panhandle."

"Well, let's get it and get out of here."

At home the next morning, I take my coffee and walk to the edge of the pond. A brisk wind, the tail-end of winter, tugs at my hair, and I pull my jacket around me.

Marlboro appears at the back door.

"Hey," I say. "The Reeds seem to be moving. They have a big van in the driveway." I take a deep breath and fling out my arms. "Can you imagine moving from this place? I love it here. I love my pond, my porch, my decks, my ducks, my house. I love my . . ."

Marlboro grabs me and pulls me inside. "No I can't imagine moving. This is paradise, silly. Now go get some shoes on."

Upstairs, I pull on boots, thinking I'll walk down the street and see what's up with the Reeds. Moving? Nobody in her right mind would move from here. In fact, nobody in her right mind would move period. I know. I've done it a couple of dozen times.

After moves to three houses in Eighty Lakes, Greg moved the family back to Texas. To Wichita Falls, of all places. He said, "Mother's calling and I have to go," meaning that he'd been made an attractive offer there and couldn't wait to go back as a successful leader to his hometown, where, he liked to say, he'd grown up on "the right side of the tracks and the wrong side of the river."

On his first day at work as chief of the schools, Greg reached into his desk drawer and brought out a court order that had languished there for several months, long enough for the previous occupant of that office—clearly a man with a fierce self-preservation instinct—to find another job and get out of town before the fur began to fly. The order demanded that the schools be desegregated with all deliberate speed, meaning, in this case, within the next two months—before school opened in the fall. Greg jumped in and began executing the order, an act that rendered our family's stay in Wichita Falls mercifully brief.

Some thought Greg a courageous man with noble principles; some thought him arrogant; some naive; one gave him an ink drawing of Don Quixote for his office wall. Racism was a fact of life in this part of Texas, and the last thing most of the locals wanted was somebody acting as the conscience of the community. Here, people sent their young sons to fancy summer camps at which the grand finale on the last night, as parents came to collect their sons, was the burning of hundreds of crosses on a hillside as the campers sang "The Battle Hymn of the Republic."

Greg, who had invited a black man to lunch in the dining room of Eighty Lakes Country Club for the first time in history, was an integrationist and an educator who agreed with the law and intended to follow it. He was bent on seeing the country's public schools desegregated. Peacefully. And he intended to start right here, even though a mongrel School Board fought him tooth and nail, going so far as to unearth an old lynching law buried in the books at the courthouse to frighten the black community into staying "in their place." Within weeks, the city was polarized.

"You don't look like a nigger lover to me," a man at a dinner party said to me one evening as I stood in front of a fireplace with a glass of wine. Hardly in my thirties, and not much given to public confrontation, I was baffled. How did one answer a statement like this? Furthermore, I recognized the man—the rich boy I'd had one date with in high school; the one who was having a swimming party to which I was the only one invited.

"And how does such a person look?" I replied finally.

"Oh, well, certainly not like you. You're much too pretty; you have too much going for you." The man looked me over from top to bottom, then leaned toward me conspiratorially. "Jacy, how did you get yourself in this position? You could have had anyone, married anyone—guys with money to burn."

I looked at him: "Do you mean, what's a nice girl like me doing trying to help the black kids in this city get as good an education as *your* kids are getting? Is that what you mean?"

He staggered back. "Well, now I didn't mean to start a big argument, I was just making polite conversation."

"*Polite?* You call that a *polite* opening? What school of manners did you go to? Excuse me, please." I moved away and went off to find Greg, who was being berated by one Lorna P. Dukey, an obnoxious woman in sequins, and a well-known school board hanger-on.

"Who gave you the right to practice social engineering on our children?" She was shouting. "The next thing we know, those people will be wanting to date our daughters!" She pointed a finger in his face.

"It's the law," said Greg. "Separate but equal is inherently unequal; it's the law of the land."

"Not in Texas it isn't."

"Dinner! Dinner is served," chirped the hostess, ringing a little glass bell.

The guests trooped to the table glaring at one another.

At the First Presbyterian Church, we received no better treatment. It, too, was segregated, and when I tried to bring a group of black children to a Christmas service, we were blocked at the door.

"These are our guests," I said. "They are staying with us over the holidays," which was true. "I want to bring them into the church and let them hear the carols and see the nativity scene."

"You can't come in with these people," sniffed the church official at the door. "Now step aside and let the members here get through."

I marched out of the First Presbyterian Church of Wichita Falls, Texas, and never went back.

For two years, the town was in a uproar over the integration of the schools, a fight heavily fueled by the majority faction of a divided school board. Greg grew thinner and testier. I was in graduate school and working as an instructor, which helped me keep my sanity. Also I focused on keeping the children calm.

Paul was not yet in school, so I hired Jewel, a young black woman, to care for him at home a few hours each day while I was at the university or doing volunteer work. Once, when I took a group of social work students on a visit to a day-care center in the black community, I was brought up short: There were Jewel's two young children. What is this all about? I asked myself. Jewel has to farm out her own kids, so she can take care of mine? The irony of the situation struck me as ludicrous. From then on, when Jewel came to care for Paul, she brought her children with her, but they could play only inside the fenced backyard, because several neighbors complained.

Greg frequently brought home older black students who were on the verge of getting into trouble. They had dinner with the family, got help with their homework, and sometimes stayed overnight. Greg thought giving them special attention and exposing them to what he called "a normal family life" would be a good influence. I wasn't quite sure where Greg got the idea that ours was "a normal family life," since I saw my own life as one of repressed desperation. I often wished for more privacy and fewer mouths to feed, fewer kids of any hue to take care of. I had my own homework to do, classes to prepare for and papers to write. But I couldn't argue with Greg. He was right, actually: if we could keep even one kid from messing up his life, or ending up in jail—where more than one of the boys who visited us were already headed—the effort was worth it.

One morning I was in the kitchen while four-year-old Paul played in the side yard. I looked out the window just in time to see my small son flat on his back on the sidewalk, wailing loudly. I dashed outside and picked him up. "What happened, Paul?"

Dose boys. Dey push me down. He pointed to two large white boys, about junior high age, running swiftly away in the direction of a busy freeway nearby.

"Why, Paul? What were you doing?"

Nuffin. Jist standin' dere. Dey say, 'Your daddy's messin' up the schools wif dem nigras' and push me down.

I held him close. "Well, they're out on the freeway now. Maybe they'll get run over."

Paul pulled away and looked up at me, tears streaming down his puzzled face. *We don't want 'em to get runned over jist for pushing me down, do we Mommy?*

I took him in my arms again. "No, of course, not, baby. Mommy was just mad at them for hurting you. We don't want anyone to get hurt." I kicked myself: Even a toddler had a better notion than I about the proper balance of crime and punishment. This life must be getting to me.

I had an eight o'clock class to teach at the university the morning after the school board ousted my husband. The board meeting had started early the evening before, but around midnight, after a shouting battle between warring board factions, Greg was fired. I was up late reading and heard the announcement on the radio, so when Greg came dragging in, he needed only to supply details. About dawn, he took a sleeping pill and went to bed.

I paced through the house until time to get the kids up. Then I got them ready for school, explaining to them what had happened and preparing them for what kids might say at school. At the same time, I fended off reporters and phone calls, crank and otherwise. When I finally walked into my English class, the students, who had heard little but school board news on the local radio station while driving to class, looked at me uncomfortably. Some avoided my eyes altogether.

"Yes, it's true," I told them when they were all in their seats. "The school board has fired the best school chief this city will ever have. A brilliant man. A fair man. A man who believes in equal opportunity for all people, regardless of color. Now, turn to page eighty-five and let's discuss the excerpt from *Babbitt*."

Later that day I took my orals and defended my thesis on *Religious Symbols in the Works of James Joyce*. Finally, I called Mother and asked in a voice trembling with rage and exhaustion: "Mother, can the kids and I come see you for a few days? I can't stand this place a moment longer." While we were away, and Greg was in Dallas looking for another job, someone threw a stink bomb through the dining room window and stuck an open bag filled with fleas in our mail slot.

The school board bought out Greg's contract. I insisted that we take the windfall and go to Paris. *Something* positive ought to come out of all the expended energy and grief. And thus did I—fifteen years after I had first packed to go—walk along the Champs Élysées eating strawberries. Gorgeous, big, bright, juicy, red strawberries. It was not altogether as I had planned, with three tired children in tow. And Gene Kelly didn't leap out of shrubbery to greet me. Jean-Paul Sartre and Gertrude Stein and Albert Camus were nowhere to be seen, and I was not invited to a single salon. But I *was* in Paris, and I made it my city. "Existence before essence!" I shouted from the top of the Eiffel Tower. Then I climbed back down and came back to the States, determined to figure out what the essence of my existence was to be.

I had no home, generally or specifically, to return to. After the hideous episode in Wichita Falls, the heart went out of me. Though there were some good and courageous people there, and still are—and I never want to forget that—the general mentality in that part of Texas was so discouraging: racism overlaid with a veneer of piety and self-righteousness, bloated affability masking a smug meanness of spirit. The entire country, in fact, seemed all screwed up: How could we have killed a president and a peace leader, sent young boys to die in Vietnam? Our leaders has tossed body count, racism, sexism, greed, patriotism, and religion into one big pot and stirred it until it boiled over. How could an individual live with integrity in a country and a society that had none?

I couldn't bear it. The only realistic way a mother of three kids could figure out how to protest, was simply to refuse to buy into the madness of it all, to refuse to participate in the greed. Accordingly, I sold or gave away everything we had accumulated, except our books and the most basic items of living. We rented a small house in Dallas to live in while we tried to collect ourselves. Greg took a new job as a top administrator of the Dallas Independent School District. The day we moved in, Greg had to go away on business. I began the chore of unpacking and putting the house together.

The kids ran in and out, sometimes helping, while I opened the packing boxes on the patio and hauled stuff inside to put away. I did this for about two days, bringing in take-out food, focused on trying to get the house in liveable shape before the kids started to school.

Carrie came home from visiting neighbors, and was reading in her room, when she began to get sick. She complained, took an aspirin, and lay down to take a nap. Paul came home from across the street and began crying with a headache. He lay down on his bed. I continued to line the cupboards with insect-repellent paper and put dishes in the shelves. I noticed that the paper had a faintly odd odor to it, but it was hardly noticeable. Ben came in later, watched TV for awhile, then said he felt sick to his stomach and went to his bedroom.

After organizing the kitchen, I strode up and down the hall putting things away—towels, bathroom stuff, bed linens. I was in and out of the kids' rooms and noticed, vaguely, that all were taking naps, but their lassitude hardly registered. The door to the patio—where the packing boxes were stored—was open, so I moved in and out of the house for several hours.

It was late in the afternoon of the first or second day we'd been in the house (time grew a little foggy for awhile there) when I noticed that the kids were not up running around, looking in the fridge, flipping the TV channels. I noticed that, oddly, the TV wasn't even on at all.

A strange quietness surrounded me. I walked down the hall and looked in to see both boys asleep on their beds. Ben never slept! And Paul looked so pale. Ben's face was turned to the wall, and he was curled in a fetal position. Paul's mouth was open, and he was snoring a little, his eyes open a slit and rolled back in his head. These things registered, but not too clearly. I went on to Carrie's room, and she wasn't there. The house was dead still; my head felt funny. In the bathroom, I saw Carrie passed out on the floor in front of the toilet, as if she had gone there to throw up but hadn't made it. I felt vaguely as if I were in a Rod Serling movie.

I picked up Carrie and got her back to bed. Then I remember stopping again by the boys' door and looking in on them, half relieved that they were quiet for a change, but my head was in a fog. Back in the kitchen, I decided irrationally that the odor of the insect-repellent paper in the cupboards was poison. I began to hallucinate. *This paper is killing my children,* I muttered and began pulling it from the shelves. Plates and glasses crashed onto the floor as I pulled out the shelf paper. Nobody waked up. Suddenly, I could not see. It was as if a film had fallen over my eyes. Everything around me was dark and still. I fancied that I could smell the killer shelf paper enveloping me like some alien vapor. I was in the twilight zone. Something was sucking me into a vortex . . . I was going crazy . . . *my kids were dying.* I was on the floor on my hands and knees unable to see. The phone, I thought, the phone. Where is it?

I recalled a wall phone between the kitchen and dining area. I crawled to the area and began to climb my hands up the wall to feel for the phone. An outlet, a wire. Suddenly, there it was—the phone! Now, what was I to do with it? I knew no one in this city. *My kids were dying, and who would I call?*

I dialed the operator. "I am . . . I just moved to Dallas . . . I don't know anyone. I need a doctor. I need help. My children and I have been poisoned. Please help me."

The operator asked the address. "I don't know a doctor, but there's a drugstore near you. Just a moment."

In a few seconds a druggist came on the line. "I don't know," I said. "Just moved here . . . know no one. . . . . poisoned . . . . kids dying . . . . I'm blind . . . please help . . ."

"Where exactly are you?" he asked. I told him as well as I could. "I'll get someone there," he said. "Hang on."

I don't know how long it was, but a doctor came to the door. I heard the knock but I couldn't get there. I opened my eyes but couldn't see. I still smelled that paper. I began to crawl to the door.

I heard it open; footfalls came toward me. "What's wrong here?" a voice said. I remember feeling the cool hard wood of the floor against my cheek. *Someone is here; now I can die.*

The doctor shook me. "Who else is here?" he asked loudly. "Tell me." I raised my head. "My kids . . . bedroom . . . boys . . . Carrie . . . back room . . ." I fell to the floor again.

He shook us all awake and got us into the living room. "I think you must have food poisoning," he said. "No, it has nothing to do with 'poison' shelf paper." He gave us pills and water. He slapped our cheeks. "Now, don't get dehydrated," he said. "I'll send a home nurse here every six hours to make sure you get enough liquid. She'll be here right away and stay with you for awhile. You'll be okay." He made a phone call and left.

The nurse came and fed us liquids. Water, cokes, ice tea. "Just keep drinking. Doctor says you'll feel better." She came that night and had us up and walking around the yard. The fresh air seemed to revive us; my sight returned briefly. She came again the next morning, and we had all passed out again. She shook us out of bed and made us drink through straws. When we fell over, she propped us up and gave us liquid. She walked us around outside. Then she left.

The second or third day—I lost count of time—I called my mother in Thalia. No answer. I called Greg's mother in Wichita Falls. "We are very sick, and I need help," I said. "I don't know what's wrong, but Carrie is passed out in the hall again, and the boys haven't moved for hours. I don't know how many. I can't see and can hardly hold my head up."

I crawled over to the sliding doors of the patio and inched them open. Then I pulled myself outside, hunching along like some demented Caliban, and put my face against the stones of the patio floor. I felt better almost immediately. This house is killing us, I remember thinking. I have to get the kids out. I hauled myself back through the door and down the hall. I took Paul, the smallest, first, dragging him off the bed. He was barely conscious. Creeping along together we got outside to the patio. I went back for Ben, and then Carrie—dragging them down the hall and out the door, half-crying, half-whimpering. The image of a mother dog rescuing her puppies flashed into my head.

On the patio outside, the temperature was in the high 90s. Inside, the house was air-conditioned, but we felt better in the heat. Within a few hours Greg's mother and father, Trudy and Will, bustled in with liquid and food. I was not hungry at all, but my limbs felt like stone. Trudy put me to bed. I remember lying there imagining that I was the Sphinx with massive, heavy, concrete limbs. Then I remember nothing at all . . . until . . .

Something roused me in the night. I will never know what. Mere survival instinct, maybe. I pulled myself out of bed and again half-crawled down the hall. My eyesight would come and go. I saw Trudy, in a pink nightgown, passed out near a bedroom door. Will was asleep on the floor. In the living room, Greg, still in shirt and tie, was in a deep sleep on the sofa. I didn't know when Greg had arrived, but I couldn't rouse him.

By this time I was sure the house was cursed, so I pulled my body to the phone and called the operator to get an ambulance. *"Everyone is dead or dying!"* I screamed. *"Hurry, please hurry!"*

Within a few minutes I heard the siren. Then knocks at the door. Then people walking, men talking. I lifted my head and saw my kids, one by one, carried out the door. Carrie's little sun-tanned arms dangling down; Ben's strong, active body, now limp; Paul's eyes turned in on themselves. These images registered, but I could not move. Then I saw a white-coated man carrying Trudy in her pink nightgown out the door, followed by a man holding Will in his striped pajamas. Greg in his suitpants and dress shirt, tie awry, went by in the arms of a burly man. Then they came to the kitchen for me.

We all lay on stretchers in the front yard. Sirens blared, red lights flashed. It seemed the world was filled with raucous, confusing alarms. Somehow I found Ben's hand. Then we were all lifted into the ambulance. I remember thinking with a fuzzy horror: Are we going to be on TV like this? *New school chief arrives in city. Dies in front yard.* Even half-dead I was horrified of headlines. Wichita Falls had snake-bit me for sure.

At the hospital, I recall seeing Greg in a wheelchair. He was being rolled to a desk to register us, but he couldn't speak. His head had fallen onto his chest. I think I was walking by this time, but don't remember exactly. I do recall telling the desk person that my family was dying, to take care of them, and I'd settle it up with her about the insurance later. I think I was screaming. They put us all together in one big room. Doctors and nurses hovered over us. They gave us liquids, and we lay there for how long I don't know. Little by little we began to feel better. I remember opening my eyes and seeing little skinny, darling Paul sitting up on the white cot, yawning and looking around as if asking: How did I get here? We awoke gradually, first one and then another. We mumbled at each other a little, wondering what was wrong, why we were here. The kids were surprised to see their grandparents, and especially laid out on cots as they were. They were the last to rouse themselves.

At some point a doctor came in and looked in our eyes with a light. "You're very lucky," he said, patting me on the cheek. "We sent a city inspection team to your house. You've been getting lethal dosages of carbon monoxide from a water heater in the hall. The heater was not plumbed properly, and all the toxic air was being filtered into the house. I'm surprised you're still alive."

So that's why we felt better lying on the patio, I thought later. Each time I went outside, I began to get my sight back; then lost it again inside. At this time, I had never heard of carbon monoxide poisoning, and the city inspector confirmed that such incidents were very rare. Well, I thought, I had sprung from my mother's womb eager for rare adventures, but this was a little more than I'd bargained for.

The hospital made arrangements for us to be moved to a nearby motel. "You must not go back in that house," the doctor said. I gave him the name of the owner, who came to the hospital and, horror-stricken, apologized. He was having the water heater replaced even as we spoke. A few days later, after the house was inspected again, we moved back in. But I refused to unpack further. It was a killer house and my kids weren't going to live there.

Our next house was a lovely suburban ranch in North Dallas, with a sweeping lawn and a swimming pool. When the kids saw this one on our housing search, they had to have it, and I felt that I owed them one. The only moral I was able to draw from this melodrama was discouraging: *The world can't sustain for a moment the revolt of a mother.* But I wasn't totally broken yet: for the three years we lived in that house, we sat on the floor, because I had given the chairs away and had no intention of replacing them. *I was still standing up insiiiiide!*

The next city Greg moved us to was Keating, Ohio, a lovely old-world city of more than a million people on the Ohio River. I was dragged seething. I had just got a faculty appointment at a Dallas college and had registered to complete my doctoral work. Greg didn't ask my preferences, however. He had been offered an attractive job as chief of a large city school system, and he intended to take it.

"Just six months, that's all I ask," I pleaded. "I'll stay here with the kids, start my new job, and you can go up there and see if this one is all it's cracked up to be. You know how these jobs are—so volatile. There's no sense in uprooting the kids again, if it's just going to be like the last one—divided school boards, mean-spirited people—a nightmare. If you really like it and think it'll be a long-term thing, then the kids and I will move up there."

"No. Wherever I go, my family will go," Greg insisted. "I won't break up the family. I don't break up sets."

Sets? What were we flatware? A matched Formica dining ensemble? "It's not breaking up the family, Greg, It's trying to preserve it; it's trying to keep some continuity for the kids—and for me. It won't be that long."

"No. If you won't go with me now, then I won't go," he said petulantly. I could see his bottom lip stuck out like a five-year-old's. "I'll just stay here in this miserable job. You know I can't stand reporting to someone else. In Keating, I'll be the boss. I'll be able to make a difference." His voice rose defensively: "I'm doing this for the family, Jacy; it'll be a great opportunity for them and a great step up in my career."

"What about *my* career?"

"You don't have one." This assertion, as with all his assertions, was definitive. Final. He saw my eyes flare and then crush. He lowered his voice. "Some day when the children are raised, you might want to start a career, but not right now. The children are the most important things in your life. Your main job is to take care of them and to be with me. I need you. I can't do this job without you beside me; without my family waiting for me at home each day. It's what I live for." He put his hands on my shoulders. "If you don't go, I won't go either."

I felt as if I lived in a terrarium, a closed system with a limited amount of air and nutrients. If one plant grew too large, it took up so much space and oxygen that the other plants shriveled or died. I went to Mother.

"Mother, I don't think Greg's being fair. Is it too much to ask for him to let me stay here for awhile? Do something *I* want to do for a change? Is it? I want to write. I want to teach. I want to finish my doctorate, get my credentials. I helped him finish *his* education. I put my life on hold for that. Now, why can't he support *me* a little? Do you think he's being reasonable?"

"No. But then, what man was ever reasonable?"

"Mother, how is it that he always puts me in a situation where I'm the heavy? I can never win with him."

"Win?"

"It's not winning so much, but you know what I mean. It's that I want to have an equal say in what we do, how we spend our life together, how we raise our kids. It's *my* life too. *It's my only life,* and I've already spent fifteen years of it marching to his drum beat. Really, all my youth!"

Mother smiled. "Jacy, you're still young."

"Yeah and knocking myself out to try to reserve a tiny little bit of my life, *my life,* for me. *I've already given the rest of it away.*" I began to cry silently. "I am so frustrated, Mother. If I say I simply won't go, he'll turn down a job he really wants. Then I'll always be to blame for ruining his life, and I'll have to hear about it for the rest of mine. If I give in, here we go, moving across the country again. Setting up a home again—and I know who will have to make a home, make friends, get the kids settled. God, the last move nearly killed us all! Literally. I've *forgotten* more friends and neighbors than most people ever *make.*"

Mother grabbed me and pinned my arms down by my side, as she used to do when I was a toddler working myself up into a tantrum. Calming me down.

"Where's all your Zen stuff, Jacy? Remember, it doesn't matter. Nothing really matters. Step back and take that long view, you're good at doing that."

I sniffled and calmed down a little. "I know. It's just hard. It's even hard to play a game with yourself that no one else knows the rules of, just to keep yourself calm."

"Jacy. I don't know what to tell you. Yours is the cry of women from time immemorial. They follow their men on pioneer trails, or wherever the men want to go. If the women don't want to go, they buckle under anyway, because they're women; because they see the whole, not the part; because they have children to consider. The men always tell them it's best for the family, but it seldom is. How do you think you got to Thalia? Do you think your great-great grandmother would have chosen this place to live if it had been up to her? Do you think she would have selected it for us—for you and me, if she'd had a choice? It was selected *for* her. Her *life* was selected for her. Knowing this doesn't make your situation any easier, but whatever you decide to do, Jacy, you know I'll support you. I *love* your children, I *like* your husband—sometimes—but *you are bone of my bone.* What *you* want is what I want for you."

I hugged her. "I have to think of everyone else first. You're the only person in the world who thinks of me first! Everyone needs one person like that."

A few days later, Greg went off to Keating to accept the job. He returned jubiliant. It was a great city; he loved it! "It's conservative, but people are Taft conservatives—civilized. These aren't rednecks. They don't have the same attitudes about integration that people do in the South, in Texas. The city is old; the houses are old and beautiful. It's a wonderful place, and you'll love it."

Once more, I tried to impress on him how important it was for me to stay a few more months in Dallas, but he wouldn't listen. So I caved in.

"I *knew* Jacy would do what was right," Greg announced to Mother exultantly. "She always does."

When I looked back on this episode several years later, I knew it was a turning point in our lives. I would always admire what Greg stood for, but living with the tyranny of a good man and his good causes, when one's own feelings and desires are not taken into account, was not a life I could put up with forever. He would deny it, and did, but he and his desires came first; his kids came second, his wife was there to hold it all together for him, make it work.

Greg should have been a monk, I thought. A reformer obsessed with a higher calling has no business marrying and begetting a family. The Catholics had it right on this point: if you're going to be married to loftiness for life, be a priest.

"I'll go with you one more time, Greg. But if this job doesn't work out for you, for whatever reason, I won't go with you again. You're too self-righteous, too domineering. You want me to make the center hold for you, so you can go out and do whatever you want to. Well I'm tired of being the pivot. I'm tired of being John Donne's *damned fixed foot of the compass*, holding steady so you can run around me in circles changing the world—*making no show to move, but doth if the other do. Dull sublunary crap!*"

Greg stared at me, his mouth unhinged. I always pulled odd bits of things into my arguments that left others speechless so they couldn't come back at me.

"I have some ideas about change, too, Greg," I continued. "Principally, change about women and the way they lead their lives; principally about women getting slotted into rigid roles; principally about me. You're so focused on everyone else's civil rights that you're making a slave of your wife."

"A slave, oh sure. A slave with a closet full of shoes and two cars in the garage." This time he had me, he thought.

"Greg, you don't even see the paradoxes, the contradictions. You may think of yourself as a liberal, a social reformer, but at home you're a dictator. You want to be Martin Luther King, and you act like Mussolini. You don't see the gray areas that other people see; you don't know how to compromise."

"No. Of course not. Compromise is not in my vocabulary," he spat out with contempt. "You're either for me or against me. You're with me or you're not."

"That's what I mean. That's radical, not rational. That makes you the ego-center of the world. You're taking on a big political job, Greg, and you're not even trying to develop some political skills."

"I am *not* a politician, I am an *educator*," he said emphatically.

I sighed. "Just remember what I'm saying, Greg. I'm serious."

Greg's face softened: "Oh, come on, you'll love it. You're always a spoilsport. I'll be able to make a big difference in peoples' lives, in kids' lives, I can change the direction of American education. This is a big arena. You wouldn't want to kill my chance to serve the nation's kids, would you?"

I turned away; nothing had seeped into his thick head. It was hopeless. As I began to walk away, Greg gave my fanny a playful slap. "I've made plane reservations for us to go up and look for a house. They have great houses there."

And so it went. And so *we* went. Two other events further knocked the wind out of me like double punches to the solar plexus. Clearly, I had dug myself into a hole I could not climb out of: One, a scholarly journal selected my thesis to be published. Unfortunately, the editors assumed I was a man, and credited my work to one *Jason Farrow*. Two, I presented my paper at a literature conference and directly afterward two nuns from a university in San Antonio approached me and offered me an assistant professorship on the spot.

"I'm sorry," I felt my mouth working, words coming out of it like little white puffs of smoke. "But I'm moving to the Midwest with my husband and family. I won't have time for Joyce and Yeats anymore."

The very first time in my life I had gained recognition as a budding scholar—the thing I wanted most in the world for myself—*the only thing for myself*—I drove home, bawling my eyes out all the way.

Then I began packing. Again.

I had climbed out of that hole eventually. But it had taken a long, long time, years of muddling through, migraines, ulcers, a lot of heartache. And then I'd had to take some pretty scary risks to wrest control of my own life from those who wanted to run it.

But I found that it's possible to have a marriage that is not a terrarium or a twin-footed compass. My marriage to Marlboro is more like . . . what? . . . like a jazz ensemble, with the two of us taking turns playing the bass—keeping the heartbeat steady—while the other plays a riff.

I envy people who got it right the first time, but clearly Greg and I had not. Maybe nobody did in the fifties. Maybe it took nearly forty years for men and women—wives and husbands—to get it right: now Greg is married to a professional woman who lives five hundred miles away from him. Ironically, they have the commuter marriage he had not permitted me. The educator had been educable after all. *Sartor Resartus.*

"Meet me at the Mill Pond Inn for lunch," I call to Marlboro as I head down the road. "I'm going over to see what's happening with the Reeds; then take a walk."

The Reeds have one of the old Victorian houses on the Mill Pond that I have always admired for their charm and funkiness. But the admiration is from afar: I don't want one. I've had a big old house before. A mansion to end all mansions, in fact. A splendid house with a billiard table on the tapestried mezzanine—twenty-seven rooms, featuring a ballroom with a Venetian glass chandelier on the top floor. A gorgeous, sumptuous, carved, gilded and overblown house. A house to die for.

And, come to think of it, I nearly had.

9

F·E·R·M·E·N·T

"Truth is stranger than fiction." I think that old chestnut is truer than we know, because it doesn't say that truth is truer than fiction; just that it's stranger, meaning that it's odd. It may be excessive, it may be more interesting, but the important thing is that it's random—and fiction is not random.
—Toni Morrison

I MEET CATHERINE REED as the small woman bangs out the door with a lamp in each hand. "What's going on here?" I ask, taking a lamp. "You're moving, I take it."

"Yes, Graham is being transferred," Catherine says unhappily. "The defense industry is about shot, so to speak. I hate to leave here, but at least he still has a job. That's more than can be said for a lot of people. About sixty were let go last week."

"Well, you won't miss the taxes. Where are you going?"

"Washington for awhile, then I don't know." Catherine looks off in the distance. "It's so hard on the kids, you know. Susan has been crying for a week, and David is in a black mood. They don't want to leave their friends, this neighborhood."

"If it's any consolation, they'll be okay in a few weeks—as soon as you're settled and they've found a friend apiece," I offer. "Somehow the kids adjust better than the mothers, especially if we have to leave a job, as you're doing."

"I know. I don't know where I'll land, if anywhere. I've been with my law firm for five years, and they've given me a good severance package, but after a year, who knows? I don't think it's right to expect Graham to build my world for me. But the cards seem stacked against me; every time I get something going for myself, some change in his life takes over and redirects mine."

I shake my head. "Things have changed so much, and then again they haven't."

"Am I *wrong* to want something for myself?"

I put my arm around Catherine's waist. "Let's get this stuff moved."

We make several trips through the house, carrying armloads of stuff to the van. Kids run in and out. Movers tramp dirt on the carpets.

"Come tonight for dinner," I call, standing at the bottom of the long curving stairway. As Catherine answers, the sun hits the stained glass window at the head of the stairs, reminding me of the house in Keating—a great fortress of a house, built by a beer baron at the turn of the century. In the early seventies, Greg and I were able to buy it because the Hadleys, an elderly couple who had lived there since the 1920s—were in mortal fear of "the neighborhood turning." A black family had bought a house down the street, and a mixed-race couple had been spotted looking for a home.

"We're too old for this," said Mr. Hadley. "Maybe you young people can put up with all this social mixing, but we can't."

We assured the Hadleys that we would take excellent care of the house, and the older couple moved to "a gated community" in the suburbs, leaving us with more than two dozen mahogany-paneled rooms, six working fireplaces, three gold-leafed chandeliers, one oval music room complete with clouds and cherubs on the ceiling, and an entire house filled with furniture built in Bavaria and shipped directly to the mansion some seventy-five years before.

Besides feeling seduced by a mansion fit for a Stepford wife, I felt squeamish about the circumstances surrounding our good real estate deal. I called Mother:

"Mother, it doesn't seem right to profit from someone else's prejudices. In this city black neighbors are *persona non grata;* the world is not the way it should be, and I'm eaten up with guilt."

"Jacy, what did I tell you about guilt? Forget it! The people want to sell this house. They will sell it to *somebody*. You're lucky you got it cheap. And if it helps at all, you might just recall that the neighborhood will have a fair neighbor in you, and the community is better served than when the Hadleys with all their silly fears and biases were there. So forget it. Enjoy the house, enjoy your life. And for heaven's sake stop analyzing everything to shreds."

"Analyzing things to shreds? You're someone to talk," I mumbled.

The Lilac Hill house was beyond elegant, but I had to admit in my secret heart that it was not my kind of house. I felt deeply stupid walking around barefoot in this place and answering the door in my shorts—attire that had been comfortable and appropriate in the Dallas house, with its patios and decks that were as much a part of the house as the living room—or more so. This house was dark and formal and cried out for someone who loved polishing. Polishing the heavy sliding doors into the library, polishing the stained-glass windows, polishing the gold lavaboes, polishing the carved mahogany dining table seating twenty, polishing the handles on the big front door. Polishing was not my idea of a good time, or even of time well spent—if it was *my* time. Maybe if I were older, I kept thinking— sixty, fifty, even forty. But here I was still in my mid-thirties, with hankerings to do *almost anything but polish*, anything but be a caretaker. I longed for simplicity, for sunshine, for a porch to sit on in my cut-offs and read Russian novels, not all these towers and mezzanines and curlicues.

I had grown through the fifties and sixties—decades that had kept blacks in the back of the bus, gays in the closet, and women in the kitchen—and sometimes in the abortionists' back alleys. It was the seventies: blacks and gays were my colleagues at the university, women were going to school and work, and abortionists had only to duck intermittently as they dashed into their clinics. Jeans, sandals, love beads, Indian pottery and African rugs were in. My students wrote "Fuck the war," on the blackboard. I told them I despised the war too, but that they, unfortunately, were protesting with a mixed metaphor.

"Look guys, you're smarter than this. You can't literally do that to a war, so think of a more accurate way of expressing yourselves."

"But the war's an abomination."

"In the eyes of whom?"

"God and man."

"Then tell me that and substantiate it. But don't tell me to fuck it. That's not literate."

In the middle of a social upheaval whose intent was something on the order of a classless society, I was embarrassed by my ostentatious house. Only a short time before, I had sold or given away a houseful of stuff.

"*It owns me*, Greg. I don't own it," I'd complained. "I would never have struck this bargain in life—to be owned—if I'd been bright enough, early enough to understand what things were all about. *Things get in the way of my trying to think.*"

And now, here I was again, the things and stuff mounting—more and more of it—beautiful, expensive, no doubt about that—but *stuff*. "The better to own you with my dear," I mouthed into the rococo hall mirror made in Bavaria in 1888. "You belong in Mad King Ludwig's castle."

I was also laboring under an irony: just as my life demanded that I face the growing domestic expectations that came with the house and Greg's high-profile job, I was immersing myself in the burgeoning Women's Movement. I read as if inhaling, nodding, *yes, yes*: Virginia Woolf, Simone de Beauvoir, Marilyn French, Adrienne Rich, Susan Brownmiller, Kate Millett, Maya Angelou, Toni Morrison, Ntozake Shange, *Ms. Magazine*. I sat up in bed one night when I read a line by Eleanor Holmes Norton: "On the road to equality, there is no better place for blacks to detour around American values than in foregoing its example in the treatment of its women and the organization of its family life."

Yes, yes, yes! I bounded out of bed. *Here* is where my own cause lay—not with futilely fighting institutional racism and self-serving school boards—but in working where my heart was, working with *women*, working *on* women, beginning with *myself!* The more I read and talked to women, the more I found similarities in the Women's Movement and the Civil Rights Movement. Working for equality for women would help *all* women.

I joined a consciousness-raising group and encouraged women and student groups to join the Sisterhood. I wrote articles, made speeches: "Class supremacy, male supremacy, white supremacy— it's all the same game!" I exhorted, quoting something I'd read the night before. "If you're on top of someone, the society tells you that you are better."

As my introduction to an important women's group in Keating, Ohio, in 1976, I was asked to make a speech as the wife of the superintendent of schools in a conservative city. I spoke with increasing zeal. So much had been dammed up inside me for so long that I was like a spigot that once turned on could not be turned off: "Without a model for what I am attempting to do, I often feel like the character, Maria Wyeth, in Joan Didion's novel, *Play it as it Lays*, who scrawled across her life: NOTHING APPLIES," I began.

"That novel has no 'normal' characters, no norm against which the reader can measure other characters. Life is depicted as a game with no rules. Anyone can play any way she wishes, but any lessons learned ultimately do not apply to that game, for the game is never the same twice—nor does it apply to anything else. Didion's Maria (pronounced like the word that means 'fate') says: 'You call it as you see it, and stay in the action.'

"Maria's position illuminates a central problem for changing women in a changing society: Nothing Applies. There is no frame of reference into which we can plug our emotions, our intellect, our talents, our need for companionship and our need for independence, our need to nurture others and our need to gain a measure of recognition for ourselves, our desire to raise a healthy family, and our desire to pursue our own private interests. Where is the norm against which we can measure ourselves? What are the rules of the game?

"We don't know what we're supposed to be these days, so we don't know what we are. We are defining ourselves in a thoroughly existential way. We are the first women like us.

"I just read a study by Carol Tavris and Toby Jayaratne, a survey that determines women's attitudes about their lives. An amazing 120,000 women responded. The most significant insight it revealed was that an overwhelming percent of these women, between the ages of twenty and forty, lead very conventional, traditional lives: they are married, have children, do not work outside their homes, call themselves political moderates, and acknowledge a religious affiliation. And yet, these women harbor very unconventional attitudes about their lives, the roles they have accepted, their status in society, and what they want for their daughters. A surprising number are discontent with their lives and would eagerly accept another role definition.

We are insecure and anxious because NOTHING APPLIES to the condition in which we find ourselves. Take a look at us here today: we are better educated than any women, and most men, in history. We are intelligent, accomplished and skilled. Why should such a woman restrict herself to cleaning her son's muddy boots, mopping up after the family, getting three meals a day, and generally, as T. S. Eliot says of the neurotic Prufrock, measuring out her life in coffee spoons?

"It is virtually impossible for a girl or woman to attend school for a dozen or more years without running the risk of becoming interested in something. To completely renounce her own interests in the interest of an ill-defined 'happy' or 'adjusted' family is an outrage. This may lead to an 'adjusted' family, but it just as often leads to a 'maladjusted' woman.

"And yet, neither is it right for children to come home to an empty house. Mother may be 'fulfilled' but the kids need attention. Remember: the moment you have a child, your turn is over!

"Two demanding jobs—one in the home and the other in the office, are too much for many women to handle well. A housewife hasn't enough to occupy her mind; a housewife with a full-time job has entirely too much. And part-time jobs of any content are virtually nonexistent. So what to do?

"If a woman has help? But where is that help to come from? Husbands and fathers have not been socialized to do things women now do automatically. They don't know how to be alert to potential emergencies in the home; they don't know how to avert a tragedy by simply turning a saucepan handle to the back of the stove, moving a glass dish a fraction of an inch, hiding the bleach. As Jean Kerr said humorously: a mother can't anticipate that her child may eat the daisies. A father, who hasn't even noticed there are daisies on the table, is far less capable of anticipating such events. The skills that many women have would, as a matter of fact, make her a very good executive—if she had the credentials, that is.

"A housekeeper, cook, maid? But what woman who truly believes in women's liberation wants to be liberated at the expense of another woman's servitude? If liberation for women is to be fair, shouldn't that liberation be across the board?

"When NOTHING APPLIES, how do we know what is coping, and what is copping out? I sometimes see working mothers condescend to housewives in offensively overt or subtle ways, making them feel guilty or incompetent. Conversely, I see housewives castigate working mothers in an attempt to make them feel guilty. We cannot seem to let each other be.

"Our mothers, grandmothers had a frame of reference for judging themselves: a woman of good character is responsible for caring for her husband, home and children; she unselfishly subordinates her needs and desires to theirs. That woman, then, is fulfilled.

"And yet, novelist D. H. Lawrence, more than forty years ago, had this startling comment about Lettie Tempest, in his novel *The White Peacock*. When Lettie decides 'to abandon the charge of herself to serve her children,' the narrator says:

> Having reached that point in a woman's career when most, perhaps, all, of the things in life seemed worthless and insipid, she had determined to put up with it, to ignore her own self, to empty her own potentialities into the vessel of another or other, and to live her life at second hand.
>
> This peculiar abnegation of self is the resource of a woman for the escaping of responsibilities for her own development. Like a nun, she puts over her living face a veil, as a sign that the woman no longer exists for herself; she is the servant. . . . As a servant she is no longer responsible for herself. . . . Service is light and easy. To be responsible for the good progress of one's life is terrifying. It is the most insufferable form of loneliness, and the heaviest of responsibilities.

"Our grandmothers and mothers did not read these words, of course. But we have had liberal access to books, so it is not so amazing that we feel in a double-bind. A woman growing up in the earlier easy-answer value system and into the no-answer one of today has a foot in two worlds, a very tenuous stance. Even the Colossus of Rhodes fell down.

"What is courage, character, integrity? Are these words defined by our ability to live at second hand? To escape responsibilities for our own development? Or do we define them by being responsible for the good progress of our own lives? By risking terror and loneliness and criticism?

"A final reason we may feel ambivalent about our lives is that we have to take a stand. In taking a stand, you align yourself on the one hand with those some see as strident bra-burning women of The Movement; or, on the other hand, with passive, professionally inept women who consciously choose the subordinate role. These attributes are by no means general for either group, but our society tends to label the most radical element of any group as representative of the whole.

"For the past six years I have taught both undergraduate and graduate students. Many undergraduate women are choosing very different lives for themselves—moving headlong into professions, marrying late or not at all. Some have very definite goals for themselves.

"But also typical are their personal essays that say something to the effect that the young woman is planning to be a doctor, will study and work hard to be a doctor—that is, unless Steven decides they can afford to be married this summer, in which case she will not be a doctor at all, but will instead be Steven's wife and live happily ever after.

"I fairly weep when I run across young women like this. How will they feel ten years hence? If the marriage to Steven lasts, will the student later realize she allowed herself to be 'had' before she was even aware of what there was to have? If the marriage to Steven does not last—and if we are to believe statistics about teenage marriages, it will not—who will she be? Steven's ex-wife. Maybe the mother of Steven's children. And certainly an unskilled college dropout.

"At the other end of the spectrum, I see women between the ages of thirty and fifty returning to the classroom. Recently, I received a letter from a forty-five-year-old wife and mother of four, who wanted to enroll in my class. Her letter reads in part:

I don't know if I can keep up with the rest of the students or not. I really don't know what I'm good at, except running a house, and taking care of kids, and sometimes I wonder about that. I don't feel like I ever get finished. I would like to finish just one thing—a book, or a paper, or a discussion. I don't know what I will be able to do in your class. I'm afraid I will look like a fool, but I'm willing to risk that. Do you think there is room in your class for a used mother?

"When I read that, I swallowed my heart. Of course there is room here for a used mother; in fact, a used mother teaches the class!

"We do not have a relevant history from which to learn. In our existential searches, we must define what is important to us, and that definition often takes the form of reconciling opposites. F. Scott Fitzgerald once said that the test of a first-rate intelligence is the ability to hold opposed ideas in the mind at the same time and still retain the ability to function. The man, Fitzgerald, didn't make it. These words came from his collection of sketches, 'The Crack-Up,' describing his psychic collapse.

"Perhaps women can't make it either. But gaining a capacity to live with ambiguity, to suspend judgment about ourselves and each other, and to maintain equanimity while living with unanswered questions is, it seems to me, the biggest challenge women face in a world where Nothing Applies.

Thank You.

When I finished, the women looked at me as if they had just observed the collapse of the Hoover Dam. Such a torrent of words had washed over them that they sat stunned into silence. I sat down. Then slowly, one by one, the women filed out of the room, staring at their feet.

Well, I've done it now, I thought. Ripped my britches, as Daddy would say. Made them all hate me or think I'm nuts. When I got home, I folded myself into the lotus position and meditated all night. "Dear Buddha, dear God, dear Whoever's out there, please forgive me for being myself. Please forgive me for being some kind of deviate, some genetic sport who doesn't know her place, please forgive me."

Next day, I was contemplating getting personal fill-in-the-blank stationery with the words "Please Forgive Me For _____" at the top, when the calls began: *What you said is true. You said what I've been thinking. You put my secret feelings into words.* By the end of the day, I'd received sixty-two calls.

I wrote to Alex on Earth Day:

Dear Alex,

I have to tell you a wonderful thing. My friend Jim, who lives in Texas, celebrated Earth Day by getting a vasectomy. He has two children, and he says that we have an obligation to the environment not to do more than replace ourselves. This is such a courageous thing to do in Texas. Even my mother gasped at the news and said, "Well, I salute him, but don't tell your father. Being able to make babies is such a mark of manhood with his generation that I don't think he'd understand it."

I continued teaching and didn't know whether to laugh or cry when phone callers to my home muttered apologetically, "I don't want to bother your husband since I know he's so busy, but would you tell him . . . ."

I needed help, and despite my philosophical antipathy toward not wanting to ask another woman to take up my slack, I couldn't find another option. Well, I thought as I put an ad in the newspaper for a live-in to help with cooking, laundry and kids, I would never ask another woman to do something that I would not do or have not done. Which left me a lot of latitude. *A lot.* The ad drew a dozen phone calls. Women came, and one by one, I sent them away.

Nancy looked good on paper, claimed she loved to cook, and her references were glowing, so I hired her. A week later, however, Nancy arrived with her attack-trained dog, Bullet. My kids had a dog; had, in fact owned a series of dogs, cats, canaries, parrots, finches, hamsters, white rats, rabbits, and other creatures ranging in degree from bad to worse on the house-broken continuum, and I was not overjoyed to welcome Bullet. But I was at the bottom of the list of applicants. So Nancy and Bullet moved in.

Then the horror stories began:

"Mom, I'm sorry to call you at work again, but Nancy put a padlock on the door to the pantry so we can't get anything to eat after school."

"Mother, Nancy said she didn't feel like taking me to my piano lesson today, and she's lying outside taking a sunbath *in your swimsuit!*"

"Hey, Mom, you won't believe this, but Bullet bit the mailman today and chased Mr. Gardner down the street when he came to deliver firewood."

I gave Nancy two-week's salary and sent her packing. The day she left, my swimsuit disappeared.

"Mo-ther!" Carrie was on the phone. "Nancy came back saying she'd forgotten something and took my orange beanbag chair off in the back seat of her van! She said Bullet wouldn't sleep anywhere else!"

Lettie was next. A gracious elderly black woman from Alabama who had come to Keating to visit her daughter and decided to stay, Lettie took good care of the children and was a wonderful cook. But Lettie's grandsons stole our house key from their grandmother's purse, broke into the house and took TV sets and other items. Lettie, heartbroken, went back to Alabama. I went back to the want ads.

Wanda was brought to us by a man from the hill country who owned a funeral home. He sang her praises as a superb cook, a great housekeeper, a lover of children, and a sweet-natured being of the first waters.

"Why are you letting her go, then," I asked, after Wanda had gone outside to get acquainted with Carrie, Ben and Paul. He said his kids were growing up and didn't need her, but he wanted to help place her with "a good family."

The kids fell in love with the tall, good-looking, twenty-four-year-old Appalachian woman, who was strong and athletic. She was shooting baskets with Ben in the driveway when I called her in to hire her. The funeral director brought Wanda back a few days later, and thus began one of the more bizarre episodes in the life of my family.

"I'm gonna make ya'll some goulash like we cook in the hills," Wanda announced on her first day in residence. This gourmet treat, as my family came to learn much to our discomfort, was the only dish Wanda knew how to make—and this one not very well.

Dear Alex:

Well, here's another Wanda story. You've already heard that when we told her she could decorate her rooms, she picked out wallpaper with horses and dogs on it, and while we were out hung the paper herself. *Upside down.* It is always a little disorienting to visit her quarters: after huffing up three sets of stairs you behold half an acre of animals with their feet struck straight up in the air.

You've heard how dumbfounded we were when we discovered that Wanda couldn't read or write a lick, which explains why she could drive the kids to school okay, under their direction, but got lost coming home each day, and why she couldn't follow a recipe or take a phone message. You've heard that one day I came home and found her hiding in a closet "because the radiators were playing *Fiddler on the Roof* and people in ball gowns were dancing all over the living room." And you've already heard that she sees Jesus floating over her bed each night.

But hark! even stranger doings are afoot.

First, she took the kids bowling one night and met a guy. He came to see her a couple of times and seemed nice enough, a fellow from India studying engineering at the university. Then one night when we were all away, she took Greg's car and disappeared for three days. We finally called the police, who found the car parked in front of a two-bit motel. (Very good for his reputation in a city whose major newspaper is always looking for a reason to beat up on him.) Wanda wandered home on the third night, saying she couldn't remember where she had been or how she got home.

During the next week, when I talked to her about her behavior, she told me that she "blacks out" when "men get too close." She does this because Jeannie, the funeral director's wife is "a whore and a bad woman." She tells me a long story about Jeannie's father touching Jeannie in "bad places." She says she saw Jeannie give birth to twin babies in the bathroom and flush them down the toilet. She says Jeannie made Wanda do bad things like drink beer and pick up men in bars . . . and on and on. She began speaking of herself in the third person.

Wanda also told me that she'd run away from her cousins "who was rapin' on Wanda when she was just a little tyke." She said Wanda had married her uncle when she was sixteen, but when "Uncle Red tried to touch Wanda, she run away and hid in a basement for a long time and didn't have nothing to eat but spiders and bugs."

She began acting more and more peculiar: One night I dressed to go out in a red cocktail dress, and when I came downstairs she began crying hysterically, "No, no, take it off! That's a Jeannie dress. You'll do bad things in that dress!" The next day, when I dressed in a navy pantsuit to go to work, Wanda tells me approvingly. "*That's* the way good girls dress; like that."

Then one night, while the family was away from the house, Wanda went through my closet and took all my clothes that were not navy or black, built a fire on the floor of her room upstairs and burned them. She had a roaring fire going up there, which we could see through the windows as we drove in the driveway. We called the firehouse and had it put out, but had we not arrived at that moment, she would have burned the place to the ground. She was hysterical when we brought her downstairs, crying and apologizing and saying Jeannie made her do it.

That episode made it clear that Wanda was not only unbalanced, but very dangerous. This hurt me terribly; I couldn't go to sleep that night, so I sat up talking to her. She told me that Wanda had burned all Jeannie's clothes to protect us because she loved us, and "Jeannie just makes trouble."

What became clear to me was that she had two quite separate personalities: Wanda, who was a good girl; and Jeannie, who was bad. Wanda kept fighting Jeannie off, but Jeannie would sometimes "come out," and take over. Wanda also told me weird and gory stories about Jeannie lying in caskets at the funeral home and letting men "touch" her "there." At my prodding, she told me that the funeral home family had taken her to a doctor. He gave her pills, but she'd run out of them a few weeks before. She got a little book out of a drawer and gave me the doctor's phone number.

Next day, I called the funeral home owner. He confessed contritely that he'd brought Wanda to us because he *had* to get her out of his house . . . he was worried that she couldn't take care of herself . . . she had a mental problem, and he'd tried to get her help, but she'd become more dangerous to his family, and especially hated his wife Jeannie on whom she had once turned with a butcher knife, so he had to get rid of her. When I screeched at him for bringing her to us and endangering *my* kids, he apologized abjectly, but said he didn't know what else to do.

I came to understand his position perfectly.

Wanda's doctor told me that their relationship was privileged and he could tell me only that she suffered from a "character disorder," and that she should not be living in our house.

"She's dangerous then?" I asked

"What I said was she should not be living in your house."

"What should I do then?"

"Pack her bags, and put her outside and do not let her in again."

"How can I do that? She can't read. She can't take care of herself. She has no car, nowhere to go."

"Just pack her bags and put her outside. *Now!*"

As a civic leader in Keating, Greg was not without influence and resources. Oddly, though, doctors, psychiatrists, social workers, hospitals, city service organizations fell away quickly when faced with taking on a problem like Wanda, which required immediate resolution. Further, we were told, we couldn't put her in an institution to keep her from getting hurt, because she had to commit herself. We approached her about this, but she flatly refused, saying she had been "in one of them places before where they put metal things with wires on my head and buzzed me." She wasn't going back.

That night, Wanda ran away. We changed the locks and were careful for the next several weeks that the kids were never left alone.

Later Wanda called and said she was living in a "dormitory with a lot of other girls" across the river in Kentucky (a place well-known for its casinos and prostitution), and that she wanted to come for her belongings.

She had lost about twenty pounds, bleached her hair, applied some violent-colored lipstick and had herself tricked up in a push-up bra and a tight fake leopardskin jumpsuit. She kissed us all and left, saying she had a great life and loved the other girls she worked with.

After she was gone, the kids, starry-eyed, rattled on about how "beautiful Wanda looks, just like girls on TV," while Greg and I sat stunned. She *did* look, we agreed, a bit like a sexy new country singer. We haven't seen or heard from Wanda since.

And now I am back to looking for someone to help me with this monster house. Every time I get someone who's supposed to help me, I end up having to help *her*. What am I doing wrong? Please advise.

Love, Jacy

After Wanda, there was a couple from Haiti, Jubal and Letricia. A strict vegetarian, Jubal's idea of a dessert treat was baked acorn squash. Ben and Paul made barfing and hacking noises when he set it before them. Each day when I came home from work, I had to hear about how Jubal was starving them to death on pine nuts.

After Greg and I had been away for a few days, leaving the kids in the care of the couple, our children corroborated one another's weird stories about the "spiritual group" Jubal and Letricia had introduced them to, urging them to join. I was spooked by the cults that seemed to be hatching right and left during this period—some friends were even then going through a long and expensive "deprogramming" effort with a teenaged daughter who had got caught up in the People's Temple of Jim Jones.

I was about to let the two go, when Mother came for a visit, bringing a side of Texas beef. Jubal took one look at the bloody red slabs laid out on his pristine cooking counter and high-tailed it out the back door with Letricia in tow.

Another ad for household help brought Vera Dinkins, a small, gray wren of a woman, whom the boys immediately dubbed V.D. and announced to one and all that her nose dripped into the pan when she fried bacon. "Ugh! Eech! Barf! Nuuhf!" My stomach churned when they went into their act, but I never witnessed that particular bacon dripping, so I doubted it.

When Ben and Paul brought classmates to the house, as they did every day, Mrs. Dinkins was patient with them. Once, when I came in while the boys had the stereo on as high as it would go, I marched upstairs, switched the thing off, and asked Mrs. Dinkins how in the world she stood it.

"Oh, it's not as loud as it sounds," she offered, blinking. She also suggested that "we'd have a lot more room in the library, if you'd get rid of all them books."

Mrs. Dinkins took tranquilizers—"for my nerves" she said—which I thought, given the crowd of kids that tumbled in and out of the house on a daily basis, was probably a good idea. The house was so sprawling that sometimes visitors got lost in it for days, and I wouldn't quite know how many were around until I saw the food disappearing from the refrigerator in vast lots. The boys always had two or three friends in their rooms on the top floor—rooms I refused to visit more than twice a year to remove the pizza boxes and other moldy memorabilia from under the beds. To add to the body count, Carrie was host to Monica, an Argentine exchange student, and Barbara, a black student from New York, for two successive years. The girls were as quiet in their pursuits as the boys were rowdy.

On those days when I had to entertain, Mrs. Dinkins inevitably took a double dose of Valium for her nerves, which rendered her quite useless. Once, when she was supposed to be cleaning the downstairs rooms for a party, she fell asleep on the entry hall sofa, snoring loudly as florists tiptoed around her with flowers and caterers rushed by her with steaming food carts. When I shook her awake and told her she might be more comfortable upstairs in her own bed, Mrs. Dinkins was hurt: "Oh, no I couldn't do that, you might need me," she protested before falling back to sleep.

Another time when I was getting the house ready for guests, I found Mrs. Dinkins with a sponge still in her hand, hanging fast asleep over the edge of a bathtub she was supposed to be scrubbing.

For all her failings as a housekeeper, Mrs. Dinkins was a warm body in the house who could be roused to dim activity occasionally, so her tenure with our family lasted several years. And clearly I needed help of whatever kind. During those years the Lilac Hill house entertained leaders of all stripe, gender, color and ethnic background: A famous black jazz entertainer played my piano; a budding writer read from the first draft of *Born on the Fourth of July* in my living room many years before he finally got it produced. The only religious leader I ever really respected sat at my polished table and later went on to become Cardinal Bernadin in Chicago. A wacky mayor brought his new bride to sit in my porch swing only shortly before he was cited for visiting a prostitute and paying her with a credit card. This man went on to become Jerry Springer, controversial talk show host. A baseball player who ate my steak and snow peas later went to jail for gambling. A well-known doctor demonstrated his Heimlich Maneuver in my living room. Staid professors whose Hush Puppies rested under my table later leapt into the flower power age at Big Sur. A magazine editor touted his new creation, *Hustler,* and his right to freedom of speech.

On my porch new feminists dumped their husbands, and proper businessmen declared themselves to be in favor of "free love." It was a time of ferment and social experimentation, a time of radical prose, hippie art, and political dissent. Wearing my fashionable long Indian print dress and sporting my "Afro," I observed all this with interest, sometimes with surprise at the subterranean quirks and passions festering beneath the surface of a conservative community.

And many years later I watched with great glee as the hate-mongering, right-wing publisher of the city's morning newspaper was sent to jail for bilking older people out of their life savings and American taxpayers out of millions of dollars in a celebrated savings and loans scandal. That man was never invited to sit at my table.

10

E·N·O·U·G·H

Risk! Risk anything!
Care no more for the
opinion of others, for
those voices. Do the
hardest thing on earth
for you. Act for yourself.
Face the truth.
—Katherine Mansfield

WHILE I ATTEMPTED to deal with the chaff from the political buzzsaw at work on Greg, Alex wrote from Eighty Lakes, responding to the Wanda letter:

Dear J,

I could not believe the episode with Wanda/Jeannie. It seems to me that I've read of a new book coming out, or to come out, about a woman with multiple personalities, much like you describe. I'll see if I can find it for you. I've never heard of anything like this before. What a weird life you have. It seems that nothing is ever simple for you, though I know you undertake everything you do with the best intentions. Maybe you should be more suspicious of peoples' motives sometimes.

End of sermon. I don't want you to be any different; I'm just thinking of how you might protect yourself better. Meanwhile . . . I have good news:

I got accepted! I am finally in law school. Barry wouldn't pay for my tuition, because he doesn't want me to go back to school. He said I was "too uppity" as it was. With the kids about to be on their own, I think I am going to move out of my comfortable home, which I love, and get an apartment. I don't think I can live with B. any longer and still give the time I need to my studies. Besides being his housemaid, I've always kept all the books for his company. And, this is a man who expects a hot meal each night when he comes home from the wars.

I have been captivated—compelled, what's the word? by Watergate. I have always sneered at housewives whose lives are determined by their soap operas, but I now realize that it's only the content of the program that is the difference between me and them. I am incredibly fascinated by the un-folding process. I confess I have some of the lynch mob reac-tion toward the White House, and I am able to excuse too readily the bias and stupidity of the investigators.

But, like you, I watch with horror and fascination as one outrage after another is divulged. I'm not sure my attitude is one so much of cynicism as it is fatalism. I think I have al-ways been more of a Calvinist than you. I remember those long philosophical discussions across my kitchen table on the nature of man, and I have always leaned toward the black Calvinistic view. The response to the Calley trial reaffirmed for me that the primitive, corrupt, perverted instincts are over-laid with only the thinnest veneer of what we choose to call "civilization." We have institutionalized insanity, not just in the U.S. but everywhere.

I'm teaching three sections of *Comp and Intro to Lit* this semester to support myself, and I'm used and abused. I am paid as part-time, but teaching a full load. I could bitterly complain, but they would just give the job to someone else. For two years I have been teaching a full load at the college level and have yet to make $4,000. Put this together, my be-ing too penniless to even come to visit you, with Barry's buy-ing an obscene Mark IV Lincoln—huge, flashy, ostentatious, and costing $6,000. I can't imagine why he thinks we need this item. It reminds me of an essay by Norman Mailer. His thesis: the new car does not get the girl; the new car *is* the girl—automatic everything, a block long, and thoroughly ri-diculous. We fight bitterly over money.

Women's lib has a great deal to say about these prob-lems, but I find myself steering away from discussions on the subject, especially with a man, and hate myself for being a white, female Uncle Tom. It is all too threatening, I guess. I am repelled by the histrionics of the movement—bra burning, men's bar stuff, but it outrages me when CBS reporters ask Bella Abzug where she got her hat, rather than questions of real substance. Bella handles herself well, segueing into discussions of issues. She wanted to speak to the convention on the abortion issue, but was not allowed to.

I wanted to stand up and cheer when you wrote that you had started a women's group. I was afraid you'd think the whole affair simply silly and frivolous. I was pleased as well by the *Ms.* address on your letter to me. I can't tell you what that small matter represents to me.

Well, I'm furious with Barry for taking my money and buying that hideous car. Since I don't believe in a god up there who is plotting my every move, I have taken up Chinese fortune cookies as a substitute; they are far less complicated too than the I-Ching.

After a Chinese dinner last night, my cookie came telling me that there will be "Fresh work in new scenes, much discussion and planning." Like most religions, this new faith is the result of a certain logical cause and effect. I believe the fortune cookie has at least as much to offer as most religions I have tried. So far I haven't gotten hung up on a personal deity associated with the messages therein, but I have read somewhere that a California housewife grinds these out in her spare time, and frankly, that deity seems as good as any.

Love, Alex

As Alex gasped in the thin air of first year law school—"It's like having a deadline to climb the Himalayas; all it takes is sheer exertion, more stamina than brains"—I tried to keep my cumbersome ark afloat. Greg's work had become increasingly onerous with school board squabblings, racial tensions, a daily morning newspaper that took pleasure in pitting blacks against whites, and vice versa. Greg couldn't seem to take positions radical enough for the left-wingers or reactionary enough for the right-wingers.

Carrie punched one of her teachers in the nose for making disparaging remarks about her father, thereby jeopardizing her standing in at least one social studies class. As the boys grew noisier and more athletic, Carrie and her friends, in the remote reaches of high school, grew more and more private. Once when I overheard the girls talking about another girl's sexual explorations, I was caught off-guard. Focused on the liberation of downtrodden and abused women of an older generation, I had paid too little attention to the concerns of younger women.

Pro-choice and *Pro-life* were terms that had not yet permeated politics in the Midwest, though Greg and I argued bitterly about abortion rights, coming to an utter stalemate about the matter and soon ceasing to discuss it altogether. I could not for the life of me understand why he couldn't see that this particular right to choose was *basic* to a woman's gaining control of her own body and, therefore, her own life. *Basic. Basic. Basic.* I was vehemently *pro life—the life of the woman who already existed on this planet, in this universe.* Greg insisted that as a "family man" he could never sanction "the murder of children." Let him bear them, then, I thought. He doesn't know what he's talking about.

Times had changed enormously since I was a naive high school girl in Thalia, the only comparison I had against which to measure my daughter and her friends' teenage lives. One day I stepped over Carrie as she and her friend Rod lay prone on the library floor working on a health assignment for school; poster board lay before them, and colored pens lay around them. Her assignment was to draw and label all parts of the male reproductive organs, and his was to draw and label all parts of the female reproductive organs. At first the scene made me gulp and raise my eyebrows. But then, after sitting a while in the porch swing thinking, I decided it was a far more healthy way of learning this information than I had been exposed to. That is, having no information at all and carrying that to my marriage bed.

Some time later, Carrie told me that one of her classmates was pregnant. No different from half a dozen of my own classmates, I thought, except that they had married the drillers, or riggers, or football players, or rodeo cowboys and got stuck in a dead-end place with a bunch of children and, usually, a philandering husband to boot. Some of them were dead already. Those who weren't were depressed, bitter, and looked twice their age. I could not think of one happy woman with whom I had been a girl. No, clearly Carrie's friend, who had an appointment for an abortion, was better off.

"I'm going with her, Mom," Carrie said firmly.

That same day I received a long letter from Alex, who was undergoing similar experiences with the girls in her family.

Dear J,

This will bring you up to date on the latest in the Roberts household. Short version: Barry's niece from Nebraska, Judy, age eighteen, became pregnant and came here for an abortion. She is staying with us a few weeks; maybe she'll stay several months and finish high school. Peter totaled my little Spitfire on the way to school, but wasn't hurt. Gillian (now seventeen, can you believe it?) is on a camping trip with some girls, and I don't want her to grow up. Further I have determined that I am probably just on the verge of emotionally becoming nineteen myself. Get the June issue of *McCalls* and read the article "Men in Crisis" or something like that and just substitute *she* for *he*, and you have a clear picture of where I am at the moment.

Beth, my friend from L.A., arrived here in the midst of Judy and her abortion. Then Beth's boyfriend Rick came, and I wondered how to sleep them. They've been living together for two years, but in my house, with my kids here? I didn't know. As I was fretting, Gillie comes in and offers her bedroom to the couple without a hitch. So I have in my conventional suburban house one young woman recovering from an abortion, and one set of unmarried lovers sleeping in my daughter's room. I don't know what to make of this. None of us mentioned the arrangement, but I'm sure someday the matter will come back to us in some form or another.

Judy comes from a very small town in Nebraska where both she and the boy grew up. Her high school class totalled nine. Her parents are determined to help her escape the local pattern of girls marrying early, usually pregnant, and growing up ignorant and small town. But this girl has absorbed too much of this mentality already.

I suspect you know a lot more about small town mentality than I. This is my first introduction to this life and its utterly provincial character. Judy has also been dominated by a strong-willed mother and father. She has the emotional maturity of a thirteen-year-old. Since she's been so docile and easy to manage, her parents assumed she was more mature than she is. It was only when the boy entered the picture that they saw how easily dominated she can be by whoever is closest to her at that moment. Sending her here was a last-ditch effort to give her a life where she could be on her own, find out who she is and what she might become.

I imagine you could tick off a dozen cases like this from Thalia, where a girl or boy made decisions too soon which stunted their lives and led them to repeat the pattern of that rural society. How in god's name did you ever escape it? I am awed by the will and energy it takes someone to do that. You made it; my niece didn't.

Which reminds me, I saw *The Last Picture Show* and loved it. I am recommending it to my classes and anyone else I see. Can we ever have been so cruel (yes), so passionless in sex (yes) so naive and knowledgeable at the same time? The poignancy of the boy was marred by a few things that were overdone, but overall I thought it was a good/great movie. The freshmen I teach in this small church-related college were "grossed out" by the sex scenes. A boy asked me why I liked the movie and looked puzzled when I held forth on "the death of innocence" and so on; then he told me that if I wanted to see a *really great* movie I should go see DeMille's *Ten Commandments*, which has been resurrected and is alive and well here.

Gloria Steinem talked at the college, along with Margaret Sloan, a black woman also editor of *Ms.*—an outspoken, dynamic, irreverent feminist. Their stated reason for going the college circuit was to puncture the myths that are rampant about Women's Lib. It's exhilarating to hear someone on a public platform say things I have been thinking and feeling for years but afraid to say. Steinem on stage is cerebral, speaks in a slightly nasal, small voice. She's clever, witty and intelligent. Some women friends and I bought them a late-night dinner after their evening appearance here and both women are very natural and unselfconscious.

Several women are putting together a discussion group; I hope it's not just a bull session. I am ready for a consciousness-raising session, much as I hate the image they represent. I don't like the fact that I respect so few women; I don't like the fact that I know so few out of my own narrow area of interest. I think all of us have a great deal to learn about each other, how we have coped with the indignities of something like carrying two-thirds of a college professor's teaching load and being paid one-fourth of his salary. I am not on a down-with-men kick, but I am definitely on an up-with-women binge.

Steinem called women "men junkies." We want a man at our side but don't care too much which one. This got a big laugh. She also said we are now becoming the men we wanted to marry. I loved that.

Love you too,
Alex

It was such a pleasure to hear from Alex. I needed friendship and support more than ever now, for Greg was really in trouble.

A school board election had changed the composition of the board, and Greg no longer had its whole-hearted support. "Forced busing" had become a divisive issue as well as Greg's promoting alternative schools as a way of integrating students. Do these things never get resolved?

The entire family had been involved in Dallas, where I had enrolled the boys in Dunbar, an inner-city elementary school with a ninety-five percent black student body, and had gone with them each day to try to bring the idea of cross-racial transfer to the consciousness of whites. *Somebody needed to put themselves on the line instead of all the abstract pontificating that was going on.* Eventually thirty white families joined with us in voluntarily busing their kids to Dunbar. Most kids had an enriching experience, including my two sons, (Ben in the fifth grade and Paul in the second) though I concluded in a follow-up study I did about the project that the younger you put the races in school together, the better.

When we arrived at Keating and enrolled our boys in an integrated school, Ben, just off the Dunbar experience, had come home shouting: "Hey, Mom. It's a neat school. There's even some *white* kids in my class!"

Paul informed us with some impatience: "Sure the school's okay; what did you expect?" And added, digging into his pocket, "Can I call Richard over—this guy in my class? I've got his number right here."

Ben asked, as I knew he would, "Is Richard black or white?"

Paul couldn't remember.

But in Keating a new school flap erupted every day, often egged on by reporters, and Greg was lambasted routinely in the reactionary, *Keating Enquirer.*

Further, I had my own downer. The Ford Foundation people who had reviewed my proposal about the Dallas integration attempt in Dunbar School asked me to come to New York to discuss it with them. At the luncheon, the group of Foundation men listened to me politely, but as I was leaving, I was escorted to the elevator by a courtly gentleman who said, "Your proposal is impressive, but I believe it's the consensus of the officers here that it is your husband who should apply for the grant and conduct the research, not you."

"*Why?* He had nothing to do with this!" I was devastated. "It was *my* concept. *I* planned the project and carried it out. *I* oversaw it. It was *I* who rode that school bus with those children every day and monitored them on the playground. *I* did the study. *I* wrote the proposal. *It's my work.*" I could feel my face growing hot; my voice rising. It was a serious project, and it was mine!

"But your husband is the educator in the family, the one with the credentials," said the Ford officer, ushering me into the elevator. "Maybe he would like to give us a call."

I was furious. Why did Barry get his pricey car when Alex worked twice as hard as he did? And why should Greg get a chance at a funded study that *I* had conceived and carried out? Why did I let

Greg bring me here to this overwhelming house and all these social obligations, when I just wanted to finish my education, so I could have some "credentials" myself? Why was I constantly stuck with the scutwork of living? Why did life demand of me things in which I had no interest and little skill, and deny me work where I could use my talents and passion?

I was becoming increasingly radicalized. I needed to put some of my frustrated libido to work in a creative way, so I came home from work early one day and sat down at my typewriter.

THE LIBERATION OF MRS. SHRIMPTON

John Charles Henry Shrimpton said he thought it was fine if his wife wanted to get a little job somewhere. He said she needed a little stimulation aside from the Waldorf City Symphony Women's Committee, and he could see, certainly, that driving car pools and scooting over to the A&P really were not very fulfilling. He said, yes indeed, he would cooperate, and he would speak to the children about cooperating. Certainly. Of course. If that's what his wife thought she wanted, no problem.

Todd, Gina, and Georgette said that would be fine. Sure. Todd agreed to try to remember not to leave his sneakers and knee pads under the kitchen table, and that he'd try to remember his bus quarters each morning, so he wouldn't have to call Mom to pick him up. He said he would really try to cooperate because at fifteen he was old enough to see that there were five people in the family, and ten rooms in the house, and only one Mom to go around. And of course she couldn't pick up everything all the time and drive to three different schools twice a day, especially if she was going to find a little job somewhere to stimulate her.

Gina Shrimpton agreed that thirteen was certainly old enough for anyone to remember to unplug her electric curlers in the morning before school so they wouldn't smoke and melt the top of the walnut dresser again. And yes, she thought she could remember to pack her own lunch each night before she washed her hair, but she would *not* pack lunches for the two monsters because she refused to be locked into a *gross* domestic role, and her mother should certainly sympathize with that.

Georgette Shrimpton said yes, she could remember to hang up her coat and not to leave her dripping boots in the front hall, and of course a ten-year-old knows what a clothes hamper is for—what did they think she was anyway, a baby? and she would remember that clothes went in it and not boots and mittens, and she would certainly do her part because Mommie needed a little help if she wasn't going to be home like always before.

Even Mr. and Mrs. George Edward Shrimpton of Akron, Ohio, who called on the occasion of their daughter-in-law's thirty-fifth birthday, told her that they were delighted she was going out to look for a little job somewhere because after all her children were in school now and could certainly be responsible for catching the bus, and of course their mother needed to broaden her horizons and do a little something stimulating, and certainly it was important that she didn't just let herself go like some people they could name, as long as the children and John Charles Henry, of course, didn't suffer from it. And certainly *they* knew that *she* knew where her *first* duty lay. After all, she had a good head on her shoulders, and they were just sure everything would turn out ok, but they would call in a few weeks anyway, just to see how things were going, and to remember that they were very very proud of John Charles Henry and his little family.

So John Charles Henry Shrimpton's wife scooted over to the A&P and bought two hundred dollars worth of food and put it away in the pantry, remembering to put half of it in the old refrigerator in the basement where the children usually forgot to look, assuring herself that all the apples and cookies wouldn't be eaten up in two days. Then she called the Waldorf City Symphony Women's Committee and told them that she was resigning since she had served on that committee for ten years, and she was going to look for a job now that all her children were in school.

The Women's Committee thanked her for her many years of service and expressed sincere regret that she would no longer be meeting with them on the first Wednesday of every month, and as payment for her dedication beyond the call of duty they sent her a plant from Fritz the Florist with a Styrofoam lyre and a red bow stuck down in it on a pointed stick and a note that said, "Good Luck to You in Your New Endeavor."

Then she called Thor and Lance and Alhambra's mother, and Victoria's mother, and Jim, Ed, Howard and Ronnie's mother and told them that she would no longer be picking up Thor, Lance, Alhambra, Victoria, Jim, Ed, Howard and Ronnie on Mondays, Wednesdays and Fridays, and that her own children would be riding the bus from now on. All the mothers were surprised and a little disappointed, but they were very understanding and said sure they understood and wished her good luck and hung up just a little too soon.

Then Todd, Gina, and Georgette's mother called the PTA and told them she would be taking an extended leave of absence, and she called the Giraffe Unit, Hilltop School, and told them she would no longer be able to be volunteer tutor. Then she took two cardboard boxes of material from the League of Women Voters over to the wife of Franklin Adams, John Charles Henry's colleague in the APKO Manufacturing Company, and left it on the Adams's front porch.

After this, John Charles Henry's wife called the HANDY-HELP AGENCY, the MOMMY'S DAY OUT AGENCY, and six women who had placed individual ads in the Waldorf City News. She spent three afternoons interviewing housekeepers, sitters, mother's helpers, and middle-aged ladies looking for something to do after their children had grown and left home. She eliminated the two who came in high heels and white gloves introducing themselves as English nannies. And she found surprisingly few women of any age or emptiness of pocketbook who would agree to greet her children after school, give them a snack, begin the family's dinner, keep the neighbor children out of the house and off the phone for an hour, and see to it that Georgette, Gina, and Todd practiced their piano, clarinet, and drums respectively. She finally settled on Mrs. McDonald who had hair dyed the color of carrots in frozen TV dinners and who brought along her standard poodle, Boots, principally because Mrs. McDonald was the only applicant who would agree to take the job at any salary.

Mrs. McDonald had one eye that wandered and a nervous tic with her mouth, and she didn't appear to be overly bright, but she had raised seven kids of her own, yes indeedy, and she had excellent references—glowing ones, in fact—and the mention of drum, clarinet and piano practicing didn't even make her blink; in fact, she declared she adored music, and that Todd's drums were really not as loud as they sounded. So Mrs. McDonald was hired to work between 3:00 and 6:00 each afternoon.

After this, John Charles Henry's wife cleaned the ten rooms of her house from attic to basement, brushing ancient cobwebs off the light fixtures, waxing all the floors and shampooing the rugs, paying special attention to the front hall and stairs. She fixed the broken doorknob and soaped the sticky drawer on her husband's desk and replaced all the light bulbs whether they needed it or not. Then she put a new washer in the faucet in the kitchen so it would stop dripping, and she trimmed all the hedges and lubed the car.

Then she took her giant economy-sized box of TIDY*KLEEN and washed everything in sight. She ironed the curtains and hung them back up in the bedrooms and baths, washed and picked all the lint off the bathmats, and zipped the throw pillows back into their washable covers. Then she cleaned Todd's and Gina's and Georgette's rooms, dumping all the chewed gum balls and Tootsie Roll wrappers and old valentines and broken plastic things from cereal boxes out of their drawers, and she filled a big bag with old clothes for the Goodwill truck. Then she took the smelly old hamster cage in which no hamster had resided for months out to the garage. She then washed and shook and pressed all the clothes in the closets, steaming iron-on patches to the jeans knees as she went along.

After all, she was going to liberate herself, and she wouldn't have time to think about all this housework after she took a job. By the time she had finished filing John Charles Henry's important dog-eared scraps of paper, creased credit card receipts, and other tax memorabilia in an accordion file and rearranging his drawers and matching up his executive-length socks, the two hundred dollars worth of food from the A&P was gone, including that in the basement, and the kitchen floor was covered with crunched Sugar Pops and splashes of purple Kool-Aide.

The morning John Charles Henry's wife realized she had just used the last egg in John Charles Henry's breakfast omelet, she accidently dropped a full box of Cream of Wheat on the kitchen floor. This accident caused a noticeable erosion in her habitual good humor. So she told John Charles Henry and Todd and Gina and Georgette to please clean up the mess the best way they could, and she went to her bedroom closing the door a little more noisily than usual.

After the children had left for school, forgetting their bus quarters, and John Charles Henry had left for the APKO Manufacturing Conference in San Francisco, forgetting his undershirts, she emerged from her bedroom in a navy and red plaid suit and black pumps, carrying a black shoulder bag containing the leads from the HELP WANTED ads from the Waldorf City News. As she walked through the kitchen, headed for the back door, she kicked the Cream of Wheat box across the room with a little more vigor than necessary.

For the entire week that John Charles Henry was gone to his conference, she left the house in her navy and red plaid suit. On Friday, Carla Shrimpton returned home triumphantly as Assistant to the Assistant Advertising Director of Flagg's Department Store. Just as she pushed open the door, the people from Giraffe Unit, Hilltop School called and said they had not been able to replace her with another volunteer, and Carla told them tough luck or words to that effect.

On Saturday morning, just as she discovered she would again have to scoot over to the A&P, John Charles Henry returned from his conference in San Francisco and entertained her with stories told at dinner at *L'Etoile*, and regaled her with the account of how his partner, Franklin Adams, had been practically mauled and molested on the dance floor by this brassy career woman-type in a bar in North Beach, and . . . well . . . the bar where the guys always go to relax after a long tiresome day in important conference meetings of course . . . but how Franklin Adams wasn't having any of this pushy broad, and how he and old Frank had spent every night in their hotel rooms reading their *Gideon Bibles*. Honest to God.

After John Charles Henry presented her with the imitation silver pin shaped like a roadrunner with imitation turquoise eyes that the company had given as favors to take home to the little woman, Carla announced that she was now the Assistant to the Assistant Advertising Director of Flagg's Department Store. John Charles Henry thought that was fine, just fine, and kissed her warmly, and said he hoped the new job would be stimulating, and not to worry about him or the children suffering, and that he, of course, would cooperate in any way he could, but that right now he had to get down to the office to read over some papers because he could never get any work done in the office on work days, of course, with people interrupting him all the time.

For the next three months, Carla stepped out her kitchen door every morning at 7:30, just before the children left to catch their buses and John Charles Henry left for his office. As she breezed out the door she called to Todd and Gina and Georgette to run water in the Cream of Wheat bowls so they wouldn't be welded to the breakfast table when she got home from work; to put the milk away; to try to find socks that matched better; to take the note to the teacher about field trip permission; to remember their nosedrops; to come straight home and practice, and not to forget their quarters and lunches. She called to John Charles Henry to turn off the lights, to lock the doors when he left, to leave the key under the thing on the porch so the milkman and Mrs. McDonald could get in, and to watch out for the cat's bowl the kids had set just outside the back door.

And for three months, Carla got sincere raves and fulfilling pats on the back from the Assistant Advertising Director of Flagg's Department Store for her clever ad copy and creative layout designs. And Carla was exceedingly stimulated.

One evening after Todd and Gina and Georgette's mother had just finished making Gina's lady-in-waiting costume for Wimbleton Junior High's production of *A Midsummer's Night Dream,* and was scrounging in the clothes hamper for the other knee pad to Todd's football uniform so she could wash it for his game, Mr. and Mrs. George Edward Shrimpton called from Akron, Ohio, to inquire about how things were going with their liberated daughter-in-law and her understanding little family.

Their daughter-in-law answered the phone and told them, yes, she loved her job, and yes the whole thing was beyond her wildest imaginings, and yes, she didn't see how she could possibly be any more stimulated, and yes, she did make a little bit of money—enough to buy some new carpet for the front hall, and a couple of silver candlesticks for the dining table, and a new walnut dresser for Gina, and new tape deck for Todd, and a new coat and wristwatch for herself.

And John Charles Henry came on the phone and said everything was fine, just fine, and his wife was terribly stimulated and had even lost quite a lot of weight, ha ha, and that everyone was cooperating beautifully, and that nobody was suffering yet, and that he himself had even taken the dishes out of the dishwasher that very evening, and how did they like that for cooperating, ha ha, and that he was making a little trip to the East Coast this week for an important APKO conference where he expected to be named Executive Vice-President, and that their grandchildren would now like to come on the phone and say hi.

Then Todd and Gina and Georgette came on the phone by turns, with only a little snatching and grabbing, and told Grandma and Grandpa Shrimpton in Akron, Ohio how nicely they were all cooperating, and how—well, riding the bus wasn't all that great especially when people fought and Todd got a bloody nose, and how, yes, they usually remembered their quarters, but if they didn't they just called Mom at work, and how neat it was to come home in the afternoon and get their own snacks because Mrs. McDonald was usually napping, and how Todd was gaining weight and really looking big enough to play on the first team since he'd discovered the old fridge in the basement where Mom stored extra food, and what a blast it was the day Gina forgot to turn off her electric curlers and Mom had to rush home from work and push Gina's melted dresser out on the patio after the milkman had reported to a neighbor that the house smelled funny, and how they all really loved the new carpet in the front hall and how it looked so much better than the old one until Georgette had run down the street that was being black-topped and then walked all over the front hall on her way to put her clothes in the hamper upstairs.

And then they all came on the phone all at once and told how some friends had just given them four new hamsters and how they didn't even have to buy a cage for them since they already had an old one in the garage. Then Gina told what a gas it was when the police came out to investigate when Mrs. McDonald took off with Mom's coat and wristwatch, and the silver candlesticks from the dining table, and Todd's tape deck, and how the police checked out Mrs. McDonald's references and found they were all her seven daughters and sons who had just got her out of an institution of some kind and were trying to find a job for her just when Mom had been looking for some lady to come from three till six.

And then Georgette snatched the phone to tell them that the only reason she ran down the street they were black-topping was because Boots was running off with one of Todd's sneakers he had left on the back porch since he wasn't supposed to leave them under the kitchen table. And then Todd came on again to tell them that yes, he sure had remembered about the sneakers, and he certainly was doing all he could to cooperate since he was old enough to understand that Mom needed a little stimulation.

Then Mr. and Mrs. George Edward Shrimpton expressed delight that things were going so well and allowed as how they always knew people could work things out to the satisfaction of all concerned if they just cooperated, and how it was really simple for women to go out and fulfill themselves without anyone suffering if there was just a little give and take like they were sure John Charles Henry was encouraging.

Then they all said goodby, goodby and rang off, and John Charles Henry and Todd and Gina and Georgette discussed how they would all cooperate about which TV show to watch tonight and which to-morrow night and so on, since it was so much simpler for all concerned when they all cooperated.

And John Charles Henry's wife scooted off to the A&P to pick up a few groceries before it closed, keeping in mind that she must get paper lunch bags and carpet shampoo and hamster food and ten dollars worth of change in quarters.

I sent copies of my story to Mother, Ellie and Alex. Ellie sent me a postcard:

To Jacy, *alias*, Carla Shrimpton, *alias* John Henry Shrimpton's wife, *alias* Todd, Gina, and Georgette's Mother. In reverse order I'm afraid. Your story is so true and good. How did you have time to write it between all that's going on? I've managed to realize at last that the trend is toward women's liberation! Hooray!

Love, Ellie

I sent a card in return:

Dear Ellie,

Thanks for your note. I'm sure you've been at the same place as Carla et al. How did I have time to write the story? This is what I've discovered: Writing is like sex; you've already done most of it in your head before you sit down at the machine.

Love, Jacy

Alex sent a recipe.

Dear J,

Here's a recipe for Aggression Cookies: Throw the usual stuff in a bowl, stir it, then dump it out on the kitchen counter and pound the hell out of it.

Love, Alex

I replied:

Dear Alex,

And furthermore (*pound, pound*) the only thing housebroken around here is Mother. And furthermore (*pound, pound*), I've always wondered why it's called the "Master Bedroom." And furthermore (*pound, pound*) remember what Marlon Brando in *The Wild One* said, when someone asked him what he was rebelling against?

"*Whaddya got?*"

Love, Jacy

Mother wrote a letter.

Dear One,

I know I'm not supposed to do this, but when you write stories, I can't help but take them in a personal way; that is, I think of you personally in the situations you describe when I read your characters, especially your women characters. And this last story bothered me. All these years I've been glorying in my little chick having flown the coop and got herself out of a provincial environment that was not nurturing to her, and then I see—or suspect that—she has herself caught in a very double bind. How do reasoning human beings get themselves at such an impasse?

Your work, which is supposed to bring you relief from housework, seems to be draining. Why don't you give it up? Why don't you go home, lie in bed and read at least one magazine a day, and one book a week, and demand that someone pamper you? You've spent too long pampering everyone who's come on your radar screen for the past fifteen years, plus catering to your husband—who sounds to me like the proverbial guy who jumped on a horse and galloped off madly in all directions.

If this sounds like a non-liberated mother, just be glad that you have someone concerned enough with your welfare to risk bucking your disapproval to say so. Moderation does have something to offer by way of longer life and serenity. And I'll bet it was some candle maker who extolled the beauties of the "lovely light." The general run of butchers and bakers—and even brilliant and energetic daughters—would do well to light one end at a time.

So saying, she beat a hasty retreat back into the dark ages.

Anyway, I'm glad to hear from you and learn you're still in the land of the *free(way)* and the home of the *brav(ado).*

I had a fleeting thought the other day while driving somewhere. I thought maybe life works like this: God gives us an overriding need (for money, love, beauty, procreation, ambition, recognition, etc.), and then gives us just enough gifts to fall short of the need. So we are always *almost* there. But we can never *quite* achieve what we think we need. I recall Saul Bellow's Henderson the Rain King, who cries: "*I want, I want, I want.*" Maybe this is the cry God planted in all of us, and then to test us, he never gives us what we need to attain what we want. I guess I am a hopeless Christian, no matter how the details of religion confound me. (I love the phrase I just wrote *hopeless Christian*—an oxymoron if ever there were one.) Maybe none of this makes any sense, but these flights of fancy keep me amused.

By the by, I have an appropriate epitaph for you: *Here lies Carla. She found herself at last.*

Love, Mother

I replied:

Dear Mother,

Well, "you're the one who borned me," as Paul used to say when I scolded him. And now I know why you borned me in January, the month of Janus, that gargoyle with one face to the hearth and the other to the door.

I think Carla and I are pivoting more and more toward the door. I had a row with Greg the other night over some way he insisted I *ought* to feel (can you imagine the presumption of telling someone how she *ought* to feel?), and I told him: The only difference between *marital* and *martial* is where you put the *I*, and my *I* is about to make a major shift. (Oh, I am becoming rhetorically gifted in battle.)

He didn't think it was funny.

Love, Jacy

Frustrated as I was with my own situation, when the wagons needed to be circled, the residual pioneer stock within me emerged. In fact, my urge to circle the wagons, to protect the good guys on the inside from the batterings of the bad guys on the outside had compelled me for a good part of the past twenty years to close ranks with Greg. We had lived under seige for nearly as long as we had lived together, and so fierce was my need to protect him that my function in this marriage had been reduced absurdly to doing just that.

Relief from assault from the outside would doubtless give this union little excuse for being. But the wagons were very much in need of circling now—perhaps for one last time. Greg's stewpot of troubles with this school board had come to a boil.

I was standing on a ladder helping a cabinet maker install bookcases next to the fireplace in our bedroom when Greg called.

"Send the decorator home," he said.

"Why? We're not finished."

"Yes, I think we are—at least I am."

"What do you mean?"

"I mean I think I'm finished here in Keating. I'm either walking or they're pushing me out."

"Who?"

"The school board, the guys downtown, business interests. Seems integration isn't good for General Motors, so to speak."

"Greg, you mean you've lost your job?"

"Or quit it."

"Well, come home and tell me about it. Come now. I have to go pick up Carrie, but I don't want the boys to be here long by themselves."

Greg came home as we were being beseiged by the media. I called Thalia.

"Mother, it's happened again. I don't know what you'll hear or read, but Greg is leaving his job in Keating. It's complicated, but after the school board changed in the recent election, the majority came to feel that Greg has moved the schools toward integration too far, too fast, so they want him out."

"Jacy, are you okay? The children?"

"Yes. I may want to bring them and come home to Thalia for a few days, just to get out of here. It's a zoo. We are crawling with sleazy news apes and rubberneckers and have no privacy. The kids are getting brutalized by some astoundingly unethical reporters, who pump them about their father's mental state. Who would beat up on little kids? It's appalling. Anyway, I just wanted you to hear it from us. I'll call again soon."

After nearly two weeks of being badgered by the *Keating Enquirer*, I sat down and wrote a five-page letter to the editor, in which I discussed the ethics of one Chris Klampit, reporter, quoting verbatim from what he said to our children, for example:

"Has your dad been worried lately? Lots of people are mad at him. Do you think somebody might hurt your dad? Has he shouted a lot lately? If you don't tell me, I'm going to write something bad about your dad in the newspaper."

On the advice of attorneys, I didn't send it, but it made me feel better and left an on-the-front-lines record of a family under media seige. In this case, our kids were paying for our precious freedom of the press. It was coming out of their hides.

Greg submitted his resignation. For days our house was filled with supporters, friends wanting to express their outrage, wanting to help. A group came together with a proposal: they would personally pay the legal costs and support Greg and our family for as long as it took, if he would sue the bastards and show the right-wing blood-suckers once and for all that they can't get away with bullying people.

Greg approached me: "What do you think? Shall we take them up on it?"

"Are you kidding? Be their sacrificial lambs? This is *my family*, Greg. These are *my children*. They have been battered enough. Why should we offer ourselves to be publicly flailed? Can you imagine how long we would have to put up with the kind of brutal stuff we've been suffering the past few weeks? Every detail of our lives would be up for grabs for as long as it took to settle this suit."

"But it's for a good cause."

"Oh, Greg. Your causes are *always* good. But your family gets butchered. Nobody really cares about that, about *us*. It's always about people *proving* something. It's about power and ego and making people bend to someone's will. And can you imagine what it would feel like to have our friends paying our bills? You've got to be kidding. Every time I bought a pound of hamburger I would wonder if I shouldn't be a more prudent shopper and save our friends some money. Come on. This is nonsense. If you want to be a martyr, go ahead. Personally, I've always seen a close relationship between martyrdom and narcissism, and I want something better than either for my kids and myself."

Greg took a job with the Cleveland School District, appointed by the courts that had taken the system over when it had refused to integrate voluntarily. Now he would live in a "gated community" himself, just like the Hadleys from whom we had bought the spec-tacular mansion on Lilac Hill—one in the inner-city of Cleveland with iron bars on doors and windows, and an armed guard accompa-nying him when he left the apartment; the guard would sit outside his door when he was within.

Ben stayed in Keating to finish high school. Carrie went off to college. After one look at the armed guards that would accompany me into my future, I took Paul and moved to New York City. It wasn't easy to leave a man whose life was in the service of a worthy cause, but I had my own worthy causes to think about. It wasn't clear just *what* had "broken up the set," but it was broken up all right.

Fitting nicely with my mood, I was met with the biggest garbage strike in the city's history.

PART III

11

Tell me, what is it you
plan to do with your one
wild and precious life?
—Mary Oliver

E·S·C·A·P·E

"WELL, LOOK AT our move like this," Graham Reed says to Catherine as he holds a glass of claret up to the light over my dinner table. "Everyone on Long Island is just a paycheck away from North Carolina." The others laugh.

"Yeah, and who would move *there*?" I say. The group knows quite well that the shores of that beautiful state are attracting hordes of New Yorkers fed up with excessive taxes and utility costs.

The Reeds share a farewell drink with Marlboro and me, then say goodbye and trudge back down the hill to their last night in their home on the Mill Pond. Marlboro puts the dishes away, as I wander upstairs to the library, thoughtful and a little sad, as leave-takings always affect me. I glance idly at the shelves that house my journals. Buried in them, amid scrawls in the many different inks of many different days and moods, are the seeds of ideas to explore or stories to uncover.

I pick up the books at random and flip through them, pausing for a moment to smile over sections describing what Marlboro loves to refer to as "Jacy's excellent adventures in Gotham City." The early passages of my New York City entries seem to take on the tempo of a speedboat, different from the leisurely notations of previous years. The first entry is dated April 7, 1976 and titled

SUFFICIENT FOR THE DAY

Paul and I live with Dr. Leonard Taubman, cousin of a Keating friend, who arranged this on hearing I was moving to Manhattan homeless. (Cousin Len just lost his wife and has huge apartment near Museum of Natural History. He'd welcome woman in the apartment with his two little girls, especially one with a young son to keep the girls company.)

This place is spectacular—exterior and entry like a cathedral; slender white spires. Inside: eighteen-foot ceilings, ten enormous rooms. Looks out on tower where Margaret Mead has office. Len has bedroom near front; girls, Leela and Sharon, thirteen and ten, have rooms off his. Len has psychiatric office in one wing, but seems clueless about handling his daughters. I become their advocate. Not that I need more kids, after those troops in the Keating house, but the girls are sweet, lost, and miss their mother.

Paul and I have two rooms in back. Mine has big windows and looks out over courtyard. I've been here a week before Len tells me tearfully that his wife didn't die from illness; rather, it was from this very room that she threw herself out this very window onto this very courtyard, killing herself. I sleep lightly on her very bed after that.

SPOT THE PSYCHIATRIST

Len is a strange man. Each day when I come home from job-hunting, I find him, head down on the dining table, brooding, sometimes crying. He wants to talk about his problems, which seem to me deep and severe. How can he counsel patients when he is so screwed up himself? He's in pain and asks my advice on everything from how to handle his finances to how to keep Leela out of trouble at school. I am drained by him, especially since I am worried about not having any money or job myself. Paul is in PCS, a performing arts school, studying music and doing well, but I need work. NYC, it seems, isn't panting for another freelance writer.

Besides, the day after we came, bringing nothing from the Keating house but a trunk filled with Paul's things, my typewriter, jeans, sweaters, and one job-hunt outfit, the cap falls off my front tooth. Each morning, Paul stands at the bathroom door laughing, as I stick the cap back on my tooth with super glue. Once, to his great amusement, I stuck my finger to my tooth and thought I'd have to go around with my forefinger in my mouth for the rest of my days. I can't afford to have the tooth fixed until I find a job. I can't find a job with this hole in my face. So what else is new?

WHY I DO NOT EXIST

After twenty years of marriage, I do not exist. I do not have a name that doesn't belong to someone else. I do not have a credit card in my own name. I do not have a bank account that is not "joint." I have no savings. I own nothing. *Nothing.* I brought five hundred dollars with me, from my last paycheck, and that has to last until I find work.

Though I do not exist, I can still perform motherly duties: Len tearfully asks me to go to Leela's school and talk to the teacher about the kid's apathy. *Sheesh!* I'd be apathetic too if my mother had jumped out a window, and my father was an unraveling basket.

OUR SECRET GARDEN

Last night Paul got up to go to the bathroom and noticed a light on in a hall closet. He went to turn it off, and found row after row of little green plants growing in egg cartons under a bluish glow. Next morning, when he told me about the secret garden, I was flabbergasted. I look in, and sure enough: dozens of marijuana plants. I decide not to mention this discovery to Len, but to get us out of here as soon as I can. Then, when I go talk to the teacher about Leela, I find that one of her "misbehaviors" is smoking pot on the steps in front of the school. Well, no wonder. Her father has his own pot farm.

RENTERS

Len tells me all his clients have deserted him (I'm supposed to look surprised?); he is broke and must rent out all his other rooms. Every day new people arrive: a mountain climber with all his gear; a belly dancer; a guy who seems to ride motorcycles for a living; a psychiatric nurse—well, that's appropriate for this looney bin. *Where does he get these people?* They all stake out a place in the one fridge for their special yogurt and wheat germ and Amstel that nobody else can touch. The girls have nothing to eat if I don't buy it, and I am close to penniless. I am not paying rent here—my original barter

being to make dinner and help the girls with homework for our rent—
but soon Len tells me that he is going to rent out Paul's room, so Paul
must move in with me. For another week Paul sleeps on the sofa in
my room. Then Len rents my room out from under me, so Paul and
I move to sofas in the living room. Is Len telling me something?

BEHIND THE GRIMY GLASS

I have some silver bracelets with me and a special Squash Blos-
som necklace I love. Paul and I walk back and forth in front of a hock
shop, casing the joint. I've never been in one and don't know how
they work. We walk in. The irony of my middle-class life and my
presence here is not lost on me as the burly man with a cheap astro-
logical sign hanging from his neck agrees to give me 200 bucks for
my precious necklace, which I can "redeem" if I miraculously find
400 bucks before he sells it. As I leave stuffing the money in my
jeans, Paul points out that the hockmeister is placing my *objet d'art*
in his grimy window. NYC was my Hope diamond; unfortunately, it
came complete with curse.

NIGHTMARE

I hear her scream again. Nightmares. The third time this week.
Without pausing to throw on my robe, I dash down the hall and into
the bedroom and take Leela in my arms.

"What is it honey? Tell me about it. It's okay, it's okay."

I pull her toward me and feel her hair wet with sweat against my
thin gown. For the third night in a row I sit with her in my arms,
rocking her back and forth.

"Tell me. That'll make it better."

Leela shudders, shakes her head, flipping the ends of the long
damp hair in my face. "Mommy," she says. "It's Mommy again. It's
always Mommy."

"What about Mommy? If you tell me, we can make it go away."

"No, it'll never go away. Dad told me. He told me I'd have dreams
forever."

I see that she has wet the bed again. Thirteen years old and still
wetting the bed every night.

"Come on. Get up. Let's get you a dry gown and change the
bed."

She lets me lift her thin body off the bed, strip her, and pull a clean gown over her head. She stands shivering, white and small, saying nothing. I rustle around in the chest, find clean sheets and smooth them over the bed. Leela stares at the wall above my head, impassive.

"Now, lie back down here. I'll sit with you for awhile."

She lies stiffly, her eyes on the ceiling. I massage her hands and arms until her body relaxes and her eyes finally close.

Len is in his office, slumped over his typewriter, asleep, just the way I'd found him when I came home from my job-of-the-week, transcribing the rambling tapes of a very bad novelist *manque*. I shake Len until he rouses, groggy, I suppose, from marijuana.

"Didn't you hear Leela screaming? She's been doing this all week. She's having nightmares, and they're frightening her to death. She needs help."

Len looks at me sleepily. "Yeah. She screams a lot at night. Just ignore her. She's sick you know. Was born sick. There's nothing anyone can do about her, so just ignore her. She'll stop screaming and pass out after awhile."

"But Len, she wets the bed, too, and she's a teenager—next week she'll be fourteen. Three nights in a row I've changed her bed. I've been wanting to talk to you about this, but you're gone in the mornings and asleep when I come home. Do you always sleep at this typewriter?"

"No. Sometimes I sleep on the couch there. He indicates the long hard couch covered in a gray flannel material, the couch he used—before his clients deserted him—for therapy sessions.

"Len, she wasn't born sick.' You know that. She needs help. If you can't give it to her, you need to find it for her."

"Leave her alone, do you hear me!" He grabs my shoulders and pushes me toward the wall. "She's sick, sick, crazy sick. I'm the doctor! What are you? A secretary playing doctor?" His lip curls.

"Len."

He softens his tone. "She'll stop soon. I think having you in the house has set her off."

"*Me*? My god, I'll leave then. Right now. This child is in pain." I start to go.

"A woman has not slept in this house for over nine months until you came!" he said. "You disturb her, your presence. She's subconsciously identifying you with her mother who spoiled her badly—ran to her every time she peeped. Just forget her."

"Len, I can't forget a little girl who screams like that at night. It's not human. She needs help."

Next morning Len is inordinately jolly in the kitchen. "Here, Sharon, we'll make you some eggs. Bring the frying pan." He ruffles the hair of his youngest daughter. "No patients today; let's have some breakfast."

Sharon goes for the eggs. "I heard a bunch of noise last night," she says, rubbing her eyes. "Here, Jacy, hold these for Daddy, please."

I obediently take three eggs.

"Like a real bunch of yelling. I got up once and looked out the door, but I couldn't see anything, and the yelling had stopped."

"Probably those bastards next door," Len says, jerking his thumb toward the kitchen window that faces the side of a welfare hotel, where down-and-out night owls play rock music all night and throw beer cans and bottles down the air shaft.

"No it wasn't," I say. "It was Leela. She has nightmares and needs some help."

"Leela's sick." Sharon says flatly, cracking an egg in the pan. "Born sick, just like Mother. She'll never get well. Dad said so, and he's a doctor."

CYCLOPS AND NOBODY

I go to a bank to borrow money to move Paul out of this zoo. All I have for ID is an Ohio driver's license. The banker with a patch on his eye like the Hathaway man (*is this for real?*) peers at it closely, as if he'd never seen such a thing before. "This is all?" he exclaims haughtily. Greg and I are not yet officially separated, but I will not draw on our joint account. I came to New York to be independent, and I'll be damned if I'll go crawling back because I can't hack it alone. So what do I do? I call Daddy and ask him how to establish a credit record. He tells me to take out a loan at the bank in Thalia. He will co-sign; then I should put the money in a New York bank and begin to pay back the loan as fast as I can to build my own credit. Then I can apply for a credit card.

LIFE'S LITTLE IRONIES

I love it. Here I am with three half-grown kids, calling my Daddy for help in gaining my *independence.*

BORN FULL BLOWN FROM HER OWN FOREHEAD

Before I do the bank dealing, I need a name. If I'm going to be independent, I need a *new* name. I don't want Greg's name, and I have outgrown Jacy Farrow; there's not much of that girl left in me any more. I go through all the names I like, starting with the family, and settle on Daddy's mother's maiden name. I like the idea of taking a woman's name, though there's no denying that you only need to look back far enough, and you'll find a man behind every woman's name. I like my grandmother's name, *Sarah Davis Cleveland*; it sounds strong and honest. Then I add my Aunt Celie's name, she is also strong and honest—but I drop the diminutive. Ceil. *Ceil it is!*

I call Alex, now in law school, and ask her how you change your name. She calls a few days later: "Just change it. There are ways you can do it officially, but they take time and cost money, so just do it yourself. Start using the name. Have it printed on your checks. When you get a job, have your paychecks made out in your new name. Then write the Social Security Administration and tell them you have a new name, and this is it. Pretty soon, *your new name will be you.*"

So *Ceil Cleveland.* I love it that you can just call yourself anything you like, reinvent yourself, be anything you want—except maybe a silk purse if you're a sow's ear. I feel like Jay Gatsby, who was forever reinventing himself. Who knows, maybe someday I'll pass through the Valley of Ashes under the eyes of Dr. T. J. Eckelberger and get to live on the North Shore of Long Island myself!

East Egg, West Egg, all around the square. *Fat chance.*

A SUMMER PLACE

Home at last! Or at least for three months. Answered an ad and found a perfect place for the entire summer. Near the Soldier's and Sailor's Monument in Riverside Park. Two floors and a courtyard garden. Artists Moss and Helga live here and have filled it with color and light. They go to Cape Cod for the summer. Moss built the spiral staircase to the second floor himself. I can't believe our luck. Paul has his own suite upstairs, and I have bedroom and study on the first floor.

Step from the kitchen into a garden with wrought-iron tables and chairs. *Heaven*—and it's *ours*. No crazy shrinks, no belly dancers.

PAUL'S BROADWAY DEBUT

"I don't do much; it's not really a pivotal role," Paul protests when I make too much of his being cast in the revival of *The King and I*. He is right. As understudy for both Louis Lenowens, British son of the famous Anna, and the Siamese Crown Prince, he mostly holds things, sings and salaams. "But I know all the lines," he says. "Everybody's lines and songs." He looks hacked: "I guess by the time I get to be a principal, I'll be old enough to do Mr. Brynner's part, so I might as well be ready."

HOW NOT TO BE A STAGE MOTHER

Stay as far away from the Uris Theater as possible. I do. I go to the opening night performance and party at the Raga afterward, then stay entirely away. At the party, Paul approaches with the star in tow, and I rise to meet the King. Brynner is not very tall. I had, on seeing him twenty-six years earlier enact with Gertrude Lawrence the role he now revives with Constance Towers, thought him to be gigantic— huge, bronzed, an oiled and bald Goliath. But then, I was not very big either, twenty-six years ago, and was quite prone to crushes on handsome actors. He is still handsome—and courtly. He kisses my hand and tells me what a "fine son" I have. I do not faint.

EEEKKK!

Paul goes to school each day, naps in the afternoon and is on stage at night. Even so, he's still only eleven, so I have to pick him up in a cab each night after the show. He is often starving, so we stop for a late supper. Once he orders trout, which comes with the head still on. "I can't eat something while it's staring at me," he says, cutting off the head and hiding it in the bottom of the bread basket. The waitress goes to and fro as we eat. A bit later, we hear a great commotion: *EEEEEEKKK!* screams a woman. *There's a fish head in my bun basket!!!* Paul and I continue to chew silently; I'm becoming a good actor too.

MY TYPING TEST

Each morning I get up and start with the phone calls. Want ads. Leads. Every time someone mentions a name, I write it down and call that person. Funny how easy it is to get to even famous people— editors, ad execs, CEOs even. (You call at lunch when the secretary is likely to be out, and the boss is lunching at his desk and answering his own phone.) *Not* funny how none of these people seems to need a writer, editor, designer, or as they say here *concept person.* If there's anything I have an abundance of, it's concepts. *Please hire me!*

My money is running out. I decide to try for a job as an office temp. But on the way, something funny happens. It's raining buckets, and of course all the cabs have gone to the moon. I am dressed in my only decent outfit and huddling under a crippled umbrella somebody left in the apartment. A man in a blue jogging suit keeps *up-streaming* me. (In NYC that means hopscotching over wherever you're standing to get closer to the corner, or the place the cabs are more likely to stop.) I move toward the corner; then he moves ahead of me. I go around him, then he jumps over me. *Checkmated in the rain!* He is in position just as a cab pulls up. He runs for it, opens the door, prepares elaborately to get in, and then with a wonderful Sir Walter Raleigh sweep of his arm ushers me into the cab. Surprised, I look up to thank him and fall into the crinkling eyes of Robert Duvall. *The* Robert Duvall. *Gulp,* I say articulately. He smiles, helps me into the cab, closes the doors and waves till I get out of sight. I want to hang out the window and shout at him: *Do you need a gopher? A coffee girl? I've had lots of experience serving others!*

At the temp agency: "Hon, sit over there, there's dozens ahead of you." I sit, shaking myself dry. I sit and sit. Two hours later, I'm led into a room with ancient typewriters lined up on a long desk. I'm given *The Gettysburg Address* to copy and a stop watch that Mr. Tinker, my monitor, sets for sixty seconds and plops down beside me. "When it rings, I'll hear it," he says. "Stop typing. I'll know if you cheated, honey."

I have a hard time getting the paper in the typewriter, since the brand is wholly unfamiliar to me, but it's a good thing I know *The Gettysburg Address* by heart, so I don't have to look at the copy. I beat around on the lunky old typewriter, muttering to myself, and try to fight the quickbrownfox to a draw.

Then I go for my dictation test. Here I sit: an assistant professor with two and a half college degrees who can read all necessary words in three languages, and I'm jerked around like I'd just failed my GED. *Mr. Tinker!* I want to yell. *Do you realize I won the Texas Interscholastic League Typing and Shorthand Competitions three years running?*

I get a placement at the Blue Blazer Ad Agency, which will give me work for a couple of weeks, but I slink out of the temp office in my damp skirt wondering what kind of victory I have won. Does humiliation build character?

NOTE TAPED IN JOURNAL

Dear Jace . . er . . Ceil,

Your life sounds like a nightmare with New York City going down the tubes and all that garbage on the streets. Sometimes it's hard for me to figure out why you left that gorgeous house in Keating, and your beautiful things. And you did have a lot of friends there and didn't have to hock your turquoise for food. (*That* one was really hard for me to picture.) But then something happens like this week, and I know why you left home.

Artie's whole clan came for dinner this week—well, just twenty-one of them, including his nine brothers. You would be aghast at how my husband and the men in his family behave. If you have any doubts about what real male chauvinist pigs are, just take a gander at the original breeding ground. They all came in here honking around, plopped down before the TV and did nothing except every once in a while grunt at each other, while the women fell all over each other in my kitchen fixing food for them. How did we come to this pass? We do all the work; they sit around and then order us about. I worked my fool head off for days for his family reunion—cleaning, shopping, cooking, and of course getting the kids to everywhere they need to go. Then while I'm running around waiting on the tables, he comes into the kitchen to tell me he thinks the turkey is a little overdone. I guess this is the first time he has looked at me today, because he stops dead in his tracks and says, "Go take that blouse off this minute, you look like a prostitute!" I had on the white voile blouse Mother made me for my birthday, and of course I had a bra on under it. I was flabbergasted. It must be what Mother calls the *fundie* in him. He thinks he has a corner on the moral majorities of the world.

Love, Ellie

GOOD NEWS/BAD NEWS

The good news is that Paul has been cast as a principal in *Shenandoah*. The bad news is that it's going on the road, so he will tour with the company all summer, and I'll miss him desperately. Greg has taken a leave and will chaperone. Carrie and Ben are in college, but will take turns, during vacations, relieving Greg of tour duties. If I don't get a job soon, I'll take my turn with this, too, but I can't tell you how much I *hate* being cast as stage mother. I love the theater, but the idea makes my skin crawl. Paul plays the son of Ed Ames.

LOOKING BULLISH

Good news! The only person I know in New York City, a writer with Texas connections, (who is moving away, so I won't know a soul), called with a lead on a job. I got it! The man, James Phillips, is a well-known financial adviser, quite famous, who offers investment information and publishes a financial newsletter. I am to be his editor. I told JP (what everyone calls him) that I had to take a long weekend this summer to go to the Midwest to see my son in a stage performance. He said, okay, no problem. Eighteen thousand dollars! I can't believe it. I had to teach three college courses a year for six years to make that. Maybe there *is* a light at the end of this tunnel that's not an oncoming train. I start work tomorrow.

LYDIA: RAW DATA

Bad news. Since I've got this big apartment, I need to find someone to help pay the rent. I put an ad in the *Voice* and get a few callers; nobody just right. On Saturday comes this knock on my door. A woman just a little older than I has ridden a bike up from the Village to look me and the apartment over. Her name is Lydia, and she is small, wiry, intense, with dark eyes and long black hair. She would be almost beautiful if she'd lighten up a bit. She has a PhD, teaches high school English and writes for the theater at night. She's plugged in with off-off-Broadway people and has had a couple of plays produced at *La Mamma.*

I'm taken with her energy and intelligence, and clearly she is taken with the apartment. She lives in a rent-controlled studio she doesn't want to give up, but when she read *"garden apartment"* in the ad and knew she was stuck in NYC all summer, she got curious. So I rent her the second floor until Paul comes back, while she rents out her own downtown apartment. The apartment culture in NYC, especially in these scarce times, has a life of its own. A garden apartment has been known to hold a warring couple together for years.

TRULY BEARISH

More bad news. JP is a monster! Today he threw a heavy glass ashtray at me for opening a window. He missed me, but hit a lamp then demanded that I pick up the pieces. He screams at the staff, comes down to work in his bathrobe and slippers in the mornings and doesn't dress till noon; will sit at his fancy French desk and shave with an electric razor. Yesterday I saw him turn a table over on the quaking knees of a secretary, because she failed to put *Esq.* after a lawyer's name on an envelope. No one who works here can bear him, except for one woman, Cheryl, who is his mistress. She sometimes stays with him upstairs. Maybe I'm just not sophisticated. Besides which, being his "editor" means following him around all day with a yellow legal pad, writing down his every disjointed utterance. This man is a total jerk and a nasty one at that. If Len Taubman's place was a zoo, this is a bestiary.

LETTER TAPED IN JOURNAL

Dear One,

Well, you are indeed having some adventures, aren't you. Are you happier now? (I am not being flip; I suspect that you are, *and bully for you!*) I *kvell* with anyone who has gumption, and you sure have that. Go for it, my dear. I know you must be going through enormous upheaval, but remember what Nietzsche said, *The chaos within you gives birth to a dancing star.*

Escape

Since my birthday, I look in the mirror and my face seems to soak up makeup like an old wall. I refuse to have a wrinkled soul, however. So I wrote this:

Limerick at Sixty-Eight and Holding
I really am very conservative,
Think proper nutrition imperative,
Organic is prime,
But at this point in time
I'll settle for any preservative.

Birthdays are a time for reflection, I guess. I have recently begun to look around me at my quiet, orderly house, at the floor with its patina of little feet, the scarred centers of the stairs that I somehow never got around to mending; they remember your footsteps and those of the other children, and I miss you all. When I lay down on the bed today to take a nap, I looked at the yellow counterpane, and had a little *frisson*—isn't that a lovely word?—it contains a shiver in its very sound, as I thought, well, that's what rest is for, to *counter pain*. Funny the meanings buried in words that we usually don't see, or hear for that matter.

My mind is a butterfly bush these day; ideas flutter around it looking for a place to light. But when they do, it takes all afternoon to get them settled down, and just now your father thinks the world is out of joint because an old heifer wandered off somewhere and he can't find her, so I promised to go out to the ranch and help him look. Then maybe he can sleep well, counterpane or no. The TV is blaring (your father is growing deaf, my dear) with some infernal soap opera, the nefarious plot of which simply reminds me of what Pascal said: *All human evil comes from man's inability to sit still in a room.* Of course, I would've added *"a woman's too"* but then M. Pascal lived a long time ago, and I think it unfair to hold him to our current standards. Don't you think?

I've read and re-read your letter about that very unpleasant man you are working for. How do people like that get in such prominent positions? (*Whatever happened to kind?*) Jacy,

Celie, Ceil, whatever . . . you really do not need this abuse. I think you might reconsider that job. Now I will butt out.

So you won't think New York has a corner on the crazies, I'm enclosing an example from our weekly Sheriff's Report, copied *exactly* as it appeared in the *Thalia County News*.

Sheriff's Report

The sheriff's office has had a busty two weeks. They responded to approximately 44 miscellaneous calls that included 1-theft of gas, 1-girls acting up, 2-livestock on Hiway, 1-burned out car in pasture with tags removed, 1-car in a bar ditch, 2-possible drunk drivers, 1-wreckless driving, 2-deliver message, 1-assist citizen, 1-dog ran over on purpose, 1-attempt to locate, 1-funeral escort, 2-burgulary of a residence, 1-request for patrol, 1-family disturbance, 1-open door at gym, 1-dumping an animal carcass, 1-loose dogs killing geese and ducks, 2-burgulary alarms, 1-abandon dog, 3-suspicious persons, 1-dog bit, 1-kids mooning, 1-pipe found missing, 1-escaped monkey, 1-criminal tresspass with his wire cutters, 1-pubic intoxication, 1-pigs in ditch, 1-phone solicitation, 1-reptile removed, l-woman screaming, 1-roof-sprayers on fraud, 1-peeking in window, 1-possom under house, 1-attempted welfare, 1-chickens ran out in street, 1-loud disturbance with a fight.

Now I would call that a very *busty* two weeks, wouldn't you? The sheriff must be exhausted, what with corralling all those animals. We had a Mayfest here, which may account for the rampaging and mooning and screaming at reptiles. I don't know how to account for *the pubic intoxication.*

Love, Mother

THE INSIDE SKINNY

For the first time since she moved in, Lydia and I sat up half the night talking. She is extremely intelligent, sometimes brilliant, awfully eccentric. Her only modes of transportation are her legs and her bike. She rides her bike to work, then comes home and runs six miles each day. She is very thin, her muscles almost stringy. I ask her why she runs so much, and she says she does it so she won't have a period, so she won't get pregnant. I don't understand this, and she tells me that if a woman has only a small percent of body fat, she will not menstruate; therefore, she has a built-in contraceptive. I'm not sure I believe this, but she may be right. However, since she's lived with me nearly a month, and I've seen no man in her life, I'm not sure what the big threat is.

Anyway, she goes on to tell me that she grew up in a small town in the Mississippi Delta with five brothers. She slept upstairs in one big room with all her brothers, and several of them had sex with her from the time she was thirteen or so. She liked it, couldn't wait till bedtime, and after she learned the dangers of this activity figured out her own way to avoid getting pregnant.

Then one by one, her brothers left home—she was the youngest—and she had no reason to run anymore, so she got very fat. She ate everything she saw, making up for all those hungry years, until she weighed about 300 pounds! Her father thought she had gone mental, so he put her in a state asylum, even over her brow-beaten mother's objections. She stayed there for six months and put on another fifty pounds.

I listened to this with my mouth hanging open. New York people just about blow me away. I haven't met a *normal* one yet. But, truth to tell, they all seem to come from somewhere else. In fact, I don't think I know a native New Yorker.

It dawned on Lydia finally that the only way she was going to get out of the asylum was to stop eating. So she did. And started running around her room, and up and down the halls, working all the fat off. "I wouldn't sleep for three or four days," she told me. "I'd just run around and around my room."

The next time her father came to see her, she had lost one hundred pounds. He kept telling her that when she weighed 135 she could come home. She stopped eating altogether and worked out six hours a day and soon weighed 135. So she went home. There, she said, she was so unhappy she knew that she'd start eating again, so she ran away to New York City.

"Why New York City?"

"Because nobody knows me here."

At least we have this in common.

Escape

Lydia took three degrees from City University. "I finished my BA in three years, my MA in one, and my PhD in three more," she told me. "At the same time I was living in a posh apartment on Central Park South, working as a high class call girl with someone whose name you'd recognize, but I pledged not to say. I worked my way through college and graduate school using my cunt as much as my head," Lydia says proudly, twisting a hank of her long black hair around her wrist and running a pink tongue slowly across her upper lip.

Clearly, I've been too protected. I'm practicing up on absorbing information without looking shocked. Now I know why so many New Yorkers have no affect: *nothing* makes a dent in them anymore.

One of Lydia's students ended up on Rikers Island, so she successfully lobbied city hall to let her go there and teach him. From there, she began to teach a bunch of inmates on a regular basis. *New York Magazine* ran an article about her and her work. *This* work, that is—the work she can talk about.

OPEN HOUSE

Across from me on the cross-town bus is a young mother with her son who looks to be about four years old. He is engaged by the landscape outside the window. We stop at a light and his mother says:

"Look, Jeffy. See. The house has no front."

I am fascinated, too. An entire apartment building in the early stages of being torn down has had an exterior wall removed. You can see the apartment partitions, the fireplaces, the wallpapered rooms, the sinks and kitchen cabinets. It's like looking into the back side of one vast doll house without the furniture.

"Ohhhh," says Jeffy. "I see the toilet. They left the door open."

Everyone within hearing smiles, and the bus pulls away from the light. Then Jeffy looks up at his mother thoughtfully.

"But, Mommy, how do they keep the cockroaches out?"

A New Yorker for sure.

A VISIT FROM GREG

Greg takes a hiatus from being roadshow parent, and comes to see me. I haven't seen him for six weeks or so, and I must say—

sadly—that I find his visit an intrusion, even though he's bought tickets to shows and made reservations at terrific restaurants; things I could never afford to do. Clearly he sees this as a reconciliation.

Nothing is clear for me. I don't know a lot about what I'm doing right now. I have a miserable job, a kookie roommate, no money, no friends. But what has made me most uneasy throughout this transition turmoil is that I don't miss Greg. I thought I would miss him when I came here; that I just needed to gain some independence, learn to live alone as an adult, which I'd never done before, learn to use my wits. After I'd done that—taken a breather from him and all the responsibilities that life with him entails—I figured we might renegotiate. But the odd thing is I haven't missed him for a day. I hardly think about him. I prefer to be alone. I don't know what to make of this, but I feel very sad about it. Maybe I've just been overwhelmed for so long that being left entirely alone, even being lonely for a change, is refreshing.

"I have a surprise," Greg says one morning. I look up from my coffee and the *Times.* "While you were at work, I called some real estate agencies, and have set up some apartments for us to look at. I've thought about this for a long time: I'm willing to move up here, live where you want to live. I can always find work." I am baffled (in the strictest sense of the word, Mother would say: *tied in knots*). Why can't he understand that it's not *here* I particularly have to live, it's just *living on my own terms* that I need? I try to act enthusiastic.

We look at apartments all over the city. Greg goes for the East Side scene with people in tennis whites hanging out in the lobby, or else the buildings with courtyards filled with strollers and kids' trikes. "We can bring the furnishings from the Keating house here," he says. "It'll be just like home."

I cringe and seek out dingy downtown places. Greg is appalled. "Why would you want to live *here*?" he croaks, gesturing at the Soho walkup, the warehouse loft, the artist's *atelier* that I find charming and whimsical.

"Because I've *lived* in the other places, Greg."

"But how would we entertain here? When I find work, we'll have to do that, you know." I roll my eyes. "Oh, we'll have it catered," he says. "We'll have a decorator and a caterer. I've put in some calls to people I know here; I have lots of contacts. I'll have a good job before the fall."

"Greg, I was reading the other day, and I ran across something Arnold Bennett wrote a hundred years or so ago. He said, *Being a husband is a whole-time job*. I don't think you're ready for that."

"What? I've been a *great* husband. What do you mean?"

"Well, maybe it's just that *I'm* not ready for that, or for being a whole-time wife either. Can you believe that for the last couple of months I've *loved* having no one to come home to? No one expecting anything of me. No one to give me anxiety because I might be late, be detained, or might have found something interesting to pursue and decided not to come home at all. I just need to be alone, for the first time not having to live up to someone's expectations, to sort through and figure out what I want to be when I grow up."

I knew that was a mistake as it came out of my mouth.

"Oh come on, how old are you?"

"Okay. All I'm saying is I've *been* the little lady, the supportive helpmeet, Captain Ahab's wife, the devoted mother. I've paid my dues. I've spent twenty years paying my dues."

"Captain Ahab's wife? He was a nut case, an obsessed man."

"And *now* I want to *do* something else, *be* something else, but I'm not sure what. And I just want you to know, Greg, that I don't know what I want, but it possibly may not include you."

"What do you mean *not include me*? You're *my wife* for Christsake!"

"Dylan Thomas said, *I learn by going where I have to go*."

"You are crazy. Perverted. A wife doesn't talk to a man like that. And can't you say anything on your own without quoting somebody?"

"Sorry. Probably not. There are very few female birds that sing. I want to learn to be one of them. And right now I don't know how. I feel like Philomena. For so long in our house *yours* was the only *voice*, the only *will* in residence. Mine didn't develop. I don't want to live like that. I want to direct my own life; then I have no one else to blame if it doesn't turn out as I want it to."

"And how do you want it to turn out? You're biting off a whole lot, Jacy. How do you know you won't fall on your face?"

I hate the way he uses my childish name, when I've told him half a dozen times that I've changed it. He refuses to recognize that I have grown in any way.

"I don't. But I'm not scared. I'm really not. I'm not afraid of living, and I'm not afraid of dying. *I'm just afraid of living someone else's life—a half life.* I'm determined to grow, Greg, wherever it leads me. *Determined.* What was it William James said? You can overcome a lot of fetters by the sheer force of the will?"

"William James, huh? Are you sure it wasn't Henry or another of your pals?"

"I'm sorry but no, I'm not. I'm tired of apologizing for being me. Greg, there's a point to be made here: you think I'm showing off when I haul out quotes and things. This is just the way I *think*; the way I *am*, dammit! If it bothers you, find someone else. Just stop trying to change me, or belittle me."

Greg went away in a frenzy of threats and blames. He left a note on my typewriter—this time not the Will in case my behavior should make him die in his sleep, as he used to do after we'd had a disagreement—but a note: *You are a slut.*

OMINOUS—FOR HER

JP is a fraud. He put me—*me*—in charge of his financial newsletter that people all over the country pay good money for. Subscribers also are entitled to one personal financial letter and one personal phone call to JP each month. A lot of them are elderly, live in Florida on fixed incomes, and write to ask him how to invest their life savings. I am put in charge of answering them. I, who until last month didn't know a bear from a bull. Of course, I have no idea what to tell them, so I go to JP. "Say anything you want to," he says, waving me away. "Say oil, say commodities, say gasahol." *Gasahol?* "These people are depending on you to help them invest their life savings, JP. I need to give them an informed answer, and I don't have one."

"Say commodities then."

"JP! What commodities?"

"I'm busy. Figure it out for yourself."

I talk to little old ladies on the phone, and they cry and say they have lost all their money. I talk to angry old men. My blood pressure soars. I take home reams of investment materials to read, hoping to educate myself so I can tell them something sensible. It's hopeless. I have no background in investment counseling. I finally tell callers to write their questions down and put them in an envelope addressed to JP with *Confidential* written on the front. When I see the letter come in, I give it to JP myself and can only hope that he will open it himself and answer it. But I never see the letters again, so I don't know what happens.

Frequently, in the middle of a meeting, which he likes to take early in the morning at his breakfast table, as he sits in his dressing gown, he will pick up one of the three phones beside him and yell to Cheryl to "Meet me upstairs, right now!" Then he will leave and not be seen until noon. Each week I've been here, another staff person leaves. I have become friendly with his driver, Roy, and the accountant, Bailey. Bailey tells me that I am not crazy, that "JP abuses everyone, so they will leave before they understand just what he's up to." I can't bear it here much longer.

HUMAN FLY

Manhattan is such a fantastical place. A guy named George Willig climbed up a tower of the World Trade Center—climbed up on the outside yet. The thought of it takes my breath away. He got fined $1.10—one cent for each story he climbed. Nothing like this ever happened in Thalia. But then, there *is* the Sheriff's Report.

SMALL BLACK ANGEL

Marcella invites me to go to the theater with her. We see a piece by Nzotake Shange about what *Colored Girls* do when *Rainbows Aren't Enuff*, have a late supper at a little piano bar on Broadway, and then Marcella heads downtown. I dash for a bus going uptown, grabbing my token from my pocket. Either I take the wrong bus, or they change the announced route, which happens fairly often, but by the time I realize I'm on the wrong bus, we are deep into Harlem, and I have no idea how to get home. I reach into my pocketbook for my wallet, where I keep a bus map, and find that my wallet is gone.

This is serious. Where can it be? Even more serious, I don't have cab money, and I don't know what bus to take home. I speak to the bus driver.

"I'm on the wrong bus, and I've lost my wallet. Can you give me an ad-a-ride and tell me how to get back to Riverside Drive?"

He pulls a transfer from the roll and sticks it out to me, saying, "You're all messed up, sweetheart. You can't get there from here."

"Well, I have no money, and I need to get home. Can I get a subway near here?"

"Naw. Not around here."

"What can I do then?"

"Lady, I don't know, but you got to get out of here, we're going to the yard." He lifts his voice: *"Going to the yard, all out!"*

I get out of the bus and stand on the street. It is 1:30 A.M., and in the dim lamplight I see papers blowing all around me. One attaches itself to my leg. Everything is grimy and deserted, but I can hear male voices approaching in the near distance.

"Well, this is it," I tell myself. "I'll never get out of here. I'll die in Harlem; serves me right for my hubris." The wind whips the hem of my thin silk skirt, blowing it up indecently. I push it down and stumble. Damn high-heeled shoes. I never should have worn them.

As I stand there, sure that this is my last night on earth, a small black bird-like woman comes toward me. "Where do you want to go, honey?" she asks, putting her hand on my arm.

When I tell her, she says, "Just follow me, I'll take you to where you need to go. And don't mind them fellas coming over there. I know them and they mamma."

As they draw nearer, she calls, "Hey, ya'll. Go on home, now. It's time you be off the street." She glides me past the group of rowdy young men, turns the corner with me in tow, and says, "There's a bus comes right by here, sugah; that'll take you back where you want to go. I'll stand here with you till it comes."

My angel hovers, and I jump over the stile and get home that night.

BIG BOY ANGEL

Same night: I've been in bed about an hour when the phone rings.

"Hey, are you . . er . . . Cleveland?"

"Yes. Who is this?"

"What's your first name?"

"What's it to you?"

"I'm the owner of Delight Burgers, and somebody found your wallet in our bathroom, stuck down in the toilet tank. There's no money in it, but I thought you'd want your cards and stuff, wet as they are."

"How'd it get there? I've never been there."

"Somebody lifted it off you, I guess, and dumped it here after he took the money. Can you come get it right away?"

"It's three A.M.," I protested, feeling a twinge of distrust. What if this guy stole the wallet and is trying to lure me somewhere?

"I'll pick it up early in the morning. What time do you open?"

"At nine, but I don't have nowhere to put this, unless it's here under the burger maker. It might get all greasy."

"That's okay. It's wet already. I'll pick it up tomorrow. Thanks for letting me know."

Two helpful strangers tonight and one creep who swiped my wallet. Better than average for an evening on the town in NYC—if you don't count the jerk bus driver.

COSMOLOGICAL CONSTANT

The only thing that's certain is that the universe is a scary place. A Wisconsin judge named Archie Simonson gave a very light sentence to a rapist, saying the woman was "asking for it," by the way she dressed. One of the better minds of the sixteenth century. Then the Supreme Court ruled that capital punishment for rape is unconstitutional. And at the same time, I travel in a cab bending over, with my head down so it can't be seen from outside the car, because I seem to fit the profile of the women that a crazy called *Son of Sam* is stalking.

LYDIA GETS THE HOTS

One night when I come home from work dragged out and depressed, I tell Lydia that I can't talk, don't want any dinner, that I just want to go to bed. I do. I worry for awhile. Cry for awhile. Try to decide what to do. How can I leave this hideous job when I have no other? JP keeps me so busy and so upset all day that I can't even think about job hunting. As I lie there weeping, Lydia crawls into bed with me. She is nude. She leans over me, her hair hanging down into my face. I am startled, jump up, push her off me, and turn on the light.

"I thought you could use some comfort," she said.

"Well, I can," I say, tossing off the covers and sitting on the side of the bed in my pajamas. "But you scared me. This is *my* bed. What are you doing in it?"

"Ceil," she says lying on my bed and propping her head up on her arm. "I've tried to tell you in every subtle way, I know: I'm bisexual. AC/DC, as they say. I have a crush on you." She reaches out to touch me, and I jerk back. "I want to make love to you. Have you ever made love to a woman before?"

"No, and I'm not beginning now," I say. "Please get out of my bedroom. *Right now!*"

Lydia gets out of the bed and does a little posturing beside the door, throwing her skinny hip this way and that, which she seems to think is seductive.

"Lydia! Believe me, I am *not* interested. I have some problems to sort out, and you're just making things worse. *Get out of here!*"

Next morning I tell her that when the month is up, she must move out. I have too much pressure on me to have to put up with this too. She complains, cajoles, pleads, screams, accuses me of being "a frigid, waspy, cold-natured slut." (Why does everyone like this word?) She finally agrees to move out. "But you don't know what you're missing," she says flippantly as she flounces out the door.

"Maybe I don't. But I'm in no mood to find out now."

A CALL FROM ELLIE

"Sister, why don't you just come home? That place sounds so crazy. I got your letter about Lydia, and all I can say is you don't have to do this to yourself. You could go back to Greg; you could go home to Mother; you could come live with Artie and me."

"And his twenty-one relatives and nine helpful brothers? No thanks."

We both laugh. I ask her if she's ever had a woman put the make on her.

"Yeah, just once. It was at camp and I was about fourteen. She came to my bed, just the way Lydia did, and I didn't know what in the world to think. I'd never even had a *boy* make a pass at me!"

"Were you shocked?"

"I guess so. I remember being more sort of anatomically puzzled than anything, thinking: how do girls do it?" She laughs. "I'm still not sure; or boys either for that matter. It's a mystery I'd just as soon not explore. Were you shocked?"

"Yeah. I must say, I was. It was so unexpected. My head was totally someplace else, and then all of a sudden here are these little droopy boobs hanging over my face. The whole idea is so repulsive to me that I'm sure I'm really a raging lesbian in heavy denial."

"Sure, Sis."

-30-

Next day at work, JP calls me into his office. "Cheryl's away visiting her parents," he says. "I need some help tonight. After you've finished here, come up to my floor."

It doesn't take me long to figure out what kind of "help" JP wants.

"JP," I say. "I have to leave exactly at six today. Remember when you hired me, I told you I had to take a long weekend to watch my son perform? I promised him, and I reminded you last week that I was going today. You agreed."

JP bellows: *"Tonight! No!"* He hurls a ten-pound dictionary to the floor. Then he alters his tactics: he slithers toward me and begins speaking softly, unctuously. "Dear, I've noticed that you've been distracted lately. Is something wrong? I want to help you. Come upstairs with me and we'll talk about your problem."

God, I think. What snake oil. "No, JP," I say firmly. "I have to catch a plane. I'll miss it if I don't leave right now."

"You're *not* leaving. You heard me, *Not, not, not!*" He stamps his feet like a child. I pick up my pocketbook and move to the elevator in the brownstone that takes us to street level. I punch the button, JP stands beside me, his arm around my waist. The elevator comes and I enter; over my shoulder I tell him goodbye. He follows me into the elevator, and as the doors close, he presses himself against me, pushing me to the wall, and begins kissing me. Sloppy, old man's kisses. They make me sick.

"See what you're missing. Come up stairs with me," he mutters hoarsely into my hair.

"No, JP. I have a plane to catch."

"If you go through that door, then don't bother to come back," he hisses, backing off a little and speaking through clenched teeth. "And I was just about to make you vice president, thirty grand."

I push the door open and step out. "Goodby Mr. Phillips," I say. The door closes on him. By contrast, even the air on the streets of Manhattan seems fresh.

If I have to live in a stairwell and smell urine all day, I will never go back.

THIS IS JUST TO SAY

The note from Lydia on the fridge begins: "CC: you have a very severe psychological problem. You are afraid of yourself and your own sexuality. You *know* you love me! You just won't admit it. The idea is too out of the mainstream for you. You can't deal with your own passions, so you repress them. I'm going to Nantucket with Marie for two weeks, and when I return I will move out, unless you've had a change of heart, which I urge you to explore. You must consider therapy. Frieda, my gynecologist, can suggest someone. Her number is in my book in the counter drawer. Call her. And make this your mantra: I want to make love to Lydia, I want to make love to Lydia. When I return, you will. MMMmmmmmmmm L"

Why is it, I want to know, that everyone assumes I'm "missing" something having to do with their own crummy bodies? And why is it *my* problem when I reject them? Could Frieda's shrink answer that one? What a crock.

TOO YOUNG TOO LONG, TOO OLD TOO SOON

Ben is living in the house in Keating, going to summer school at the university. VD is still there as nominal housekeeper and cook. Greg is in and out occasionally. I haven't been back in two months but stop here to see Ben on my way to Indianapolis to see Paul in *Shenandoah.*

When I walk in the door of the magnificent house, I begin again to feel the pain that drove me from the place. Carrie meets me here, as we have planned. She wants to talk to me about the college man she is dating.

We go up to her old bedroom with its antique maple bed and the quilt with bright yellow sunflowers from a trip to Appalachia. She loves old things with a contemporary dash.

"Same old yellow radiators," I say, smiling at the cheerful color she had painted the steam radiators when she was in high school.

"Same old me," Carrie laughs.

"Yes, thank goodness. You're just a little larger version of the perfect self that I have loved for twenty years."

Carrie screws up her face. "You sound like dad. *Perfect, perfect, perfect.* I am *not* perfect, don't want to be and am tired of having that label slapped on me."

"Sorry. It's unfair. And I was kidding; I won't do it again."

"I think I'll marry him, Mom."

"Grant? Why?"

"Well, I'll be out of school before long, I don't know what I want to do with my life. Grant and I have a lot of fun together. He wants me to marry him and help start a computer business. We could move to Chicago or Wyoming or something. Computers are big now and growing. We'd be on the cutting edge."

"Chicago or Wyoming? Carrie, you're not telling me any reason you should marry Grant. Is there any other?"

"Well, he's cute," she laughs. "He looks good in his swim trunks, he smells good."

"Carrie."

"Well, if you must know, Mother, getting married is the only way I know to get to sit at the grown-ups' table at Thanksgiving."

We laugh and hug—two confused women, twenty years apart in age, both wanting to prove our adulthood, both wanting to try the world on for size, neither knowing quite how. A man is a cheap and quick way out, Carrie thinks. I know better. A man is the most expensive way out of the identity crisis all girls go through. And if the relationship is not for keeps, it is extremely painful to extricate oneself.

"Carrie, promise me one thing. No, don't promise me anything; Mother always says it's unfair to extract promises from people. One makes promises only to oneself. So don't promise, but I want you to think about this very hard: Don't marry to 'find yourself.' It will be a disaster. Marry only when you are very sure of who you are and what you want; when you know at what points you can and cannot compromise; when you are a whole, self-sufficient human being who does not *need* anyone to be fulfilled. Marry only because you have found someone you want to share your life with—*the full life you've made for yourself.*"

"Mother, that's a large order. I don't know how to make a 'full life,' that's why I'm thinking about getting married."

"I know, Carrie, that's my point. It's all wrong. You've got to be a whole person *first*. No matter what Plato said, we are not two halves of one whole madly rushing about trying to connect to the other half to complete our deficient selves. Not as individuals, anyway; maybe that image works metaphorically in a general, abstract, gender sense, but. . . ."

"Mother, what are you talking about?"

"Oh, I don't know. I have a talent for making simple things complex. The simple part is this: Just don't get married until you know exactly what you want from your life. Marriage closes down options."

"It didn't for you. You're doing what you want to."

"Oh, Carrie, look at me. I'm not having a *middle-age* crisis, I'm having an *adolescent* crisis. I jumped from child to adult, without the *angst* in between that you're going through now. I'm doing the same hard work as you are at twice your age. I just want to spare you from having to do it at *my* age. Do the hard work first when there aren't so many other people to consider or to confuse; then settle down to whatever it is you decide to do."

"Girls never listen to their mothers, you know." Carrie smiles, mocking.

"I know. But it's my job to say these things anyway."

"Dad's hurt because he thinks you're leaving him."

"Maybe I am. I don't know. It's possible. I'm trying to figure that out right now; I should have figured that out—whether I could live without him or not—*before* I married him. That's what I'm trying to tell you about Grant."

"He's so hurt, Mom. He comes to me with all his feelings, and I feel sorry for him, but I don't know what to do."

"I'm hurting, too. Do you feel sorry for me?"

"No, Mother, you're strong. You'll get over it. I don't know about Dad. He's not strong in the same way. Remember we always used to protect him when we were kids, and you helped us, so he wouldn't worry or get upset. Remember?"

"Yes. And it was my mistake. I thought it was my *role*, but it created a family pathology in which we all conspired to protect your father from bad news. I was responsible for that stupidity. It wasn't healthy. And besides, it was arrogant on my part. Who was *I* to think I could shoulder all the heavy stuff, the bad news? He probably kept things from me too, for the same reason. Doing that keeps the other person weak. It was a kind of co-dependency, but I didn't even know the *concept* then, let alone the word."

"Well, you thought he had enough to worry about in his job, and with those awful reporters after him. It's understandable, Mother; don't beat yourself up."

"One thing I've learned is that a lot of family dysfunction comes from people doing the best they know how, with all the best intentions in the world."

The room is darkening. Carrie switches on a bedside lamp. "Mother, how did your parents make their marriage work for so long? They seem happy."

"I can't speak for them, but I do know that Mother possessed a life of her own, a life in her mind, to which Daddy did not belong. There was space there, which probably saved their marriage. Daddy may have had another life, too—maybe his cowboying was that other life. He'd get out there and ride those horses, herd those cattle, and come home cheerful and pink-faced, and god knows what went on in his head while he did that. We all need space. Separateness goes a long way toward preserving togetherness. Your dad and I didn't have it."

"Why?"

"I don't know. Maybe we weren't smart enough to know we needed it until it was too late. Maybe it was because we came out of the fifties. Our life, from the first, was a role based on 'togetherness,' a vicious, pernicious kind of sentimentality, a virtue trap: we have to be good, we have to be role models, we have to be. . . . "

"*Perfect.*"

"Yeah, how'd you guess? Perfect. People are looking up to us, we can't let them down. Though your dad didn't seem as aware of it, he probably felt as suffocated, at some level, as I did. Perfection takes a toll."

"Tell me about it."

Carrie lies back on the yellow bed and props her head on her arm. I run my fingers through her glossy hair, just as I used to do when she was a child, combing my fingers through it, holding it lightly in a gossamer web, letting it fall. My precious daughter.

"So do you think you'll split from Dad or not?"

"I told you, I don't know. I wasn't brought up to leave a husband. I was brought up to hang in for the long haul. And I did—probably too long for everyone's good."

"Then you don't love him anymore?"

"Carrie, I'm not sure what that means."

"Then when you say you love me, that means you don't know what you're saying?"

I sigh. "No that's different. I love you unconditionally, deep, deep down in my heart. Nothing can ever take that away. Nothing."

"Then how's it different with dad?"

"It's a lot more complicated. People married a long time fall into patterns they can't reverse sometimes. Roles. I can't live in a marriage that's a *Noh* play—two people in wooden masks with neutral expressions on their faces, moving slowly around each other in a stylized pattern. In center stage the *shite*—the main character, always male—and of secondary importance, of course, the *waki*, his foil, both surrounded by a chorus that. . . ."

"*Mother, stop. You're doing it again!*"

"Doing what?"

"Wandering, meandering, talking about obscure things."

I reach down and pull the slippers off my feet impatiently, tossing them into a corner of the room. "Look. Why is it that when your *grandmother* talks like that—obscurely, metaphorically—you fall all over yourself thinking she's brilliant and wise and awesome. And when I do it, it's just some garbled-up kook talking?"

Carrie reaches out and hugs me hard. "Because you're the *Mom*, that's why; not the *Grandmom. Roles.*"

I invite her to come live with me, but she refuses. She's probably right: she doesn't need me right now anymore than she needs a husband.

"Mom, what are you going to do when you go back to New York?"

I think for a moment. "I am going to beat this," I say far more bravely than I feel. "I'm going to beat this through *silence, exile, cunning.*"

"Through *what*? Oh, weird."

BEN WEIGHS IN

"Ma, I don't think you're treating Dad right, he's got his feelings hurt."

"Oh, Ben, I'm so weary of having to defend myself. You've seen me run this house and this family since you were born—seventeen years ago. Did you ever see me *not* treat your dad or anyone else fair?"

"Well, no."

"Have you ever seen me scream or holler or be deliberately mean, or not try to make sure everyone gets everything they need?"

"Well, I guess not. You're just moody sometimes. And you tried, I guess, until you left. I don't think you should have left. It got Dad all upset when he needed you."

"Look, cut me a little slack, will you? I'm not just a mom or a wife. I'm a *person*, too. I need some time to do something for *me* for a change. Is that okay?"

"Well, I guess so, Ma, but what do I do with Dad?"

WHY I DON'T CARE IF THIS PLANE CRASHES

I am on my way back to NY, a miserable, mental, physical wreck. My stomach gives little lurches, and sour air puffs into my cheeks. My head aches, like someone is driving a jagged shaft of lightning through it. My skin feels like someone else's, and I am dead inside, empty, like I used to feel when the children were very small in Eighty-Lakes, and I thought my life was over. Like the times I would lie on the bed and look at the wall in a deep depression. The heart is just out of me—the energy, spirit, intensity. I'm screwing up my kids, I'm screwing up everything, but if I capitulate to Greg's overweening needs again, and the family pressures, *I'm* screwed forever: axed, dead meat. I might as well have a lobotomy. There is a little tiny kernel in me that wants to live, not be usurped. What is it Mother says? *"I'm standing up insiiiiiiide!"*

Oh God, I'm going to throw up. Looking at the paper bag in my lap just makes me feel sicker, makes me smell the vomit that's not there yet. I am going back to nothing in New York. Zero. Zilch. Nada. No job, no friends, no prospects.

Why did Greg have to show up at the Keating house? This was going to be my time with my kids. What's he doing dumping his problems on them? Humiliating me in front of my children. Another talk between us going nowhere. *The subtext always: I am guilty for something.* What? Not loving him madly? Not letting myself be browbeaten or shamed into submission anymore? You don't shame people into loving you.

What am I doing wrong? Is trying to live honestly—without faking it—wrong? Is everything a role? Can no one stand the truth? I cannot go back to that house to live. I cannot live with him again anywhere. I am just not a person that I like when we're together.

Which means I have nothing but me. Waiting for me in New York is exactly one apartment paid up for exactly one month. Then what?

I cry quietly on this airplane, sniveling into my tissue, but I want to scream. I want to yell: "It hurts! It hurts! I want to be dead!" If this plane comes crashing down at this very moment I wouldn't care. My kids will be taken care of. I don't care anymore. *I just don't care . . .*

RUCKUS AT THE CAROUSEL

As I drag my body over to the baggage area, I see a young woman weeping, trying to extricate from the baggage mechanism a bicycle with one wheel, and a man I have known slightly from a another life. He is holding the other—smashed—wheel of her bike. Should I greet him? *I must look like a ghost, the end of the world.* I start to slink away. *I am so empty, can people just see straight through me? Oh, I don't care anymore.* As he moves my way, I look up at him. "Garry? You're Garry Simmons."

The man turns: "Jacy! What are you doing here?" We talk a few minutes as we find our baggage and lug it off the rack. "This young lady," he gestures to the owner of the bike, "was seated next to me on the flight. The airlines somehow managed to bang up her bike, and I was trying to help her get it together."

We will all share a cab into the city. I am listless, limp, happy to be taken care of.

In Manhattan, we drop the bike and its owner off, then turn toward Riverside Drive. As we near my apartment, the pain begins again. I had been diverted for a few minutes, and now I have to confront the bleakness again. I dread putting the key in the latch.

"I'm going to be in town on business a few days," Garry says, as we pull up. "Would you like to go to the theater some night? There are some plays I want to see, but I don't relish going alone." *God knows how I must have looked to him. A waif, a lost soul.* I nod. He writes down my number. I fumble at the door, then fall into the darkness beyond.

Lydia is in the process of moving out. I stumble over her stuff as I head for bed. Tomorrow I will have to begin looking for work again, and then a new apartment. Tomorrow.

CAN'T BEAR THE BULL ANY LONGER

From somewhere I summon the energy to call JP's accountant, Bailey, and tell him that I have quit and to please get my final check ready for Roy to pick up. Then I call JP's black chauffeur. "Roy, I couldn't stand it anymore. I quit. Would you pick up my check from Bailey and bring it to me the next time you drive this way?" Roy agrees, and a few hours later he is at the door. "Here," I offer. "Let me give you something for your trouble."

"No, no. You earned every cent of this. We all do. Soon as I find another job, I'm out of there, too. Good luck." He tips his hat and is gone. I open the envelope: eight hundred dollars between me and a urine-soaked stair well.

I SHOULD HAVE BEEN A PAIR OF RAGGED CLAWS
SCUTTLING ALONG THE FLOOR OF SILENT SEAS

Instead, I lie here like a mud fish stuck in the bottom, my one wandering eye staring up in a glazed fashion. I can't get out of bed. Three days I've been here, not even getting up for food. The phone rings a few times. I can't answer. I hardly have the energy to write this, but it's the only thing that keeps me sane. I have no other purpose than to stay alive to write in my journal. I have to pull myself together. I have to pull myself together. I have to pull myself together. *That's* my mantra, Lydia. I have to pull. . . .

WHAT FRESH HELL IS THIS?

A great clamor at the front door. Only Lydia, letting herself in.

"Goddammit," she yells. "Why don't you answer the phone? I've been calling you for three days." She barrels into my room with an enormous St. Bernard in tow.

"Sit, Birthday!" she shouts. "Sit!" The dog's pink tongue hangs out, panting, as he explores my feet.

She turns her eyes on me: "God, look at you. What in the hell is wrong? You look like me in my *anorexic* days. That's the new word for what was wrong with me, you know. Didn't have a word for it then but *nuts*. Come on, get out of there. *Get up.*"

It's hard to say no to Lydia, though as we both know, I can and have when it counts.

"We're going to put you in the shower, then I'm going to fix you some soup, and we're going to talk. *Sit, Birthday!*" Birthday, already sitting like a lump, rolls his eyes and looks superior.

"What is that?" I point to the dog.

"My new lover. I bought him for my birthday because (pointedly) *no one else* remembered it."

"Sorry, I was otherwise engaged. What happened to Marie?"

"She's a twit. She's outta here."

"He's sort of big."

"I like 'em that way."

Lydia starts my shower, pulls clean jeans and T-shirt from my drawer, and comes for me. She reaches down, hauls me out of the bed, and holds me as I stumble toward the shower.

"Get clean now; you're a mess."

I let the shower sting my body, roll off the top of my head. I try to stand up straight, but I feel myself crumple. Then I lie down in the steamy tub and submerge myself, trying to make the world go away. *I could drown myself under here.*

I would have to do it fast, for Lydia is at the door banging. "Come out, or I'll come in there and get you, and we wouldn't like that would we?"

I dry myself, pull on the clean clothes, and run a comb through my hair. I already feel better. In the kitchen, Lydia has set the table. She has steaming soup and tea.

"Sit," she commands.

"Who? Me or Birthday?"

"You. I hope you mind better than he does. He needs obedience school."

"Who would tangle with him?" I ask, smiling for the first time in a week. "I hope he's housebroken."

Lydia tells me she's all but moved out; she'll spend one more night here, and then be gone. We talk about her Nantucket trip, the play she's working on, the staged reading another one is getting and her imminent return to teaching. Sensing my depression, she steers the conversation from anything that will upset me, and I am grateful.

Later, we share a farewell glass of wine together—"Just *one* for you," she directs. "Red wine's a depressant; has too much thingamajig in it." (Lydia knows everything.) The phone rings. She answers. "For you. A guy. Not Greg." She makes a face.

"Garry." I answer the phone more brightly than I feel.

TOMORROW TOMORROW, I LOVE YOU TOMORROW

Garry picks me up in a cab. I hope my exterior looks more orderly than my interior feels.

"So why are you here?" he asks.

"Well, it may sound silly, but I needed to try my wings all by myself, in a new place where nobody knows me. I've had a job, but just quit it, and I'm looking for another. I hope to stay here for awhile."

"Women's lib stuff, huh?"

"I guess that's the shorthand for it."

"No, no offense. I sympathize, actually. Suzanne went back and got a law degree. We're separated, and I expect we'll be divorced before the year is out."

"What are you doing now?"

"Well, you may recall, I got my PhD in history. I taught for a while, wrote some books, and for the past few years I've been historical consultant on films and TV movies. I worked on *Roots* for example, and now I'm coming into Manhattan about twice a month for a show about American presidents.

"Sounds like great work."

"It's fun, it's lucrative, it's high profile. It gives me a chance to come to the city. I've met a lot of people here."

The show we see is *Annie*, and we leave with a smile. For a brief time at least, my spirits have lifted. At "21" we have the pricey hamburger and catch up. I tell him my situation with Greg is similar to his with Suzanne, but rockier, more ambiguous. After a couple of glasses of wine, I also tell him about my experience with JP, why I am out of work, and express some doubts about finding another job.

"I met you at a university; the last time I heard from you it was from a university; why don't you try a university?" he remarks sensibly.

"To tell the truth, I never thought of it. I'm really interested in writing, so I thought my best bet was ad agencies, journalism, publishing. But I don't know anyone and haven't been able to get my foot in the door."

"Check out the New School for Social Research and see what non-teaching jobs they have. Then let's talk."

When the cab drops me off that night, I feel better than I have in months.

THE NAME GAME

Job hunting, I've decided, is like a marathon dance where you dance til you drop. But you don't stay with one partner long; the trick here is to get passed along. What you do is ask everyone you talk to for a name to call, and when you get that person, you ask him or her for a name. All you need is one name to start with. If you get that first meeting, that first lunch, and you present yourself well, then the pass-along game starts. I called the New School for Social Research first. They had no jobs open, but after I told a very nice person there what I was looking for, I was directed to a writer at National Public Radio, from there to an editor at *Publishers Weekly*, from there to an editor of *Woman's Wear Daily*, from there to the Associated Press, from there to American Management Association, from there to Chester Burger Management, from there to Philip Morris, from there to Lever Brothers, from there to J. Walter Thompson, from there to Harper and Row, from there to *The New York Times* Foundation, from there to Columbia University.

I got a lot of phone calls, a number of meetings, and several quite nice lunches out of people in these places, who, miraculously, just kept passing me along.

I guess you can interpret that in a couple of ways.

BACK TO SCHOOL

It was Fred Hechinger at *The New York Times* Foundation who took me to lunch and then passed me along to Howard Rusk at Columbia University, a vice president so new he still answered his own phone. He tells me that, yes, they are considering hiring a writer, editor, magazine journalist, and to come to see him right away.

"Tomorrow?"

"Tomorrow, then."

I stumble up from the subway at 116th Street, walk a few feet and look up at the awesome dome of Low Memorial Library, which casts a cold eye on me. I feel like Jude the Obscure. Inside, I sit in an antique captain's chair with a crest on its back, and interview. Yes, the vice president is looking to start a new journal, and, yes, I have the right background. (No typing test required.) He smiles. I smile. We like each other. Can I make a magazine to rival Harvard's? No question. Just let me at it.

I take the subway home musing: Now, who can I get to make reference calls for me? That seems to be the way it's done in NYC. *Oh God I want this job, Oh God I need this job, Oh God I've listened to too many Chorus Line albums.*

At home I call Garry. He will call Rusk. Then I think: Didn't Joe go to Columbia? My major professor in graduate school, Joseph Satin? I call him. Yes, he did, and of course, he'll call right now and tell them if they don't hire me they have a "very large stupid problem." I call in chips from everyone I know back to tenth grade. That's the way they do it here, but unfortunately, most went to ritzier tenth grades. Nobody from Thalia lives in NYC, except maybe an actor a few years ahead of me in school. Where would I find him? Call Mother; she'll run across the street to the beauty parlor and ask his mother.

A week passes. I wait. I interview at an ad agency. Two offers come through on the same day: J. Walter Thompson and Columbia University. I take the latter without thinking twice: Twenty-one thousand and benefits. Benefits! I hadn't even thought to ask. Ad agencies can be fun, but where I really belong is at a place with a big, juicy, dangerous library. I ask Mr. Rusk for a week to find an apartment before I begin work.

HUNTING AND GATHERING
I've just met a writer who's going to The University of Montana as poet-in-residence for three months. Naomi hands me the keys to her Chelsea apartment. I will send her a check as soon as I get paid. The living room windows look down onto the well-dressed mannequins in a new store called Barneys. Number 1 train just around the corner. And a dentist down the street. As luck would have it, he's a Columbia graduate who trusts my new-job story enough to begin the tooth-capping process immediately. No more Super Glue! See: some decent people in NYC. It also pays to get in tight with the Ivy League folks.

HOW TO CARRY A FUTON DOWN BROADWAY
On the back of your neck. I am moving by myself, since Paul has not come back yet. I don't have much to move, but there is this futon. It's light, but too big to fit into a cab. So I carry it seventy blocks on the back of my neck. (*He's not heavy; he's my brother.*) Finally get it to my new home and the elevator is botched. Wouldn't you know? Now I have to lug it up three flights.

CHEESE AND APPLES
Naomi leaves cheese and apples in her fridge and tea in her cupboard. Also some Valpollicello I can have, if I replace it before she comes back. A roof over my head, a futon for my flanks, cheese and apples. And a job in New York City!

THE FIRST PICTURE SHOW
Garry is in town for a few days, and we decide to burn out on picture shows. First, *Saturday Night Fever*—John Travola in his white

Escape

suit—then dinner at the Regency, where Garry is staying. We talk over brandy till two, then a cab takes me home. I like this man; he's interesting, charming, loves theater, film, music, good food, has lived abroad and brings a European perspective to everything we discuss. He is not preachy or moralistic, and though he has a very high opinion of himself, he can listen. I like the way he tucks a white napkin in his collar before he eats—British style.

WHERE GRUB STREET MEETS ACADEME

My magazine job is whatever I make of it. I am called editor-in-chief because nobody knows what to call me, and I make the title up myself and stake a claim to it. I am assigned to a dank office with a good address (the Journalism Building) and a nonfunctioning typewriter. Then I am left entirely alone.

The last part is the best. I approach my existential task with a quotation from Pascal taped to my wall: "The eternal silence of these infinite spaces frightens me." Suffering the exquisite anguish of benign neglect, I set out to create a magazine. No one tells me what I'm supposed to do, and no one gives me any objectives. I would always rather say I'm sorry than be safe, so I don't ask permission. I just set out to create a job and a place for myself.

I figure if I use my intuition and get it right, I'll add a spark of creativity to the joint; if I get it wrong, they can fire me. Both seem preferable to having someone looking over my shoulder. So here I am making things up as I go along.

PAUL WRITES

Dear Mom,

John Raitt (he's real famous) has taken over Ed Ames's role in the play. It was funny the first time. Mr. Raitt is kinda old, and he had to carry me in one scene. You know the one where I'm supposed to be asleep? Well, he picked me up, and I felt him tremble all over and stumble round. It was scary. I think we have it down to a science now, but if I grow anymore or he shrinks anymore, this is gonna be a problem. I miss you.

Love, Paul

THE NEXT PICTURE SHOW

Night two: *Star Wars,* more engrossing than I had imagined; mythic, really quite fun. Science fiction has not been my genre, but this is different, more polished, opens up new worlds, so to speak, and I guess that's what my adventure here is all about—new worlds. Or is it Garry who's fun, who's a kind of new world? Dinner after at Joe Allen. Noisy but cozy. Then we walk the streets of Manhattan talking, talking, talking on a warm, gentle night. I tell him about my job. He says call up his old friend Amatai. I wear my green hat. You should always wear hats, he says. I do, I say.

BEN WRITES

Dear Mom,

Dad is a basket case. You have got to go back to him. You're being selfish thinking of yourself. Think of him for a change. How would you feel if he committed suicide? Think about it.

Love, Ben

A LIT CRITTER

I am thinking that life is like a piece of literature—you have to work hard at it to understand its puzzles and paradoxes. If it's too cheaply won, it's not worthwhile—just a soap opera. But if it's too abstruse and convoluted, you give up: it lies on your bedside table gathering dust, while you look away. Pretty soon you don't even see it anymore; you just do your rote things. The trick is asking the right question, finding the key. Is this a reliable narrator? What is the subtext here? What did that gesture, that symbol mean? You've got to work to earn the payoff. Sometimes the process can be unutterably hard—almost overwhelming. But if you trust the author, and yourself, and make the effort, you'll be rewarded. Life is not an open book; it's a closed one that you have to pry open—and you have to have the right tools to do it.

THE ULTIMATE PICTURE SHOW

Night three: *Annie Hall.* Unforgettable. When she sings "Seems Like Old Times," Garry reaches over and takes my hand. I smile at

Escape

him like a kid: holding hands just like in the picture show in Thalia. Sweet, and no sweaty palms. At that instant I make a synapse switch from two lonely people in Manhattan who like movies and hanging out together to feeling just a little bit 'courted.' Curious what a dry palm can do. Dinner uptown at Café Des Artistes. This is amazing: here I am a waif in NYC, waiting for my first paycheck so I can afford to buy bread, counting every cent, and then a man comes to town, and I eat like a rich girl. *Seems like old times.* Schizophrenic to say the least. *Look, look, Dick and Jane. Look what boys can buy. Look what girls can't do all by themselves. Yet. Just you wait, 'enry 'iggins, just you wait.*

Garry won't be back for a couple of months. As he puts me in a cab, he places his hand lightly on the back of my neck and says, "I have fun with you. The time goes too fast. I think we have some chemistry between us." Then he pecks me on the cheek and is gone.

12

S·M·A·R·T

Each of us has a life story. An inner narrative whose continuity, whose sense is our lives. We all construct a narrative that is us—our identities. Our singular narratives are constructed continually unconsciously by, through, and in us—through our perceptions, our feelings, our thoughts, our actions and our spoken narratives. Each of us *is* a unique narrative.
—Oliver Sacks

A PRINT-OUT OF 90,000 FRIENDS

I need some help making a magazine, so I decide to look for writers and people with ideas. At the university, I ask for a print-out of all faculty and alumni and get a wad of papers with 90,000 names. Only slighter lighter to carry home than a futon. Then I set about reading, highlighting everyone I ever heard of, and calling them up. Miraculously, most are accessible. My newest best friends are Isaac Asimov and Lewis Thomas. But others give me interviews, promise to write for me, to help with story ideas: Robert Merton, Carolyn Heilbrun, Milos Forman, Frank MacShane, Arthur Ochs Sulzberger, Scuyler Chapin, Marvin Harris, Virgil Thomson, Anna Freud, Jacques Barzun, Eli Ginzberg, Henry Graff, Joseph Brodsky and yes, Garry's friend, Amatai Etzioni. Well, dear diary, you get the picture. I am high as a kite: I fly, I fly, like a diamond in the sky. Goodbye earth, goodbye, goodbye.

THE REMEDY

Daily I am surrounded by brilliant people. I never knew such erudition existed. When you grow up being the smartest little girl in Thalia, and your mother thinks you're gifted, you gain a certain sense of yourself. But *these* people—the ones I see and talk to and interact with all day. I am stunned. And I am humbled. Almost daily I recall Goethe's words: "Against the superiority of another, the only remedy is love." This remedy co-ops your feelings: in love there is no room for competition, for envy, for jealousy. I am filled with love every day. And I am so very, very fortunate.

AT THE SUPERMARKET

I am pushing my basket of groceries, following a little man with a homburg atop his white hair who is pushing his basket of groceries. He knocks into the shelves, and cans of pork and beans come tumbling down, ten, twenty, thirty cans, falling, tumbling, rolling. The little man bends to pick them up but becomes confused when more begin to hail down upon his shoulders. He stops, stupefied.

I move in and start to pick up the cans.

"Let me help," I say.

He turns to me. "I er . . . would much appreciate that."

I look up into the face of the world-famous physicist, the Nobel Laureate, the Manhattan Project, the nuclear bomb. I am stunned. My mouth moves.

"Do you know who you are?" I ask with remarkable intelligence.

"I . . . er . . . think so, yes, I am . . ."

"I. I. Rabi. You are I. I. Rabi, and you should not be bothered with pork and bean cans. Please go on, and I'll take care of them."

"You are very . . . er . . . dear . . . I . . . dear . . ."

"It's okay. Can I call you in your office?"

"Oh, of course, of course . . . er, I'm at . . ."

"I'll find you. Just remember me—the pork and beans woman."

"Oh, yes, yes, thank you, dear . . ." He wanders off pushing his basket. I try hard not to think of Charlie Chaplin.

SHORT

I call I. I. Rabi, and we become friends. His smile is very sweet. For years he calls me "The Dear Bean Lady."

DRAMA

Paul calls and says he will be back in time for school. When he gets back to NYC, he wants to audition for a living. Music and drama are his passion. I tell him about our new apartment—home for at least three months—and my new job, my delirious new life, my beautiful balloon. I do not tell him that a short time ago I wished fervently to go down in a flaming airplane.

AN INTELLECTUAL TREE HOUSE

Columbia is still an old boys club. Not for nothing do portraits of glowering men peer down from stately walls. The College is still male, an anomaly even among the Ivies. I am amazed I was hired to work here since I am female, Southern, youngish, and talk funny. Nothing about me fits the culture but my curiosity and desire to learn. One prominent legal expert from whom I attempt to get a quote looks me up and down and tells me dismissively that I am an "attractive nuisance." A professor I am interviewing pointedly stops in mid-sentence and spells a word he has just used, *oxymoron*, for me, as if I were a nitwit. In every meeting it's assumed that I will take the minutes because I am the only woman present. There are no women vice presidents and only a meager handful of full professors. But there is Margaret Mead.

I CAN'T BELIEVE I ACTUALLY CALLED HER

And I can't believe she actually invited me to come to see her. Margaret Mead has been here a long time but is not tenured. It's a scandal. From my window I can see her moving heavily along College Walk in her huge caftan, leaning on her walking stick like some Old Testament prophet surveying Sodom and Gomorrah. When I ask for her advice, she says in her wonderfully resonant voice: "You must remember, young woman, Columbia—like New York City—allows everything and supports nothing. You can succeed here, but only if you're very, very good at what you do. And no one will help you do it."

SPRINGING FROM OUR OWN BROWS: AGAIN

Mead is right. The one person here who encourages me is a woman, Carolyn Heilbrun—professor and author. After reading her book about women reinventing themselves, I call and ask her to lunch. I tell her I'm trying to reinvent myself, that her book struck me to the bone, and I'm glad to learn I'm in good company. She is sympathetic, and, I feel, the first truly reliable person I've met in a long time. "It's sink or swim here," she cautions. "If you get in over your head, don't depend on any these Columbia guys to pull you out."

LIAISONS DANGEREUSES

At nine I fell in love with the library in Wichita Falls; at thirty-nine I am falling in love with the New York Public Library. For years I've been an attitude looking for a home—one of those insufferable people the teacher addresses with a starchy: "Now students, let's not see the same hands again." Loaded with information, perpetually overprepared, I stand on the corner of Broadway and 116th hailing a cab, a Thesaurus in my left hand, a calculator in my right. Ready for anything. Except muggers.

Musing, distracted, diagramming complex sentences in my head, I turn left out of every door. I pass up my office on the way to work. The synapse snapped, I suspect, somewhere between *The Golden Bough* and *Crazy Jane Talks to the Bishop*. I underwent, as they say, synapsis. I burst forth from that little explosion a true New Yorker—not to mention a library bag lady, one of those odd creatures, heels ground off their shoes, stumbling from between the great lions heaving a Macy's bag filled with books. I am my mother if there had been a library in Thalia.

They say you *are* what you read, and I think I am becoming something wholly unrecognizable except by a few—mostly New Yorkers. I am driven to know everything. *Now. First.* And then to tell it. *Now. First.*

The obsession with knowing everything and knowing it first afflicts most severely those of us who lingered overlong in graduate school, I believe. Whether a causal relationship exists here, or whether it is simply that the kind of people who tend to linger overlong in school are people who want to know everything—a self-selected cohort so to speak—is beyond the scope of these musings. Do though, register that the question was addressed. I do not wish to be accused of overlooking anything.

I am reminded of the Harvard professor's prayer: "Dear Lord, please deliver me from the sin of intellectual arrogance, which, for your information, means. . . ."

In Texas, where I was born, people think they have to *have* everything. I was once described in a Texas newspaper as a "book collector." I thought of myself as simply a reader. In New York, which I have chosen, people think they have to *know* everything. This may be a disease that has no name, but most likely it's a case of arrested development: we are still trying to get those hands in the air first, trying to please that teacher who's been dead now for twenty years.

WHAT'S WRONG WITH YOU?

Well, at least he didn't call me a slut. That's a change.

The guy is more highly placed in the university than I, but I don't even think of that when he asks me out. I just think of the swell black-tie event he invites me to: a Diana Vreeland retrospective at the Metropolitan—gorgeous models, terrific clothes. *Think pink.* On the agenda are champagne and other bubbles—far into the night.

Then it's time for him to take me home.

"Can I come up for a nightcap?"

"Well, it's awfully late. I have an early day tomorrow."

"Not if I say you don't."

"What?"

"You don't *have* to have an early day tomorrow. Stay up all night with me, and you don't even have to come in tomorrow."

"What?"

"You heard me."

I look at him. Surely he is not meaning this. Finally I speak: "I'm sorry. I have a lot of work to do tomorrow. I'll have to say goodnight here." I hold out my hand.

"You don't even have a job tomorrow, if I decide you don't have a job tomorrow."

Dropping my hand, I pause. "Well, I guess I'll just have to risk that, won't I?" I turn the key.

The next day at work I am half expecting my office to be padlocked. It is not. A call that I'm fired? Doesn't happen. The world is as normal as it has ever been: the man greets me at the early morning meeting as if the evening had never occurred. More importantly, the creep never asks me out again.

PASSING

An employment agency I registered with when I was job-hunting calls me. I tell them I have a job and am not interested, but the woman is insistent.

"Come for an interview, anyway," she says.

"Truly, no. I like my job."

"I have a pharmaceutical company—a big time place—that wants someone with your exact profile."

"I really can't take the time off," I say.

"Well, let me talk to them, and if they're serious enough, they'll come here to see to you. They did express intense interest in your qualifications. Let me summarize: You are from the South?"

"Right—if Texas is the South to you."

"Well, your voice is certainly Southern. You were active in Civil Rights?"

"Yes."

"You worked in an inner-city setting?"

"Yes.'

"You have worked on school integration in several cities?"

"Yes."

"You've taught in college, and published articles, and worked in communications?"

"Yes."

"I know they'll love you. You have everything they want. Tell you what. I'm not supposed to send you for an interview until I've met you personally, face-to face, but I'm going to Europe this week. Send me a photo, will you?"

"Okay . . . but I have an interesting job."

Sure enough, the gentlemen who were looking for "a Director of Communications for a National Pharmaceutical Corporation based in New Jersey," call me for an interview. I wear a white suit to set off my fantastic tan.

The men seem impressed with my résumé, though a little uncomfortable it seems to me, and ask me the usual questions. Then they ask how I came to be in New York City, and I go on about being accompanied by my son, who is now in a stage show called *Shenandoah.*

"Oh," said one man, brightening. "I saw that play. I took my grandson. We both enjoyed it, and *your* son was in it?"

"Yes," I said. "He was one of the leads."

"Ahem, yes . . . er . . . yes . . . well, I recall in the plot there is a little white boy and a little black boy."

"Yes."

"And yours son was . . . er now . . . er . . .?"

I look at him stunned. He blushes. Then it hits me. Of course. *That's* why they were pursuing me so heavily. I have the perfect "profile." Even my suntan is great.

I put down my fork, stand, smile, and extend my hand: "Nice to have met you gentlemen." I nod my head with its curly Afro, and walk away.

NYC STYLE

It's called an "artichoke," my new haircut. It's shaggy here and there. Funny, as a girl in Thalia I dreamed about my job in New York City, where I would be "in the know," like the *Life* magazine girls, with a black velvet jacket and pearls hidden away in my desk drawer. Later, I practiced tossing my hat in the air and hailing a cab like *Mary Tyler Moore*. When I finally get a desk drawer in NYC, women are wearing long skirts, tall clunky boots, and heaving enormous leather bags over their shoulders. The new look. I buy a fragrance named "Charlie," some boots with high square heels, and a slim-legged pantsuit. I am practicing my striding.

ELLIE'S DESCRIPTION OF MOTHER'S DESCRIPTION OF GOD

Ellie's letter starts: You should have been here. The preacher was on vacation so he asked mother to "fill the pulpit." Well, she did that all right, but you won't believe with what. Franny Tucker nearly fell out of the choir loft when Mom likened the Trinity to a three-headed God. Mother combined some of her poetry, some of her prose and a lot of her philosophy into a real rousing sermon. I can't imagine anyone understood much of any of it, which is just as well.

She said things like: *The way to ascend to God is to descend into yourself,* quoting, she said, someone called Hugh of St. Victor. Then she said (and I'm copying from her notes): *The God who makes us live in a world without using him as a working hypothesis is the God before whom we are standing* (per Dietrich Bonhoeffer). Then she talked a lot about *the ground of our being, Theonomy, and Kairos,* and she said William James wrote about a person whose doubt disintegrated when she looked inward and said, *The Heaven that I have within myself is as attractive as any that has been promised or that I can imagine; and I am willing to let the growth lead where it will!*

Then, you won't believe this: she wound all this up with a warning that "God is not *out there.* He is not an old white-whiskered man in the sky keeping score; he is not William Blake's old Nobodaddy, a crotchety old father who showers favors on those who give the most literal obedience to a ceremonial law and moral code. Thank you. Now go home to your families and have a pleasant day."

HOUSE WARMING

I finally get my own apartment and invite Carolyn Heilbrun, the only woman faculty person I know, to help me celebrate. After a glass of wine, she makes a telling comment about how women—even well-intentioned women—deal with one another these days. "You've made a noble effort here, my dear," she says about my daring to write of feminist issues in campus publications. Then, with an ironic smile, she adds, "but when I first saw how white your teeth are, I was not sure you were up to it." We both laugh. "You shoulda seen me when I was gluing my front tooth in every morning," I say.

MOTHER JOINS WOMEN'S LIB

Dear One,

Did you know that in the Frontier Hall of Fame in Oklahoma City, there is a huge bronze plaque with at least one hundred names of memorable pioneers and only two are women: Sacajawea and Willa Cather? Somebody ought to protest to somebody about that. That is not just hearsay, more like *heresy.* I have a picture of the plaque to prove it.

Speaking of the paper you're writing about female archetypes in fiction, please include a type of woman who has the capacity to see and hear and smell and taste and touch life no matter how simple the circumstances, and better still to really experience it, before, during and after the event. With all our women's lib, let's not ever downgrade those qualities. And I was reading something the other day that struck me: it said "Men have only two categories to put women in—*saintly and po' ho's.*" What do you think of that?

Your father has nearly finished off the book you sent him, *All the President's Men*—as if they hadn't beat him to it.

It is horribly hot and dry here, no rain for two months. Remember when we had that awful drought here when you were in high school, and I put the hose into the bathroom window upstairs to drain water from our bathtub into the yard? You threw a little tantrum and said it embarrassed you because it looked like our house was taking a perpetual enema. Remember that? Well, I think I'm going to have to resort to that again if it doesn't rain soon.

I have nothing else to say, so I'll just summarize the Sheriff's Report of the week: 1-tombstones turned over, 1-overdue motorist, 1-goats eating trees and climbing on car, and 1-goats in highway. Bye.

NOTWORKING

They looked, so help me, like a group of hopeful sorority pledges in the fifties. Not since then have I seen such a gathering of gray wool and white silk, occasionally relieved by a red carnation pinned to a drab lapel. Not since then have I seen such a clutch of bobbed and shiny heads, such discreet use of blusher.

At first I thought them the Stepford Wives—but with a difference: They all wore sensible shoes. Not a sandal, nary a high heel, hardly a boot in the bunch. "Grandma shoes," we used to call them. Or "Old Lady Spencer shoes"—as worn in the halls of Thalia High by the lab teacher. Shoe salesmen called them "crocs"—short for crocodiles—notoriously hard to move out of the stores then. But now these women are shod for action.

The action revolves around exchanging business cards. With each other. The notworking, with their overdue bills at the printer's, exchange their graphic monuments to maturity with the other notworking in a tribal ritual called networking.

"It helps," said one woman, "if you put '*and associates*' on your card. Then people think you're a company."

The stars of the day—V.P.'s in corporate slots, head hunters, presidents of companies with names like *Charisma, Success* and *Manage!*—women who have lent their luminosity to the panel discussion earlier, have left hastily for legitimate business elsewhere.

On the program a few minutes before, an "image consultant" has advised us what to wear should we wish to "assure success": gray suits, white silk blouses with optional red carnations, sensible shoes. Another consultant told us what "buzz words" we should know and how to place them in our larynx.

"Even if you don't know what they mean," she said, "you should use them anyway. They impress people."

Some of these impressive words are *relevant, motivated, meaningful,* and *parameters.*

Another speaker told us how we should "fantasize" our "ultimate job" and "come face to face with risk." And another informed us that initials on our top-grain cowhide briefcases were "in bad taste," and earrings (except for gold studs) were a no-no.

My favorite panelist's presentation reminded me of a different *Network* in which the characters stuck their heads out windows and yelled about how fed up they were. This consultant has us screaming in chorus: *I have a right to know what I know! I have a right to feel what I feel!* And thus were we "freed up" and our "chutzpa quotient" raised. I found it difficult to "play down" myself, as one consultant told us to do, while yelling how I have a right to feel what I feel at the top of my lungs.

If the medium was the message, the messages were mixed. Overall, besides being thoroughly confusing, the *Day of Business Networking with Seminars by Successful Managers*, reminded me of the stories the wives of corporate executives used to tell about workshops sponsored by their husbands' companies to assure their becoming "successful corporate wives." The only difference here was that these women were learning to become "successful corporate women."

Next day I flipped through my pile of exquisite business cards and called Beatrice J. Edwards and Associates, Management Consultants.

The line was—you guessed it—notworking.

CRIME OF PASSION

I commit a crime: I give Diana Trilling's book *Mrs. Harris* a "mixed review." Mrs. Harris, of course, is the headmistress of the Madeira School who murdered her diet doctor lover, Herman Tarnower. A scandal. Lurid headlines for months. What with the media overkill, one gets embarrassed at even being curious about this case. I happened to say that in my review, to which Diana took vitriolic umbrage. Diana Trilling, widow of Lionel and ergo sacred cow of Columbia University, is seduced by the case and follows the trial of Jean Harris to write a book. I review it honestly, but without a lot of enthusiasm. Diana—still a faculty-dinner-party force to be reckoned with—calls the president of Columbia and demands that I be fired. Legacies of Lionel give me a hard time on the phone: *Do I know who this woman is?* Of course, I tell them. But it wasn't a very good book.

Provost Fritz Stern calls me into his office.

"You understand we have a problem," he says.

I nod.

"You didn't create the problem, but let us say you have exacerbated it."

I nod.

"What do you propose we do?"

I think—hard. "I gave the book a fair review," I say, finally. "It was not very well written."

"I don't argue with that, but now what are we going to do about Mrs. Trilling? She is demanding a retraction and your resignation."

"I can't retract my opinions," I squeak. "That's dishonest."

"What *can* you do?"

"I can run negative reactions to the book review in our letters section."

"Do you have any negative reactions?"

"No."

"Have you any positive letters?"

"Yes, two. One agreed with my review. The other said I was a foolhardy woman and offered me leads on a job when I lost mine."

The Provost smiles. "You're not going to lose your job, but we have to fix it. How do we do that?"

Smart

"Maybe you could ask someone on the campus who disagrees with my review to write a letter to the editor. Do you know anyone who would do that? Some people have called me . . ."

"No."

"Maybe *you* could do that?"

"No. But I suppose *you* could find someone to do that. Maybe someone in the Development Office who understands the delicacy of these matters."

I head back to the office and call a colleague. He agrees to write a letter lambasting me for my poor choice of words, if I review the letter before he submits it.

The next issue carries a letter in which I am roundly chided for many vague things concerning Diana's wretched book. I run it without comment.

I never hear from Diana Trilling again.

NOW PLAYING AT THE PLAZA

Garry is in the city. He called last week and told me to set aside three evenings and to select three restaurants: beef, fish, and French. Also, I should meet him at the Plaza where he has a corner suite overlooking Central Park.

"What's the special occasion?" I ask.

"Never mind. Use the house phone and ring me. Wear low-heeled shoes. Brown."

All day long as I work at my desk, I obsess: What's he up to? What low-heeled shoes? Boots? Loafers? Sandals? I play it safe and wear Cordovan leather flats with my cream silk blouse and long skirt.

He has left the door ajar, and as I walk in, I see him standing before me grinning. He has on jeans with knife creases, a starched white shirt turned back at the cuffs, and square-toed Frye boots. His face is very tan.

"Give me that," he says, taking my pocketbook and tossing it on the bed. "Now, open the closet."

I follow directions. Inside on a hanger is a perfect Annie Hall outfit—corduroy pants, vest, white shirt, soft, billed cap.

I pull them out, astonished; laughing, tossing them one by one on the bed, like Jay Gatsby tossing his silk shirts.

"Did you see the braces?" Garry asks, proud of himself. "Real leather braces, see." He holds up the suspenders. "I'll go in the other room and open a bottle of wine; you dress."

I follow directions well when the man has brought me the most imaginative gift I can think of. Off with the cream silks, on with brown corduroy.

I saunter into the living room touching the bill of my cap, singing "Seems Like Old Times." Garry puts his hands on my shoulders and spins me around.

"You are the most adorable woman," he says grinning broadly. "I couldn't get you off of my mind all month. When I saw this outfit in a store window, I knew it had to be you," he pauses. "It had to be you."

I try to strike a slouching pose like Diane Keaton; then slide into my favorite, Audrey Hepburn. *"Take the pic-ture, take the pic-ture,"* I call, arms aloft as if flying down the grand staircase of the Louvre. I am surely the Winged Victory, and I'm about to lose my head. "Garry. Thank you. This is so much fun." I am laughing hard. "I feel like a girl, a kid, a child."

"Your laugh, your style, your hair."

"It's called an artichoke."

"Your mouth."

He comes to me and takes me in his arms. Kissing him is like the world stopped. He does it again and again, pausing to kiss my eyes, my throat, my lips again.

"The reservation," I say breathlessly. (I was never good at breathing and kissing at the same time.) "Italian. It's waiting."

"I didn't say Italian."

I kiss him. "I know. I did. It's just around the corner, Central Park Sou. . . . ."

"Do we have to?"

"Yes. It's traditional. I buy dinner for every guy who brings me brown corduroy."

COUTE QUE COUTE

We walk to the restaurant smiling. We smile while we eat. We walk back, arms around each other, singing, "Seems Like Old Times."

People on the street smile at us. Dogs smile at us. Horses wearing flowered hats and pulling tourists in buggies smile at us. The door-man smiles at us. We return to the room, and Garry removes my pocketbook from the bed. "I'm ready for dessert," he says.

In short order, I am consumed.

WHAT THE TAPE IN THE NEXT ROOM IS PLAYING

I could cry salty tears, where have I been all these years, little wow, so tell me now, how long has this been going on?

13

Have you ever noticed
that what passes as a
terrific man would only
be an adequate woman?
—Anna Quindlen

D·I·L·I·G·E·N·T

MY COMMUTE to the university on Long Island where I now work is just over an hour each day. Usually I listen to the radio as I drive home from work, but today I can't. Some thug in a parking lot snapped off my antenna, and I haven't had time to get it fixed. Why, I wonder, would someone do a thing like that—just walk by and break something? What gives a person the impulse to destroy any vulnerable, unprotected thing he sees?

And drivers. In New York they seem to be bitten by the devil: *Eat my dust!* But I remember one blistering hot day I was driving into the city. Cars and their honking, snarling passengers were backed up on a ramp trying to enter the expressway, while even those on the expressway itself were slowed to an intermittent lurch. I saw a blue car trying repeatedly to nudge into the expressway line being just as repeatedly thwarted by drivers already there. When I reached the blue car, I stopped and waved it in ahead of me, resulting in a blast of angry horns behind me.

As I finally reached the toll booth, I pulled up ready to sling my token into the basket, when the booth man halted me, lifted the toll arm, and motioned me through. Startled, I looked up at him. "The guy in the blue car," he said pointing up ahead of me. "He paid your toll, and said to tell you thanks for being a decent person. So thanks." The booth man and I grinned at each other for a moment, while passengers behind leaned on their horns and yelled.

A decent person. We need *rewards* for that now?

Recalling that incident puts me into one of my fugue states: I dream up a plan for making drivers more civil.

What you could do is set up a program. Set aside fifty thousand dollars a year for five awards for Uncommon Courtesy. A selected group of say, five regular drivers in the state, call them Watching Drivers, maybe, would be given the charge of identifying one uncommonly courteous driver during the year. Then when each of these five Watching Drivers in their routine driving patterns came across a person going out of his way to be a courteous driver . . .

Another of my grand schemes. My granddaughter told me last week that I remind her of Lucy Ricardo. *Lucy Ricardo!* A stake through the heart! All your life you think you're Audrey Hepburn, and some kid comes along and calls you *Lucy!*

"And why do I remind you of Lucy Ricardo?" I had to ask, steeling myself. Do I wear dumb shirtwaist dresses? Artificial eyelashes? Is my hair *that* red?

"Because you're funny," she laughed, pointing. "You always have *an idea! Ha ha ha.*"

The kid didn't say "screwball idea," but that's what she meant. What are kids watching this fifties stuff for anyway? Don't they know it will eat away their brains? Lucy was a wimp; couldn't even say the word *pregnant* on TV for pete's sake. Next thing you know it'll be *pink and chartreuse. Triple-roll socks. Pageboys. Poodle skirts!* What's the world coming to?

My heart is laden with rue, so I rustle around the floor of the car with one hand, feeling for what Marlboro calls "The Tapes," as he crosses his eyes and throws up his hands in horror. "The Tapes," he says, "placed end to end, would reach from here to *All Things Considered.*" When my journals began to take over the bookshelves and climb into baskets under my desk and then into wicker trunks in the corner, I started recording my thoughts on tapes.

These tapes hold about fifteen years of my life and times, and they are tapes nobody but I can bear to listen to for more than ten minutes at a stretch, according to Marlboro. But I treasure them, and about once a year take out a few to play in the privacy of my own car.

I reach down to riffle through the cards that separate the tapes into sections in one of the carefully organized blue zippered bags I keep them in. On the way to the car, I have grabbed *Moving, Traumas, Bugs to Eliminate, Great Verbs, Fragments, Republican Allergies, Ab Ova, Toxic People, Alternate Side Parking, and Witty Riffs,* among others.

I slide *Moving* into the tape player. A strain of "On the Road Again," wafts through the car and then:

"Hello. This is CC—my new initials—speaking to you from the Barbizon Hotel for Women on September 2, 1976. I had nowhere to go when the owners of the 90th Street apartment came back from the Cape, so I landed here for a week or so. Paul is staying with the family of his classmate, Sarah Jessica Parker. Carrie and her friend Nina, from Columbus, Ohio, are visiting me. Say hello Carrie."

"Hello all you people out there in tapeland. This place stinks."

"Thank you, Carrie, for your nicely phrased sentiments. And Nina?"

"So the first time I come to New York City, and guess what? I'm staying in this place where we share a bathroom with a woman who goes out to work at night just as we are coming home. Don't tell Mamma!"

"Thank you, Nina. Your final words just happen to be the name of a nightclub opened by friends of mine on West 46th Street. Actually, the two were actors and teachers I knew back in Keating, Ohio. Small world or what? Lots of things here we *Don't Tell Mamma.*"

Carrie: "Mother! You *are* Mamma!"

"Hello. I'm speaking to you on September 12, 1976, from our new home in Liz's third-floor apartment on West 79th. Liz is away on a month's vacation to Greece. Her apartment is tiny, but pretty and cozy with chintz flowers on sofa and chairs. Geraniums bloom in the window boxes, and English ivy hangs from ceiling planters. The bed is big and puffy, but, alas, there is only one. Paul has to sleep on the sofa in the living room. Or sometimes we swap. The way it works is this: the one who gets the bed has to take the cats, Honey and Gravy, and they love to crawl over your face while you try to sleep."

"Hi. It's November, and thank god for Hannah. She is gone for the month, so Paul and I have moved into her place on West 15th until we find something else. Hannah has great taste (and no cats!), but our stay here is so brief that every day I'm searching for the next apartment. Actually, if you want to know the truth, I think all this is a great adventure. I've moved a lot, but never quite from pillar to post, so to speak. It's nerve-wracking, but funny. And Paul is a great sport. Paul?"

"Well at least I never have to make up my bed since it's somewhere different every night."

"Oops. Hi there. This is CC hanging out the window of the beautiful Alcott Hotel here on West 72nd, looking into a stunning courtyard below. Actually, it looks more like the armpit of the world. Old bed-springs, an eviscerated TV. As the ads say, 'must see to believe.' But there's plenty of space in these rooms that are too ugly to speak of. My son Paul is sitting on a repulsive green bedspread as he wraps Christmas presents. We'll be out of here in no time—headed for Keating for the holidays. Then on to West 118th for a few weeks while my friend Pat travels. She's leaving us her Toyota, too."

"Hello. It's January, 1977, and this time I have a roommate, Bonnie, to help with the expenses. We're in a large airy place with a terrace in Morningside Gardens at 125th and Broadway. Bonnie goes to Teachers College. Paul has left to go on a road tour again. There's a huge library here, but, unfortunately for my reading pleasure, it's all in Hebrew."

"Hi. Cindy and Bob, our gorgeous theater friends, are away for awhile, so I have a snazzy home in Manhattan Plaza on West 43rd. This place has the most spectacular view of midtown, right where the ball drops on New Year's Eve. I think I'd like to keep these guys in my life for more reasons than one—spectacular New Year's Eves would be the second."

"Hello. Since I last recorded our moving life on these tapes, I've made stops at the Piccadilly Hotel and once again in Chelsea. The Piccadilly is worth a mention: One day as I was preparing to brush my teeth, the maid came in to change the towels. I picked up the glass in the bathroom, and, like Tinkerbell, she flew between it and me. "I wouldn't drink from that glass if I were you," she said sternly. "It comes from the kitchen, and you know *that* place."

"Today I'm speaking from our digs on East 96th Street. After a miserable winter here during which I walked into a snow bank in my nice black boots and walked out the other side like the Hunchback of Notre Dame, with both heels broken off, Paul is back with me. So life looks up. I must say, however, that the blizzards and snows and cold have been so bad that once I was caught in the theater district without a cab or a bus, so I went in to see *Oh Calcutta* by myself, just to get warm. Well, let me tell you, I was glad I was by myself. That was one ugly play.

"Now we are living here for three months. Pat put us in touch with Sheila, a journalist on assignment in Italy. It's a great place, but Sheila is a bit somber in outlook, and her favorite color is brown. Everything in this apartment is brown—I'm talking *dark* brown—chairs, sofas, curtains, blinds, bedcovers, pillows. Even her dishes are brown, to say nothing of the towels and soap in her bathroom. After a while it gives you an attitude."

"Hey. I think I have a long-running show this time! Meaning: Barnard Professor Electa Arenal will be away until May '79 and has leased us her apartment on West 79th, along with all its furniture and books. We can settle in a little bit and stay here until Paul finishes high school. What a relief. Paul, want to say a few words?"

"Yeah, Mom, great location, cool place. I have bunk beds. Can Toby stay over this weekend?"

"Hi again. It's September '79. We had a great run in the Arenal apartment, which I'll always think of as quintessential Upper Westside. Big rooms with a great old oak table and bookshelves, and a tiny kitchen painted purple. Just right for us. Paul finished high school and, somewhat wistfully it seemed to me, sang "There's a Place for Us," at the graduation ceremony. When he caught my eye he nearly cracked up. He also won the award for creative writing. After that, he and a pal took off to Montana to visit his uncle. Since he left I've been back to the Morningside apartment for two months, and now have a long-term lease on a three-bedroom Columbia apartment on

West 115th—big, cheap, and hard to get. My name finally came to the top of the list. I'm scrounging the streets for cast-offs to furnish it. My friend Mo Stein down at NYU brought me an old door to set on filing cabinets to make a big desk. Little by little it's coming together. We can stay here, I'm told, until I leave Columbia, which may be never, since I'm taking courses here now as well as working. Paul will enroll in the fall. I'm having a little housewarming party tomorrow night to welcome myself to *my first apartment in my very own name.* (Do not ask, as my father always does with raised eyebrows, *"and what, may I ask, is that?"*)"

I reach over and hit the eject button. Enough of that. Moving uptown, downtown, across town was a great way to learn New York City. An anthropologist would have a field day. It's amazing what one learns about people from simply looking into their medicine cabinets. I count on my fingers as I drive. Twenty-one moves in nine years—sixteen in the first year alone—and probably a few I've forgotten. And now I've been on the Mill Pond for ten—the longest residency of my life, except Thalia.

For some reason, I think of the time the lights went out in New York City, when the three of us, Lydia, Grace, and I were in a small 39th Street apartment drinking Irish coffee, playing an electronic piano and singing from old sheet music: "Blue Skies," "Ain't Misbehavin'"—the oldies—and even old hymns, "At the Cross," "Onward Christian Soldiers" and "Deep River," which someone dug out. Suddenly, the dinky little piano ground to a stop. Then slowly, and more slowly, the lights dimmed and were gone. Wait a moment, we laughed. They'll come back on. But they did not.

We looked out the window to the hotel across the way. No lights. Looked up and down the street. Black. Went to the phone and called across town. "Yes, they're all out too. Must be a transformer."

Grace fumbled in some drawers and found candles. Should we stay or go home? The fellow who lives here, an old ex of hers, is out of town. We better get home.

People meander in the streets. Pitch dark. No cabs in sight. Everyone is trying to get home, off the streets. The crazies will be out shortly. We dodge people in the street who are as frightened of us as we are of them; head for curbs or the sides of buildings. After many blocks, we find a bus and cram ourselves inside. There is light in the bus and it holds twice the number of people it's built for. Someone has a transistor, which plays loudly, but we get no news. People speak more loudly than usual, make sympathetic eye contact; there is a kind of excitement, a spirit of camaraderie unusual on a city bus. People exchange information; one man passes out candles from a box.

We can't see where to get off, no street lights or stop lights, so we get off about six blocks too soon and dodge the crazies who clutter the streets along Broadway, shuffling, drinking from bottles in brown bags, whining, talking to themselves. We've left Grace off at her apartment. Lydia stops for cigarettes at the only open shop, one that sells yogurt and ice cream through a window to the street. The door is locked, and men in the store work by candle and flashlight; about four dozen people hang around the open window pushing. The shopkeepers charge $1.00 for everything—even match books.

Loud noises, sirens, flashes of blue police lights. As we cross Broadway, two cars collide ahead of us. Traffic skids, cars spin, walkers run for walkways, glass shatters.

Down the street a gang of black and Hispanic boys use chain saws and axes, tearing into the front of a store window. They pass the merchandise along to the street like a bucket brigade. The boys take radios, TV sets, clothes. They load the stuff into cars waiting at the curb. Six stores are looted in half an hour this way. We hear gunshots and run into a sidestreet. Someone is firing a pistol randomly into windows. Three men carry a console TV down the street, pulling and tugging. "It's mine." "No, it's mine!" They argue loudly. One steps back and yells: "This is my TV, I stole it, and if you don't give it to me, I'm calling the cops." No one laughs. This is serious business.

Next day, up and down Broadway, you can step around glass and garbage and buy a leather coat, tag still dangling from the sleeve, for ten dollars. Jewelry, briefcases, radios are hawked on corners. "Miss, do you wanna buy?"

The city has been in darkness for twenty-five hours. One hundred policemen have been injured. Looters arrested: 3,776.

With a few minutes left before heading north, I rustle around in the bag and come up with *Stock Taking*. What in the world could I have been taking stock of and when? I turn the tape over in my hand, almost reluctant to revisit old dilemmas. Then I think how *glad* I am that I've been a relentless diarist. How sad it would be to let your life simply slip by, day after day, without attempting to make any sense of it, without trying to put some order in the chaos. Whatever other compulsions I might have, I am thankful for these: an obsession to observe and record.

I slip in the tape and push the button. After a few seconds of static—even the static is symbolic, I think—I hear my own voice.

"It is June 28, 1978. Paul is away. I have been alone for a week, spending most of my waking hours trying to decide how to put my life together. Clearly I have to make some big decisions. I can't pull Paul around New York City much longer. It's been an adventure for both of us, but we need some stability. He more than I, actually. But it's important to me that he see me as a stable person, which is, of course, what I am, basically; what I was, obviously, for many years. The last three years have been anomalies, but I needed them as surely as any kid needs an adolescence. I don't think it's an exaggeration to say that I've learned more about myself, and other people, in the last two years than I did in the first thirty-five of my life."

I pass a slow-moving car filled with old people. Using my best *Uncommon Courtesy* manners—old people?—I do a doubletake; they're probably no older than I, they just drive more slowly in their large Lincoln than I do in my little convertible, my toy car. What is that quote on an old-fashioned sampler from Elizabeth Cady Stanton?—that my friend Celia Morris has on her kitchen wall in Washington, D. C.? "Let me not grow more conservative with age." I like that. And the one I have on my refrigerator, a *New Yorker* cartoon of two torpid women in their sensible shoes sitting in a moribund middle-aged room, one saying to the other: "I'm waiting for postmenopausal zest to kick in."

My glance falls on a tape I hadn't noticed: *Nasty*. What can this be? I stick it into the tape player, and pull onto Middle Neck Road, around the curve and into my driveway. I sit in the car listening—and, as it happens, cringing.

I flip the tape out hating myself. I had recorded an episode in which I'd been inexcusably nasty. I was probably jealous of Libby, Paul's "older woman friend." I was probably jealous as a mother, jealous as an aging woman faced with a lovely, bright younger one. Libby and I never spoke about that scene afterward, but we were both very kind to each other in the days that followed.

I do remember another conversation with Paul about Libby, some time later. Paul was working as a salesman in a clothing store between school and acting roles. When he was terminally bored, he often called me at work. I remember this one vividly:

"Hey, Mom, are you busy? Can you tell me something? I have to know."

"What's that, Paul?"

"Do you ever have PMS?"

"PMS? What's that?"

"You're kidding."

"No I'm not. I don't know what you're talking about."

"Mom, premenstrual syndrome. You know that. All women have it."

"Paul, a lot of times women don't feel too great just before and during their periods, but it's not a big deal. Nothing that needs a name, for pete's sake."

"Lib told me, the women I work with have told me it's a big part of their life. It's a big part of my life too, because I live with Lib. It explains the moods and things, the way women are."

"Paul, that is just a bunch of bull."

"Mom, it's *not*. Marilyn can't come to work about three days each month because of it, and well, they always say something about, well, it's PMS time; and Lib, she has to take her pillow and go to the sofa a few days a months, or she tells me to, because . . ."

"Oh, Paul, don't let them con you this way. Nobody feels terrific a hundred percent of the time, men or women . . ."

"But men don't have anything like this."

"Believe me, Paul. If you could think up a legitimate excuse for not getting out of bed three days each month, wouldn't you use it? If you could convince everyone that this was dictated by your sex? What a good deal."

"Well, I guess, but I don't know. This seems so important to all the women I know."

"I don't know whether you can remember this or not, Paul, but I sure can: Once upon a time men got away with something similar, or at least analogically similar. Men had convinced themselves, and women, and the world at large that they couldn't help themselves when aroused by a woman; that they couldn't be blamed for making a pass at a woman, or attacking her, or even sometimes committing rape because their bodies, their sex drive, dictated their behavior, and they had no control over it."

"Really?"

"Yes, really. Even women made excuses for a man's inability to control himself. Well, men can't get away with that now. It is not even seen as 'manly' to have no self control. What I'm saying is that this attitude, and the PMS attitude with women, is primitive—old wive's tales, old husband's tales."

"But Mom, I've seen Lib during those times, she's cranky, and can't get up."

"Look Paul, I've been working every day for over a dozen years. I have six women working for me. Not one has said she couldn't come to work because of PMS. Not one *would* even if she *did*! And one *better* not. If a woman is going to claim equal pay for equal work and all that, she has no right to pull out those old crutches and clichés. She better have something really wrong with her if she can't come to work three days a month. Phases of the moon and being crippled by your sex just don't wash. Women can't have it both ways any more than men can."

"Ah, Mom. Give me a break. I just get to understand *one thing* about women, and now you tell me it's a lot of bull."

"Sorry, Paul. Lib may certainly have something wrong with her that she needs to look into. But in general, normal women do not have to take to their beds simply because they are women."

"Well, okay. Thanks for listening."

Back home, in the library, I pick up the notebook that contains letters from Alex and settle in. Marlboro has gone to a ball game, and

I have poured myself a cup of tea. I flip to the tab marked "Dating (Late 70s)."

"A lawyer asked me out on Saturday. With less hesitation than I care to think about, given the absurd situation (an estranged husband at home, while I have my own apartment), I accepted. I feel like I'm back in high school. A 'date' sounds excruciating. I've never had any skill at light banter, and Saturday night looms like an ordeal. I am also curious and confused about man-woman relationships at my age. I would like very much to have some friends who are men. But I have never been able to make a man understand that being a friend doesn't mean romance. Why does the romantic element always have to be there? It makes me nervous. With men, if you just want to be friends, it's always an assumed rejection of them as romantic objects. I'm struggling like a foolish adolescent and wonder how in god's name a women does this at thirty-seven! Our daughters could doubtless give us some valuable advice."

Undoubedtly, I think, remembering the awkward dating years of my own middle-aged adolescence. There was Harry, the overweight professor who begged to sit in my lap and be rocked like a baby. Morris, a diabetic, carried his hypodermic needles in a blue velvet pouch and cried when I refused to help him shoot himself. He broke down, saying his wife had left him, his son was gay, and he needed a woman to help him put the world back together like it was supposed to be. I declined that job. And then there was Pete, the former quarterback, who claimed over a giant Margarita at *Caramba!* that he could not get an erection unless he had on his football helmet. I didn't stick around to verify this claim. Most middle-aged single guys were a bunch of losers.

There *had* been the British journalist with the BBC who was intelligent and good-looking as well, but unfortunately quite in love with a French beauty Françoise, whom he finally convinced to come to the states. Well, I had a good time with him for a while anyway.

I'd never been to a single's club, or actually picked up a man, but I *had* gone with women friends to a bar and flirted. I remember sitting in P. J. Clarke's over a hamburger and having a combative religious argument with a Roman Catholic man I'd met at the bar. After the hamburgers were duly scarfed, we both wandered away in mutual relief. So much for bar pickups. And then after Marlboro and I got to be an *item*, as they say, we'd sometimes pass an evening by going into a bar, sitting at opposite ends of it, and flirting our way to center, then exchanging notes on the terrible pickup lines we'd endured. We'd regale Tony the bartender with our Mike Nichols-Elaine May seduction patter.

I wrote Alex about my most embarrassing dating story:

"Gil has a spectacular suite in the Carlyle overlooking Central Park. On our first evening together, after seeing a play called *Le Club*, where women dressed up in tuxes like men, played pool, and smoked cigars—a take-off maybe on the Century Club or the Union Club— Gil ordered up dinner from the dining room, and we talked and listened to music. He is bright, and cultured, and funny—not to mention such a tacky thing as rich—and I *really, truly* liked him. But then he made a pass, so I began lecturing him absurdly on how to behave with a woman on a first date. I can't believe I did that! He's in his early-fifties and surely doesn't deserve that. Oh I am such a twit! Still acting like Jacy Farrow in Thalia, Texas, the unavailable girl. I am nearly forty years old. Will I never learn?

"As it happened, while we were having this riveting discussion, a blizzard hit the city, and all transportation ceased. Busses stopped. Cabs disappeared. Even his driver could not be coaxed from his warm bed into the frigid night. I could *not* get home. No way. The solution? I spent the night in his guest room. What else could I do after the lofty lecture? It was pure insanity—me lying in the guest room and him calling, "It's much warmer in here, darling," from his own four-poster. *Oh, to die.* I think dating brings out the silly in us no matter how old we are. Fortunately, one of Gil's excellent qualities is patience, to say nothing of a good sense of humor. When he had his driver take me home the next day, he said, 'Okay. Tonight it will not be *a first date.* You bring the salad, and I'll make the dinner. I'll send the driver for you at six.' All went as he planned, and I am happy to report that we still have a warm relationship."

"I am discovering something interesting about myself," wrote Alex, after finding the man she is still with eighteen years later, who told her: "I have nothing to give you but my truck, a bike, a kayak, and a box full of returnable bottles."

"As a long-time married woman, I always had a sneaking suspicion that I wasn't cut out to be monogamous but had been forced into it at an early age. I thought I was missing something. As a single woman, I've discovered just what it is I was missing, which has only made me devoutly monogamous. An irony: in this age of sexually liberated women, I am an anachronism. Oh well, one nice thing about being forty is knowing who you are and what you want and saying so."

About that time I was introduced to a dashing older man—the CEO of an multinational corporation based in London. After a pristine date or two, he offered to put me up in the company's suite in the Pierre so I'd be there for him whenever he came into town. The offer included credit cards and charge accounts up and down Fifth Avenue. But he demanded that I quit my job because going out with a "working woman" was beneath his dignity. I told him to keep his dignity, and I'd keep my job. I'd finally found work I liked, why would I give it up to sit in the Pierre and wait for a guy? Or even shop all day, and wait for a guy? Why was it so hard for men to understand that? I considered writing a play called *Waiting for Da Guy*, based on . . . well, you know.

Actually, some of our correspondence to the contrary, men were less on our minds than was our work. Exhibit A:

Dear Alex,

Florence (designer), Meg (writer) and I had to go to an Ivy League editors meeting at Cornell, but I had no money in my budget for the trip. So we figured out a way to go anyway. We could hire a Rent-a-Wreck for $10 a day, and we could stay together in two rooms in a cheap motel. This was all very fine, except the Rent-a-Wreck was truly a demolition, and we were panicked that its fenders would fall off in the middle of the Palisades Parkway. When you looked down at what should have been the floorboard in one place, you could see the pavement beneath us as we rumbled over it.

A further complication was that Meg had a new baby she was nursing and couldn't leave at home, so Michael came along. Michael's father was to join us in Ithaca to keep the baby while we were in meetings. All the other Ivy editors were, of course, men, and they had no idea what to make of us, clattering up there in our smoking car with our baby chairs and bundles and diaper bags. All we needed was a mattress tied to the top. This was not the Dear Old Ivy they knew and loved.

Papa duly met us, and we got him and baby situated and went to our meeting. At morning break, Meg went down and met her husband who brought the baby to be nursed. We were bending over backward to be dignified and professional. Then in the middle of the afternoon, when we were supposed to be discussing "Why Academics Cannot Write," or "The Disappearing Canon," or some such ponderous subject, a big important football game came on, and the guys rolled a TV set in and put it up on the table in the meeting room while we were still in session. This really irked me. Why should *we* be the only professionals there?

"Go get the baby," I said to Meg.

"What?"

"I mean it. Go get the baby. How dare these guys interrupt our meeting for this stuff. We have been breaking our necks to keep our personal interests out of the way! What's more important, football or Michael?"

Meg brought little Michael in as the men stared at us in disbelief—a baby in the boardroom? How dare we?—then turned their backs, hunched their collective shoulders, and pulled their chairs closer to the television set, the better to ignore us.

But we had made our point. It's a new era. Men and women will be working together professionally from now on, and the guys can't call all the shots anymore—to use a perfectly obnoxious sports metaphor.

I guess we won't really be equal until a domestic metaphor leaps to mind as readily.

14

B·E·Y·O·N·D

The manuscript consisted of letter paper, wrapping paper, programs, envelopes, paper napkins—in short, whatever would take the imprint of a pencil. A great deal of it was written with a child crawling around my neck or being sick in my lap, and I dare say this may account for certain aspects of its style.
—Agnes DeMille

"HEY, BRO," I look up from a letter and call to Marlboro who is pecking away at his word processor on the other side of the fireplace that divides the long library in which we work. "I've been invited to speak at Commencement at Thalia High School. What do you think of that?"

"I think that's wonderful and you should do it," he says. "It's important, and it's an honor."

"But what would I say? I've been away so long, I'm not sure I know what kind of kids they graduate there now, what their plans are, their dreams, the things they have to overcome. I don't know that I have anything to *quote impart unquote*. I don't want to do it unless I can say something helpful."

"Do it. There can't be that many of them. Call Ellie and ask her to find out something about each graduate. Get an annotated bio. Say something personal to each one."

I lean back in my leather desk chair, tapping my teeth with a pen: "Hey, not bad. How do you know this?"

"If you'll recall, my dear, I spoke at my own high school's commencement a few years ago. I thought it all through then and was quite a smash if I do say so myself."

"Or quite smashed. Which was it?"

"Do it. I know it's not the cast of thousands you're used to addressing, but do it anyway."

"Oh, don't be silly. The point is: what will I say? More than half the people living there now *were not even alive* when I graduated from Thalia High. My cells have replaced themselves several times since I was seventeen years old. If all your cells have been replaced several times over, are you still *you?*"

Marlboro tosses an old-fashioned art gum eraser at me. "What's scary is: You were older then; you're younger now. Quick, who said that?"

It always beats me the stuff he keeps in his roll-top desk: two-cent stamps, dry Handi-Wipes from airlines, a worn-out magnet in the shape of a Scottie dog, black jellybeans that have corroded onto Indian head pennies. "This thing looks like it's been moldering in your drawer a hundred years." I toss it back. "Somebody from the sixties—Bob Dylan, I guess."

"See, you're quick. You'll think of something." Marlboro returns to his word processor, and I know this is his final decision, if not word, on the subject. Nevertheless, I sit looking into the fire crackling in the fireplace. What should I do? I'd like to do it, no question. But not because I'm some long-in-the-tooth alum, who has "made something of herself." I would do it only if I could talk to the graduates as if they were my own kids. I've learned some important things. Even my own kids listen to me now—sort of.

It's funny: sometimes I meet people, like the couple in their sixties down the street, who have lived in the same house all their lives, raised their children there, kept the same furnishings they started out with as young married people. They've had the same view, the same garden, the same bed, and I simply can't imagine a life like that. What do the sociologists call it? *Mutaphobic?* I guess I'm the opposite: every six months or so I have to push the furniture around in my house, just to change things. I can't imagine a life without the daily prospect of change, surprise, a new challenge. *Maybe I'm weird, abnormal.* If that's the case, what right do I have to impose myself on any gathering, let alone a group of young people making their way in the world for the first time? *I'm probably just a freak.*

"Marlboro, am I abnormal?"

"You're asking *me?* Ask someone who doesn't know you so well."

"Oh, come on, I'm serious. I'm trying to think about making speeches and things."

"Oh, well then. Seriously, I would say, dear, that you're definitely within the range of normal, though you would probably drive a sane man around the bend. I would add, too, that you're a perfectionist, obsessively tidy, clearly an overachiever—though to tell the truth, I've never quite understood what an overachiever is."

"Me neither."

That was true enough. I had never understood that term, unless it meant that someone had achieved more than the sum of background, environment, and personal characteristics would predict. I remember a conversation with Mother some years ago. Funny how some things people say about you, no matter how casually, stick in your mind for years. In a conversation about somebody's success at something, Mother had commented that my successes had come from determination, brains, and looks, in that order. I was irritated with my mother's assessment, because a) she had put brains second, and b) she'd included looks at all—clearly a cheap shot.

Now, I'm not so sure. There certainly are a lot of people brainier than I. What had Marlboro once said about living in a culture where everybody was a valedictorian? It's a humbling experience, and it's my daily life. But I love it. I love *them*.

"Bro?"

"What is it now?"

"When you first went to Harvard as a skinny kid from Ohio, what was it like with all that competition in the brains department that you weren't used to?"

"Well, first I thought I'd gone to hell . . . then heaven . . . then hell. It was a toss-up. But I soon found that everyone else felt the same way I did, which made it a little easier. Not a lot."

"Well, at least you didn't have to drag a *Miss Twinkletoes* title along with you."

"No, you're quite right about that."

It's funny that girlish charms are always seen as a plus—and maybe they *are* a help in getting a foot in a door occasionally. But overall, in the kind of academic work that has been my life since I outgrew Jacy Farrow twenty-five years ago, distinctive personal style is a drawback, if anything—especially for women. Maybe that's why I chose it—casting against type wouldn't be unlike me. *Perverse*, Mother would say. Something to think about some other time. But even now I recall dear Professor Rabi once remarking about the brilliant physicist Chien Shiun Wu, who worked on the Manhattan Project, and later became a world renowned research scientist: "When she came in here she was just a little bit of a thing, so beautiful nobody thought she had a brain in her head," he told me. And another handsome young woman who subsequently got a Harvard research grant once told me: "In my class in advanced calculus at Columbia, my professor, the president of the American Mathematical Society, started the course by saying pointedly: *One hundred years ago, women could knit, but could not do math. Today they can do neither.*"

Most women suffer sexism or cuteism or ageism, or all of them, somewhere along the line. But, as Mother said, one thing I *had* been was *determined.*

Maybe that's what I should tell the graduates: *Be determined, graduates, as you face the cold, cruel world. Yuk. Hokey.* If that's all I had to say, forget it. Being determined was easy: cut the whining and just do it. *What's that you say? You have a migraine? Just throw up over there, please, and get on with it. Anyone could do anything if she wanted to bad enough,* that's what Mother had said.

And perfectionist? I guess so. At least I never quit until I got things right, or to suit myself. But ridiculously high standards about some things: I can't guess how many pages of a paper or article I'd retyped in the old days of typewriters because I didn't want the White-Out to call attention to a corrected misspelled word. *Easy* misspelled words and typos were okay, but I wouldn't White-Out a *hard* word for the world to see that I hadn't spelled it right the first time; I'd type the whole page again first.

Obsessively tidy? Probably. I learned early, when I had a houseful of kids, that I couldn't get anything accomplished unless I was organized. Learning that has been a plus in my professional life: never touch a piece of paper more than once, stack all your pink callback slips and then return them all at once; keep a carbon of conversations and correspondence; do simple tasks first and get them out of the way, take time with the complicated jobs, start with a clean desk every morning, end with a clean desk every night—all that.

"Bro, am I really an obsessive neatnik?"

"No dear, you're perfect. Now, can I please finish this sentence I've been trying to write for the past hour?"

I sigh and poke at the smoldering log with the old branding iron Daddy gave me—wrapping it in a towel and three miles of duct tape to mail it to me from Thalia, after I'd expressed a desire for it—making little sparks fizz out of the charred wood. Wood, fire, smoke, ashes, fertilizer, new growth. When would it ever get warm? The winter had been one lacerating blizzard after another for the second year in a row. Probably that hole in the ozone. And spring wasn't looking much better. The forsythia had made a feeble debut, and then the late freeze had nipped it in the bud. Reminds me of the symbol of hope in MacLeish's play, *J.B.* The story of Job all over again. Forsythia? Hasn't been much hope this spring on the fabled North Shore.

Shoot. I'd really like to do it. Like to go back and talk to the kids in my old high school almost forty years later. But how to put myself where they are now? Is Thalia still the stifling, dead-end town it was in my day? Does anyone notice? Does anyone care? I stop: In my day—what can that mean? *Now* is my day. The best days of my life are now. Maybe I should tell them that. But teenagers wouldn't understand that. They think these are the best days of their lives. They think they're on top of the world, and I'm over the hill. Kids, wet behind the years. Funny, sounds Joycean.

I pull my chair closer to the fire, get a blanket for a wrap, reminding myself of my mother—sitting, wrapped up, gazing into the fire. What can I say, what do I know? *Mother, dammit, help me.*

Well, I now *have* the life I dreamed of while lying on my pink flowered bed in Thalia so many years ago, but how many kids in Thalia now dream absurdly of coming to work as a "life underwriter" in New York City and falling into the arms of Arthur Miller—whose eightieth birthday, by the way, is being celebrated this year. Eightieth? Impossible.

And my long-ago dream of writing for *Life*—about the only magazine I knew then—makes me chuckle. Now, I occasionally have dinner with the son of Henry Luce, the man who ruled *Life* as I knew it. The man who made a magazine with a voice so interpretive that it even spoke to me at fifteen, in Thalia, the end of the world. Now, I've had a long acquaintanceship with Jacques Barzun, the legendary intellectual consultant to that magazine that was my primary connection to a world beyond Texas. Barzun, my intellectual mentor. How many kids in Thalia would recognize his name—or others I had read, re-read and tracked down to sit on their footstools at one time or another—William York Tindall, Robert Penn Warren, Leslie Fiedler, Carl Rogers, Robert Merton. Would these graduates care about knowing people who changed cultural and intellectual history? Do any of them have the passion to learn, as I did?

Staring into the fire and pulling my own "holey comforter" around me as Mother once did, I think there is almost no one living I've read or watched on film or TV—whom I admired, a big qualification—in whose presence I had not figured out a way to put myself at one time or another. Four U.S. presidents, five First Ladies, the Dalai Lama, Elie Weisel.

"Hey, Bro," I call. "Who's the most important person you've ever met? I mean, the one who meant the most to you?"

"Well, I shook hands with Winston Churchill once, but by that time he was pretty old and senile. Still, it was Winnie. Martin Luther King, I guess. And Justice William O. Douglas, he would be a contender. Why?"

"Never mind. I'm just thinking."

Would the Thalia kids give a hoot about any of these people? Or would they be impressed only with someone who can bring the latest word about Madonna, or Magic Johnson, or Michael Jackson, or Jay Leno or some Nashville singer? Some Dallas Cowboy or other? David Letterman? Maybe I could start my speech, *As I was saying to Rosanne*.

Does anyone, anymore, dream of living in Greenwich Village, or Montmartre? Is there anyone there like I was who wants to read everything there is to read, know everything there is to know, travel everywhere?

I raise my voice: "Bro, I don't think I know what to say to these kids. I don't think I can do it. I think there's too big of a gap between them and me."

Marlboro looks up: "Look, you're being patronizing. Times have changed. These kids are a lot more sophisticated than you were then. They don't have to live in the dream-state you did. They've got their own cars, phones, satellite dishes. How you gonna keep them down on the farm, after they've seen TV?"

"It's ranch, not farm. They only farm in Windthorst."

"Where?"

"Forget it. If you don't know that, you don't belong in this conversation."

"*This is a conversation?* My mistake. I bow out. My pleasure."

All I have, I think, are strong impressions. Life is like a pointillist painting: you have to get at a distance and connect the dots to see the meaning.

I sit silently, listening to a loose electric cord with its heavy plug apparatus *thunk* against the side of the house as the wind gets up. The thing has been *thunking* in a high wind for months, but like the Arkansas Traveler's roof that never leaks when it doesn't rain, this plug *thunks* only when it's too windy and cold to fix it. Tomorrow, I think, I'll go out and pull the thing down, knowing already that I won't.

Warm, content, a whole world of things to think about. I wonder what would make me any happier than I am today? See my kids more, for sure. I've been lucky in the reproduction lottery. Good kids. Maybe being able to set them all up financially, for life. That would make me happy. But then, that's probably a selfish wish, gratifying to me, but not so good for them. They need to rub against the old vicissitudes as I have done, and have their rough edges ground off in the process. *That's it: Graduates, rub against the old vicissitudes; guaranteed to make you stronger, make you better people.* Is that really true? Some fine people I know wouldn't recognize a vicissitude if it bit them. Charmed lives. What makes good, successful, happy people? Is it because positive things happen to them, or negative things?

My mind drifts back over some of the troubles—the scary ones—I've had the misfortune to rub up against. There's a difference in those and the superficial trials related to moving to New York City with a child and being broke, homeless, jobless, friendless. All those things nearly got me down only once, and pretty much in private, but one-by-one I'd fixed them. The really traumatic things were the scalding divorce, the muggings—two muggings actually, one Paul's, the other mine—and then the other, unspeakable thing. And then there was the time one of my kids got into trouble, and I couldn't do anything to help him, but stand by, support him, open my pocket-book, be brave. Those traumas were harder to come to terms with, and I'm not sure I learned anything, or had my character much improved, by any of them.

The divorce, yes. I'd learned in the crucible of it *exactly* why it was necessary.

But Paul's run-in with a mugger and a pistol in front of The Cathedral of St. John the Divine? Well, that certainly reinforced how precious he was to me, and how steely a couple of thirteen-year-olds can be. He and his pal Toby had been walking along the street in daylight when a guy in a ski-mask grabbed them both, threw them up against the fence in front of the church, put a pistol to Paul's head and a knife to Toby's back and told them to empty their pockets. When they did, of seven dollars between them, he told them to stay there for five minutes and not turn around. If they did, he would return and kill Paul's mother; he knew where I lived because he'd watched Paul come out of his building. The boys clung to the fence for at least five minutes, then ran into the apartment and sat down in the middle of the living-room floor, pale and mute. Later Paul admitted that he was traumatized more by the threat then the actual mugging. "I just thought, okay, I'm gone. I'm dying right here," he told me. "Then after the guy left, I got terrified he'd actually come after *you*."

From my own horrendous mugging I learned how like the Keystone Kops New York police can be, and what sitting in front of a Grand Jury is like. This incident occurred one summer night when I'd stepped out of a cab, walked the half block to my apartment door, and let myself into the vestibule. As I put the key into the lock of the inner door, I felt a presence beside me and looked up into the face of a young black man who immediately began to garrotte me with a cord of some kind. I'd been so startled and terrified that I broke all the mugging victim rules: screaming bloody murder at the top of my lungs, over and over again, as the man pulled me out the door and down the short flight of steps to the street. I was still screeching when he threw himself on top of me to yank my handbag from under me where I'd fallen on it as I crumpled to the sidewalk. As it happened, Paul's bedroom window was open. He looked down, saw his mother lying on the street with a mugger atop her, and ran down five flights of stairs in nothing but his underwear and little white socks.

The man fled toward Broadway with my shoulder bag and Paul chased the guy, who jumped into a waiting car. As fortune—or fate—would have it, a police car cruised along just at that moment. Paul, still in his undies, flagged it down, breathlessly telling the story and pointing out the speeding car whose red tail-lights were still visible. The police car zoomed off uptown in pursuit of the thief. Meanwhile, another radio car came blaring out of a side street and crashed into the first cop car, spinning it around to face downtown. A third police car coming from uptown, headed the mugger's car into the concrete pilings under the El at 125th Street, then hit the El itself.

Meanwhile, back at the scene of the crime, I picked myself up, dusted myself off, and limped into the apartment to the attentive care of tenants who had witnessed the melee in whole or in part—certainly they had heard the ruckus I'd made—and Paul, horrified, scrambled back upstairs and into his jeans, suddenly aware that he'd been dashing through the streets with his virtually nude adolescent body on glaring display.

Later, a fourth police car came to take us to the 26th Precinct, so I could point out the mugger in the line-up.

"Well, you sure caused a stir, little lady," said the cop, as he drove us to the station. "Three police vans was tore up before they caught the perp." He described in detail the various crashes up and down Broadway.

Paul and I squeezed hands in the back seat, and tried to keep from giggling. We were nervous and off-balance.

"So you caught the guy?" I finally managed to squeak out.

"Yeah, he's a little roughed up, big gash on his head, and a broke arm. But we got him all right."

"And you got my handbag back?"

"Yes, we're holding it at the station."

After we were ushered in to review the line-up, we peered behind the glass at four perfectly healthy-looking men, and one with a bloody gash on his head and his arm in a sling.

"Which one you think it is, Paul?" I whispered, trying not to giggle.

"Well, I have a good idea, and I didn't even get a look at his face." Paul retorted.

In the outer office, I asked for my handbag. They told me it was being "held for evidence."

"What evidence?"

"We just need to hold it overnight to check it out." The cop looked at me sternly: "I'll call you tomorrow."

Back in my bedroom, still shaken, I glanced at the mess I'd made early that morning—it seemed eons ago—when, in a hurry, I'd knocked over a can of talcum powder on my dresser, which had spilled on the floor, and . . . . yes . . . then it struck me . . . into my handbag. Oh boy. Later the police officer called and said everything had checked out all right, and he was returning my purse.

"Was it the baby powder?" I asked.

"Yeah," he said, sounding embarrassed. "Sorry to have to put you out, but it had the appearance of . . . er . . . something else."

My story to the Grand Jury resulted in the mugger's eight-year residence in Sing Sing. About that many years later, I recall, I could swear I spotted the guy on a subway. *Who could forget those glittering eyes?* Terrified that he'd recognize me, I got off and took the next train.

Had any of this improved my character? Well, not so I could tell. And neither my character, nor my temper, had been improved by another event—involving a famous astronomer I went to interview for an article. For about an hour we sat in his living room while he talked, and I ran my tape recorder and took backup notes. When I admired a mobile replica of the planetary system on a table beside the sofa, the professor said, "I have a better one in the back; come out and I'll show you."

I followed him into the back of the large apartment. As we walked into a darkened room, he made a movement as if to turn on the light, then slammed the door, shoved me onto the bed, pushed my knit dress up and grabbed the top of my stockings, attempting to drag them down over my hips. He dodged as I flailed my arms, trying to hit him.

"Quit this! Stop!"

I pulled away to the top of the bed, holding a pillow in front of me. He pulled off his chinos and came at me again.

"Stop it, you jerk!" I heard myself yelling. "Quit. Get away from me!"

Panting, he pulled off his underwear, and in his plaid shirt made a dive for me. I threw a pillow at him, then a book lying on the bed table. I tried to edge from the bed to the door, but he was on me again, pulling my hair back tightly, then tearing at my stockings.

"You like this, bitch, you know it!" He screamed at me.

"Get *off* me!" I tried to get a knee in his groin, but he had me pinned to the bed, and was shouting, "Come on, come, come!" I yanked my dress down between myself and him as he pressed himself against me hard, and I heard him groan. I felt his sweaty hair in my face as he pushed me further into the bed.

In a few seconds, he was up. "I'm finished!" he said cheerfully, and then turned contrite. While I struggled to find the door and get out of the room, he followed me. "I'm sorry. I'm sorry. I didn't mean it, I couldn't help myself," he repeated, as I jerked clear of him, grabbed my handbag and slammed out of the apartment. I didn't wait for the elevator, but took the stairs as fast as my shaky legs could.

On the street I looked down. My dress was a mess. Fortunately, a cab stood under the awning of his building, and I grabbed the door and fell in. Not until then did I cry. At home, I took off my dress and gingerly rolled it up in a paper bag. Then I soaked in the bathtub a long time, wondering what I should do. If I raised a stink about it, I would undoubtedly be hurt more than he. I decided to do nothing. Better to ignore it. Disgusting . . . humiliating. I took the paper bag with my dress in it and threw it down the incinerator.

For the next week, the man wrote hand-delivered notes apologizing, telling me he was sorry, inviting me to go on a cruise with him. He sent me half a dozen inscribed books he had written. I never saw him again except at a distance, nor did I write the article. I did keep the tape, though—dated and annotated.

I get up, poke at the fire again, then wander to the bookshelf and pull out one of his autographed volumes: "Best regards," it says. "I hope we will always remain friends." *Friends? Not likely.* I'd kept the books for . . . what? Evidence? To remind myself not to trust professorial jerks. Then I recall that Mother, on a visit to New York, had picked one of the guy's books off my shelf, read it cover to cover, and enjoyed it. "He has a brilliant way of putting science and religion together," she'd said.

I couldn't find a retort for that.

My mother; what a piece of work she was. For fifty years her words had held her family together. Then she stopped talking. But, I remember with a smile, death was not the first thing that stopped her. Once it was her daughters.

Before she died, the last time Mother stopped talking was on a visit to New York City in the early eighties. She and Ellie had come to spend a couple of weeks, and Mother was sitting on the bed hemming a bright green blouse with white embroidery, drinking hot tea, and talking. She'd segue from an item she'd read in the *Times* about astronauts, to a story Aunt Celie had told in 1925 when she sat on the lawn at the ranch looking up at the constellations in the night sky, naming them—Cassiopeia, Pliades, Orion's belt—to The Big Bang theory, to the deplorable hole in the ozone. All pretty much in one breath.

She was at it that day as Ellie and I dressed to go out and celebrate our recently arrived-at singledom. We had both just split from long-time husbands. Greg and his complicated personal missions, and Artie and his twenty-one relatives and nine brothers had vanished in nuclear family explosions of awesome dimension, leaving both of us limp. We needed a radical change of scene, so we were dressing absurdly in punk black to try out our new status on the world. This took some concentration at our age. We'd agreed to go vamping, but neither of us knew a whole lot about this activity.

I smile, missing Ellie as well as my mother. I wish my sister lived closer. We had good times together being foolish. It was nice to have one person in the world you could act dumb with, no questions asked, no judgments made. That night we thought it would be funny to pretend we were downtown people for the evening, which was about as far away from our former lives as we could imagine. But Mother kept talking about stars and creation and gasses turning into other elements, and how she had always loved math in college until at some point she'd felt betrayed, felt right back to the place where everything was relative, where your perspective made all the difference, and you couldn't say anything with certainty anymore.

She was going on in this vein, when I walked over to the bed and cupped my hand over her mouth. "Mother, stop talking. We're trying to put ourselves together here, and all this stuff about relativity and creation and God is diverting. Now, if you think I should wear this black turtleneck, just nod. Or if you think I should wear this black scoop neck, just nod. Ellie will hold up earrings, and you nod when she holds up a pair you like. But please stop talking for a minute, will you?"

Mother twitched her shoulders and gave a look of exaggerated hurt. "Okay, I just won't talk again, ever, and see how you like that," she snipped, stabbing the needle into the fabric she was holding.

Her silence was disconcerting, if for no other reason than it was so unusual. Daddy didn't talk much, and he heard even less. Like most men back in Thalia, he had little interest in Cassiopeia, the relative absolutes of physics, or creation theories. The only Big Bang he knew anything about was the one that came from the muzzle of a hunting rifle slung across the rear window of a pickup. Daddy was a good, solid man, but he couldn't compete with Mother in the "ozone hole" department. The last fantasy he'd had was about the tooth fairy at age six. Fantasy was the air Mother breathed, and Daddy's practicality, his prosaicness, kept her grounded. Mother had said that over and over: he was her rock. Without him, she'd fly off into the ether forever. But for talking and exploring fantasies, Mother had Ellie and me.

Most of the time we relished her flights, but sometimes, like right then, we needed some quiet time to get ourselves up as the blessed single women we were for the first time in twenty years or so.

"What, exactly, does 'vamp' mean?" Ellie asked, applying black eyeliner to her almond-shaped eyes.

"Beats me," I said. "Just sounds like a good idea." I blotted the white lipstick that I fancied looked stunning with my dark tan, and turned to Ellie. "This is what I intend to do: walk around minding my own business looking drop-dead gorgeous, knocking every man who comes within my aura on his ass. And then I'm going to come home to read from that pile of books over there." I gestured to a dozen books teetering on the nightstand.

My sister gave me a look. "Okay, Cruella DeVille, when do we start?"

We paraded before Mother in our wicked attire. Her lips had turned to stone. She lifted her chin, closed her eyes in an exaggerated look of haughty disdain, and tended to her mending. Ellie slid three silver rings onto her own fingers and held them up for Mother to admire. Mother turned her face away, chin at a stubborn tilt. Ellie cut her eyes at me. She can say a ton with her eyes: "Long-suffering daughter. Impossible Mother. Oh, how I adore the Silly Season." Mother examined the wall beside the bed with pointed attention.

"Hey, Mom, want me to warm your tea?" Ellie asked, nudging her, kidding her into a reply. Mother whipped her head around and looked at us both imperiously. She wouldn't be caught off-guard like that. What did we take her for? We'd told her to be quiet, and she would—till hell froze over.

I carried the teapot down the long hall of my railroad apartment, refilled it with boiling water and brought it back to the bedroom. When Mother traveled, she brought her own china cup, just as she brought her own long-handled, Lady Hamilton-patterned, silver-plated teaspoon, and her own down pillow. Mollie had brought hats. When she'd traveled anywhere in the world, Mollie carried hats with cabbage roses, hats with pheasant feathers, hats of black horsehair. One ought never to be caught without a proper hat, she'd said.

Mollie had been dead for twenty years, but her affectations lived on in *Another Form*. Just like the live oak tree in the yard at the ranch turns into firewood into flame into heat into ashes into fertilizer for crops into new growth. Just like Mother said. Just as all things change but nothing ever escapes once it has been created by that first Big Bang. Other forms. We were always alert to *Other Forms* when we were with Mother.

I poured the fresh tea into Mother's fragile, translucent teacup with shamrocks on it, which always surprised us by surviving her journeys long and short. It was sort of a symbol of Mother herself, who drank only tea. No coffee. No alcohol. But, as I recall, Ellie and I were thinking hard about alcohol at that moment. The smooth Cabernet I'd begun thinking about was rapidly transmogrifying into

Another Form—preferably a double martini. "Do you want a cookie to go with your tea?" (Mother took her cookies wafer thin.) "Or a slice of orange bread?" (Which Mother seldom traveled without—made by herself in sturdy round columns, cooked in #2 tin cans, well-greased and floured.) "Or I have a cheese Danish from Zabars." (Mother wrinkled her nose. Store-bought food was virtually inedible.)

Ellie was all decked out; tight black pants, tight black turtleneck, high black leather boots, silver dangly earrings. She looked stunning, tall and slender, her dark hair with its slice of silver cutting through at one temple. Her teeth are very straight and white. She is beautiful. We are both Amazons compared to Mother, whose delicate ankles are crossed as she lies in silence on my bed. Her hands are small and white, her eyes a sparkling light blue. A silver ringlet lies at the nape of her neck where what she refers to as her "Psyche knot" is pulling loose. Daddy is lucky. His house has been filled with wondrous women.

"You can talk now, Mother," Ellie said. "How does this look?" She did a turn in the middle of the room, her booted heel squeaking on the hardwood I'd polished for their visit. Mother looked her up and down with raised eyebrows and elevated nose, then turned back to her mending. Her rude daughters were not going to entice her to speak.

As we exited, Mother gave a mock sniff. Ellie and I looked at each other: She was dying to talk, but she was stubborn as hell. Small, radiant, silver-haired, she had a rapier tongue and a steel-trap mind. She was also funny, and a good sport. Earlier in the week, she had joined us and one million others in a long demonstration march for nuclear disarmament. She had allowed us to dress her to highlight her Native American heritage—the term just coming into preference. She wore jeans, moccasins and fringed jacket. We plaited her long silver hair in one heavy braid down her back into which we entwined colored beads. At age sixty-eight, she'd marched five miles—until we all gave out.

But the night of The Silence, after Ellie and I had bar-hopped for a few hours—undoubtedly devastating all the men we'd vamped by edging out before midnight—we came home wondering what kind of reception we'd get.

Mother was sitting just as we had left her, reading, drinking tea. "Did you girls scare up anything you'd have?" She asked brightly, as if she'd never given us the silent treatment at all. We looked at each other dramatically.

"She speaks!" said Ellie.

"Indeed. What a miracle!"

Mother gave us her best haughty look. "It's *your* turn not to talk," she said. "Now, about those gasses that escaped during the Big Bang, I'm perfectly sure that they are still in the universe, but certainly by now they have changed to Other Forms."

I smile, fighting off tears. I had *enjoyed* my mother so. How many women, I wonder, can say that? That their mothers brought them joy. *Real joy.* It was during this stay that I, a little reluctantly, introduced Mother to Marlboro. Reluctantly, because I had, after all, recently divorced a decent man, one of the grounds being that I needed some independence. I knew Mother would sniff out a contradiction immediately.

Oh well. I shrugged, and decided to bear the consequences. He was just a friend, after all. It was not as if I were going to *marry* him or anything. I had already decided that unless I found the perfect *perfect* man, I would never marry again, and I wore as protective coloration my adamant resolve that a perfect man did not exist. Besides, who would marry someone with such a ridiculous name? And especially since he had the further unforgivable personal failing of being a *football nut.* Yuk. I'd left that silly business back in Texas once and for all.

No. It was safe to introduce Mother to Marlboro. I would be depriving them both, if I didn't.

They found a common subject instantly, as I recall—something about the finer points of gasses escaping from one nuclear explosion or another, and how they were eternally and indubitably captured in a universe in which nothing is ever lost.

The matter of my needing some privacy and independence at that time in my life was the point of several conversations between Mother and me during that visit. I pointed out to her that in all my years I'd never lived by myself, and I really needed to do that.

Mother agreed, but reminded me that a few years before—when I'd lived in the big house in Keating, with too many people living in and running about, and a lazy-Susan full of crazy housekeepers that I invariably became responsible for—Mother had asked me in one of our long talks: "What do you *want* more than anything in the world, Jacy?"

I'd thought a few moments, and then replied wearily, "More than anything in the world right now, I just want to be left alone."

Then Mother had asked: "Well, what are you *more frightened of* than anything in the world?"

And I had answered, after a moment, looking a bit hacked: "I guess I am most frightened of being left alone."

It was true; a paradox, as most things are when you get right down to them. There was alone, I explained to my mother, and then there was *alone.* One was desirable, the other scary. Mother smiled. Of course she knew that. She just wanted to make sure her daughter did.

Mother had always seemed to me a specialist in moral dilemmas, being always above the fray. "Don't fight fire with fire, you'll burn down the house," she'd say. "Revenge is unworthy of you. If you let someone control you to the extent that they change your behavior to match theirs, then they've won." She also said that "an eye for an eye just leaves two blind people."

I took all this to heart, but it hadn't made my life any easier. When I turned the other cheek, as she counseled, I just got swatted twice. Furthermore, her advice was so radical that when I actually acted on it, I was sometimes thought to have a hidden agenda. I wasn't at all sure that all these lofty practices had helped me get along better in life, but oddly, I've almost always felt better about myself when I followed them. Just like Mother had said I would, of course.

I flip through my journal, and my eye lights on notes I recorded after a phone call from Carrie in 1981.

"Mother, you were right. I shouldn't have married Grant. And besides nobody in Montana wants computers, and Grant doesn't know much about them anyway, so I think I'm going to leave him."

"Carrie, slow down. Is computer aversion in Montana enough to torpedo a marriage after three years?"

"Well, Mom, if you must know, Grant's a drunk. He starts drinking in the morning and stays drunk all day. I thought as soon as he left college and all the keg parties, he would stop and be a normal person. I thought it was just a college thing, but he hasn't stopped, Mother. *One day he rode a horse up the steps and into a bar in Red Lodge and turned around and around in the middle of the floor.* Everyone in town thought it was hysterical; what a great personality Grant has and so on and so forth. But I thought it was stupid and just too humiliating."

"Rode a horse into a bar?"

"Yes, Mother. His mom and dad have drinking problems, and I think when he got out here where all the guys act so tough and macho and hang out all night together, it got to him, too."

"Well, what are you going to do?"

"I don't know. Maybe go back to Keating and get a job."

"You can come to New York and live with me. You can take some classes at Barnard—you can go free as long as I work at Columbia."

"Mother, I hate New York. It's filthy and all bombed out. Besides the girls at Barnard don't shave their legs, and I've been raising baby lambs in my bathtub all winter."

"Carrie, this is going too fast for me. Horses in bars, hairy legs, baby lambs in bathtubs, all in one breath."

"Mom, don't make fun of me."

"I'm not making fun of you, honey. I just don't know what direction this conversation is taking at any given moment. If you think you should leave Grant, that's your business. If you're really unhappy, I'd think it's almost a relief to get this a marriage over early, so you can get on with living, doing whatever you want with your life. You're smart and disciplined; you can do whatever you want to do."

"I know, Mom. But not Barnard, *pleeeze.*"

"You could learn a lot, meet interesting people. You can't imagine how I would have loved the chance to go there when I was twenty-five; you just can't imagine, and it wasn't even on my radar screen then . . . just think . . ."

"Mom. Stop. I'm not you!"

I stop, stunned.

"I'm sorry, Carrie. Of course, you're not. No more than I was my mother. In fact, I think I remember saying that to her in just those words," I sigh. "I'm just concerned about you."

I shake my head. This was a bad time with all my kids. Those times come in cycles, I think. I riffle through some pages. There should be a note about a phone call from Ben sometime around here, too. Yes, here it is:

"Ma, I'm in the hospital. I have some broken ribs and lots of gashes and stuff. I was bleeding all over."

"My god! What happened?"

"Car accident. My car jumped a curb, ran into someone's front yard. Hit the porch. I ended up in a flower bed."

"Oh, Ben. Where are you? Is your dad there? Is anyone else hurt?"

"He's taking care of the car and stuff. Nobody else was hurt. It was just me. You know those pills I've been taking for hyperactive-whatever-it-is? Well, they make me pass out sometimes. I did. Tore up my car."

"Ben, you're not supposed to drive when you're on medication."

"I know, Ma, but I didn't think it'd hurt this one time."

"When are you getting out of there?"

"Tomorrow, I think. I'm sore all over. This sucks, Ma."

"Do you want me to come there? Or do you want to come here when you get out? Do you feel like it?"

"I don't know. I'll call you when I get out. I'll go to Dad's, but then maybe I'll come see you if that's okay. Mom, could I live with you awhile? This is not working out for me."

"Sure. When you feel like it, get your stuff together and come." I try it again. I'm having trouble giving away an Ivy League degree. "Do you want to go to Columbia?"

"Maybe. I just want to get back in school and make something of myself. I shouldn't have dropped out."

"Well. That's history. Let's go forward."

"Okay, Ma. I'll call you."

Motherhood is never ending. Ellie had said there was a time when all her kids were teenagers that she had an anxiety attack every time the phone rang. There was never good news on the other end. And I remember our own mother saying, "Boys and cars, boys and cars!" with great exasperation. One of our brothers was always getting in an accident. How many cars and pickups had Daddy repaired and replaced?

I had been relieved to raise Paul in New York City, where he had no car during his teenage years. Of course, there were other dangers—muggers with guns not excluded. Yet, on the whole, he'd given his mother less grief than any of the kids in the family raised in Texas and Ohio car cultures.

I look through a journal dated 1985–86, and light on several entries recording phone calls from Paul.

"Mom, can I talk to you for a minute?"

"Sure. What's going on?"

"Well, you know last week I had the audition with this guy named Rogers, supposed to be a big producer, and I thought it went really well? It was for an off-Broadway thing by Fugard."

"Yes."

"Well, this Rogers called last night and asked if I'd meet him for a beer and talk about the play, so I did, and we had a good talk, and he said he really liked my work and wanted me for a call back, and he'd introduce me to some people."

"Good."

"Yeah, well, on the way home we were walking and talking and he said something about I'd make a good model, and

I said I wasn't interested in modeling; I was interested in acting. And he pushed me into an alley and tried . . . Mom . . . I swear, tried to kiss me on the mouth."

"What?"

"Yeah. I pushed him away and told him I wasn't interested in that."

"So what did he do?"

"Well, he got real huffy and told me I was confused about my sexuality, and if I didn't get straightened out about it I wouldn't be able to work in the theater in New York."

"Mom, can I bother you a minute?"

"Of course, what can I do?"

"Mom, can you come down here and talk to Lib? She needs someone to talk to, and well, you know, she can't talk to her mother."

"What's the problem?"

"Well, Mom. She's pregnant. And we don't know what to do."

"What do you think?"

"Mom, I love kids, you know that. I'd love to have a family someday. But I can't be a father. I'm only twenty-one. I don't even have a steady job. Half the time I'm stone broke. But, Lib, you know she's thirty-three. And she thinks she might not ever have a chance again, so she sort of wants to go through with it."

"Paul . . . I don't know what to say."

"I sort of feel like I owe it to her. I feel guilty about keeping her from other men who might be able to marry her and give her children. I've told her and told her that when she wants to leave and find another man in a better position than I am, to do it. But she won't do it. She says she just wants to be with me. Mom, I can't get married now. Mom, am I treating her right?"

"I don't know. Tell her I'll be there as soon as I can."

"Thanks, Mom."

"Mom, can we talk?"

"Yes, Paul."

"Mom, Lib said for me to thank you. She said thank you most of all for staying out of it and letting us decide. She's fine today, but staying in bed. She'll call you tonight herself. She said thank you again. She couldn't even tell her mother, but she needed another woman there."

"Mom!"

"Yes, Paul . . . . "

"I'm freaking out! Did you see the TV? Did you see what happened to the shuttle?"

"Yes, I have the TV on now."

"Mom, it was like . . . they were there, and then they weren't. Just like that. Unbelievable. I don't know what to do. I feel like a baby, crying. It was just like when Charlie died. He was standing there, and then he just keeled over and wasn't alive any more. And like the baby. It was there in Lib and then not there. And like your and dad's marriage; one day it was there, then the next it's not. Nothing stays. Love doesn't stay, people, babies. I'm scared, Mom. You can't even trust the ground you walk on, or the sky. Mom, I am friggin' freaked! It was like they stood for all of America—the whole map. You couldn't make a movie like that—with men, women, blacks, whites, Jewish, a school teacher, even someone named Smith—everybody would think it was too pat; too corny. But it was the whole map of America that blew up in the Challenger. It's like a bad omen, like pushing God until he yells *stop it*! Like the Tower of Babel. Like when will we learn? It's just freaking, Mom, freaking!"

"Paul, Paul. I know. Shall I come down there, or do you want to come up here?"

"I want to call Grandad. He's the only one I know who stays. He stays in the same chair."

15

The problem with some writers is
that they're not *from* anywhere.
—Flannery O'Connor

To rebel against tradition was
somehow to hold fast to it.
—Alfred Kazin

C·O·M·M·E·N·C·E·M·E·N·T

I LOOK DOWN at the audience from where I sit on the stage in Thalia High School and smile at my father, my aunt, my sister, my daughter, my granddaughter, and—wonder of wonder—both brothers, who sit here in the front row looking handsome and proud, waiting for me to speak. I had half expected that the last two would find urgent business elsewhere, shortly before this event, so I am especially surprised and flattered that they have come. Of course Marlboro is here too, beaming because he's convinced me that I should do this, should make this speech when I don't know what to say and that whatever it is will probably be irrelevant to these young graduates anyway. Half my family gathered here tonight once graduated from Thalia High themselves; my aunt—my mother's only living sibling—did so in 1934.

I look around nervously. This stage, this setting has changed very little. Same wooden floor, same old piano, looks like the same stage curtains even, maybe not. In any case, it has probably taken me more coats of paint to spruce myself up for this event than it has taken to get the stage in order. A big electronic screen has been added, I see, and some amplified music. The old lectern, where a school official is now speaking, looks the same. I recall how frightened I felt the last time I stood there: frightened because I had to sing that sappy song my mother had chosen about "beyond the blue horizon," frightened because I had to make a speech, frightened of what

I'd find in the big world out there after I left home. I knew I would go off to college, but then I had secret plans to move to "Green-witch Village" and become a world famous singer just as soon as possible, so I could then move to Paris and slip right into its café society. From there I would launch my career as a world famous writer, maybe with Arthur Miller's help. (I try not to show that I am laughing at my own youthful presumption and naivety as I sit up here. To help, I recall the verse Mollie taught me: *When I grow up and carry a stick and look very dignified, no one will know that it's only a trick, and I'm really myself inside.*)

A few minutes earlier, as I was walking across the school yard to the auditorium, a young girl rushed up to me with an ancient yearbook, holding it out to be autographed. "I came to hear you," she said breathlessly, "because you were Jacy Farrow, the most beautiful girl in Thalia High School. My grandfather pointed you out in this book." I stood astonished, looking at the pen the girl held out to me. "Yes, I guess I *was* Jacy Farrow once," I agreed, finally. "I don't think I am anymore." She looked disappointed. Who wants the autograph of a long-in-the-tooth woman with tinted auburn hair and a purple dress? I thought. This child wants the autograph of someone young and glamorous. So I added, looking at her "But who knows? You never outgrow your younger self entirely." I took the pen and scrawled my childhood name across my dewy childhood face. As she scurried away, clutching her grandfather's book, I thought, Well, there's some truth in that: Like Jacy Farrow, I can *still* be something of a twit when pushed too far—as Marlboro is fond of pointing out.

Does anyone here on this stage have such dreams as I did? I think, watching the graduates file in, the tassels on their mortarboards swinging in front of their noses. What turn-of-the-century bug-a-bears that they cannot even imagine now will they run up against? I've reviewed their backgrounds, thanks to Ellie, and see a few here who love to write, who work on the yearbook and *The Cat's Claw*, as I once did; one who has won several journalism contests and is off to college with a scholarship. A couple here are musically talented and will go on to study; several want to work with young children. One particularly gifted young man—perhaps influenced by living near the ruins of the old Royal Theater in a town that Larry McMurtry jokingly calls "my own theme park"—has his heart set on an acting career. (Dare I mention to him how difficult my own son, Paul, has found that route to adulthood? No, not tonight.)

Basically I see, though, that the young people of Thalia have little ambition beyond playing football, listening to country music, hunting, fishing, racing cars and riding horses, just as they did when I was a kid. Three of the twenty-nine graduates—two girls and a boy—already have babies. It occurs to me that they, as teenagers, have had a variety of erotic settings available to them; in the old days of Thalia, the picture show was about the only place teenagers could be alone and unsupervised. Perhaps that's the reason it always carried the aura of something vaguely sexy and forbidden.

Well, these three kids are already learning that there is something in the world more important than themselves, something smaller and needier and more helpless. They are likely to grow up a good deal faster than their classmates. Or else they *won't* and their families will suffer. Did anyone ever tell these kids to hold themselves above the crowd? To value their own special selves, and not to be "too available"? Did anyone tell them not to be influenced by their peers in Thalia, that teenage values are mostly silly stuff, and that they'll be grown-ups many more years than they'll be teenagers? Did anyone ever tell them to *kvell* with winners—even to take pride in the victories of people they don't like very much? That the only remedy for the superiority of another is *love*? Did anyone tell them, as my mother did over and over: *Don't quit, no matter what. Keep on keeping on. You can do it, whatever* it *is for you*? Did anyone ever tell them that nothing is lost? That they can build on experiences whether good or bad; that success is simply a small comfortable space between doing one thing imperfectly and doing the next thing imperfectly?

Did anyone ever tell them that yes *even good posture* helps sometimes?

I sit trying to think what I should tell these kids. As usual, I never know what I'm going to say until it's half out of my mouth. What can an old fogie like me, whose choices were limited so early, say to a group of kids whose choices are vast? *Just be careful*, I guess. *Stay alert*. Shall I tell them that simply to be conscious is to be confused; that no one escapes confusion or sorrow; that all the joyful and wonderful high points of their lives are precious gifts, not entitlements?

I hear my name and look toward the lectern, where a lovely young lady is introducing me. She makes me sound so terrific and brilliant that even *I* look forward to meeting me and learning my "secrets to success." Coming from her lips, the account of my life sounds charmed—as I grow seamlessly from small town girl with dreams to big city woman with family and career. It is as if Tinkerbell, who once made an appearance in girls' health class in this very auditorium, whisking her wand across our heads with the twinkly promise that "Soon you will be a woman!" is making a return appearance. How do I tell these kids that it's not quite that easy, but to *hang in there?*

I rise to applause and approach the speaker's stand. The auditorium is full to overflowing with family, friends and well-wishers of the graduates. My stomach makes its usual little lurch, as I face the crowd. I *still* get stage fright. I *still* don't like to perform.

"Good evening graduates," I begin. "Good evening parents, teachers, administrators, friends—but especially graduates, for you are the ones who have worked so hard to get where you are tonight. And you have the decisions to make about where you are going from here.

"Thank you for inviting me back home. Thomas Wolfe was wrong when he said you can't go home again. Another writer, Maya Angelou, says 'the truth is, you can never *leave* home. You take it with you—under your fingernails, in the look in your eye and the way you move your head and hips.' You also take it with you in the tone of your voice, the expressions you use, the way you sum up a situation, the very way you think and react. You carry *home* around with you in the lining of your coat.

"In the past weeks, I have been thinking about what I might have to say that would mean anything to you. As I did, old memories came flooding back. You know, they straightened out the Mississippi River in places to make room for houses and liveable space. And occasionally, the river floods these places. *Floods* is the word they use, but author Toni Morrison says that the river is not *flooding* at all; it is *remembering*. It is remembering where it used to be. All water has a perfect memory and is forever trying to get back to where it was.

"In trying to think of some words to tell you tonight, I took Toni Morrison's concept and saw myself as a diverted river, trying to get back to where I was forty years ago, when I was here like you are. Trying to think what hills and valleys I ran through—not many around here—what the light and weather and vegetation were like. Like the river, I was trying to remember where I was before I was straightened out to make room for a lot of other people, and houses, and liveable spaces in my life.

"Water seems a funny metaphor to use for memories of this part of Texas, since water was the one element, when I was young, that we missed most. We had a terrible drought when I was just your age, so the kids in my class, whose families depended on ranching and farming for a living—which was most of us—didn't have much money. But those of us who had a lot of ambition just had to figure out what we wanted anyway—with little money and no contacts. Since many of us didn't even have television in those days, the only knowledge of the world beyond Thalia that we had, the only sophistication, came from watching the picture show."

I waited a beat: "And you see what happened to *that*."

This comment gets the first laugh of the evening, and buoyed, I continue for the next twenty minutes exhorting the young Jacys and Sonnys and Duanes to grow up carefully, treat one another tenderly, and spurn greediness. I tell them that success is a dynamic thing, and that working at getting what they want is just as engrossing, just as fulfilling, just as plain much fun as finally getting it. I tell them to stay flexible, to take risks, to stretch themselves.

I tell them to keep a distance between themselves and a problem, in order to tackle it with clearer judgment, and I tell them to keep their sense of humor—always. Maybe—I tell them—I should leave them with my favorite three-step bit of Eastern wisdom:

1. Do not be deluded.
2. If you can't help being deluded, do not judge others, and do not feel guilty.
3. If you can't help being deluded, and you can't help judging others or feeling guilty, do not open your mouth.

They laugh again, so I know it's time to sit down.

"This is *your* day. Enjoy it. I wish for you more than to make a good living. I wish for you to make for yourself—as I have had the good fortune to do—a full, gorgeous, wild and precious life.

"And I thank you for helping this river remember its source."

16

R·E·T·U·R·N

Ellie: "I feel now as if there is
nothing I could not do,
because I want nothing."
Captain Shotover: "That's a real
strength. That's genius.
That's better than rum."
—George Bernard Shaw
in *Heartbreak House*

LETTERS AND PHONE CALLS. The tools of my trade. I am so lucky to have lived in an era, perhaps the *last* era, in which letters were not only a means of conveying information, but often long, leisurely modes of self-expression. My mother looked forward to receiving letters, but I suspect she enjoyed even more sitting down at her desk with a cup of tea and writing letters, often by hand, but in her later years on the word processor Daddy bought her as a gift.

Once she had copied a long passage from a book she was reading—*A Woman of Independent Means*—into a letter to me. "I write long letters," the passage began. "Sometimes by compressing and editing the events of my life, I infuse them with a dramatic intensity totally lacking at the time, but oddly enough I find that years after, what I remember is not the event as I lived it, but as I described it in a letter. I find the very act of writing turns fact into fiction."

Mother went on to tell me that she'd saved all my letters over the years. "They're in a manila envelope in my hidey hole with your name on it," she had written. "After I go on to become Another Form, this envelope belongs to you. You can follow your own growth through the letters."

She was right. Both my correspondence with her and with Alex provide a kind of *bildungsroman*—the growth, over time, of a life. Not a particularly important life in the grand scheme of things, but a life that participated fully in the social and political upheavals of an era. And my correspondence with Alex documents the evolution of two young women, burdened early by convention, who slowly learned to take their lives into their own hands.

As television usurped dinner table conversation in the fifties, telecommunications of one sort or another have taken over the job of long leisurely letters in the nineties. My home phone rings at least a dozen times a day. At the office, twice that, outnumbering letters about fifty-to-one, unless you count *e-mail*, which I don't count or even read if I can help it. If long, descriptive letters allow us to blow off steam, *e-mail* traps that steam in the heat of the moment and spews it out. More that one hot memo has had to be undone by twenty more.

Paul now leaves phone messages, since he can't reach me quite as easily as he could before: "Mom, they're writing my part out of the soap. I'm going to get hit by a train or something; they haven't decided. Basically, it's because my nine weeks are up and they don't want to commit to me or pay my unemployment. That's what they do. *As the World Turns* wants me again, but I'm fed up with soaps. They treat you like trash, and it has nothing to do with acting, anyway. Terri and I are thinking about moving to L.A. She has some Juilliard connections out there, and she can get work playing with a group. What do you think?"

Ben's message: "Hey Ma, great news! I've been accepted to Northwestern Medical School! My internship at Baylor paid off. I'll be a full-fledged orthotist and be able to help kids and old people who need artificial limbs. It's a field that's really growing. I want to come up to see you and talk about it. Dad says he'll meet me in Chicago in August and help me get settled. What do you think of that? See, you *can* overcome a little Attention Deficit Disorder if you concentrate hard enough. Having five TV sets going on in your head all the time has been rough, but working out in the gym has helped me focus all that energy that drove everybody crazy when I was a kid."

Carrie: "Mother, I just read a study by Mardy Ireland Research something, saying that up to twenty-five percent of women of every color and class prefer not to have children. Can you believe that? Obviously, they haven't seen Bethany!"

"Hey Sis. I just found an article and put it in the mail to you this morning. It's from the *Wichita Falls Times*, Tuesday, April 30, 1985, and it's called 'Judicial Oversight—When the Judge Died, Did the Panel Die, Too?' Basically, what it says is that U.S. District Judge Sara T. Hughes was still technically overseeing the desegregation of the Wichita Falls public schools just before she died, to make sure the school board continued to obey the law. The city editor of the paper was quoted as saying that the deseg order by Judge Hughes in 1970, and Greg's determination to follow that order, had split the community and caused Greg's ouster. Basically Greg is being *praised* for obeying a law that he got *fired* for obeying fifteen years before! Remember all those fleas and stink bombs in your house? I guess you made a little difference there, after all. It's a very positive article about him, and I know you'll want to read it because you've always been proud of Greg's courage."

Alex, who almost always writes, called to leave a message: "C, sorry to leave this news like this, but I have to go see the family. Joan died of breast cancer last night; the horror we all fear. Her long nightmare is over. She'd just finished another stint at Yaddo and has a new book of poetry out that I'll send you. It's called *Daughter, Mother, Sister, Muse*. Be well. I love you."

Another phone call about ten years ago brought me to the Memorial Methodist Church in Manhattan to mourn a death among another kind of family.

The theatrical voice informed me that Lydia had been killed. A bike-auto accident in midtown. Wouldn't you know that Lydia would go this way—riding her fierce bicycle in the noonday sun? Lydia had spun in front of a truck that threw her off her bike, propelling her head into the curb. She died instantly.

Paul and I joined the small group in midtown to lay Lydia to rest—perhaps the first rest her skinny, intense little body had ever known. When the leader called for testimonials from the audience, an actor gave a reading from *Green Pastures*, another conducted a Black Mass, a basso profundo from City Opera sang "A Mighty Fortress Is Our God," and Paul and I moved to the front of the church to sing "Amazing Grace" as we looked out over Lydia's gathered friends: spine-straight school teachers, black, brown and white students, all crying into tissues; shackled and guarded punks from Rikers Island, looking tough and grim; gays in leather, lesbians in overalls, and transvestites in red lips and sequined sleeves. Mrs. Wright was there— the little old neighbor lady leaning on a walker, whose rent Lydia had paid for years. And Cheri, Lydia's young man friend, was hauled in on a chain by her St. Bernard, Birthday, who sniffed up and down the aisles and then hung over the casket whining and drooling. Even Vivian, the witch Lydia consulted occasionally, brought her cat Minnaloushe in a peaked hat decorated with silver moon and stars that changed color in the lights, as the cat's eyes did.

Lydia, who had been my Vergil, my first guide through the underworld of New York City, had covered her bets with her friends: she got a send off to every imaginable hereafter.

A couple of months after Mother died, Ellie called with more bad news. My old high school friend Duane had died of a heart attack. Ellie's call set me ruminating about the last time I'd seen him for any length of time. We'd hung out together when the crew was in Thalia filming *Texasville*, posing once in jest for the documentary film maker who was curious about "the people behind the people in *The Last Picture Show*, and was trying to ferret them out. Duane got a kick out of the fact that his life had been immortalized on film.

As we talked, it was sometimes hard to separate ourselves from the lives depicted on celluloid. After all, the movie was made in *our* hometown, and there *were* all those rumors. One night with Ellie and Mac, another schoolmate, we drove over the border into Oklahoma to a honky-tonk to dance. It was the night Duane and I had discussed in the Dairy Queen, with Daddy shouting questions at us. "*What* honky tonk? Slept on *what* sofa?" Ellie and I had crept home because Daddy would ask us what we'd been doing, and I for one did not care to report, mainly because on the way back across the border Duane and I sat together in the back seat holding hands. As we joked and talked, his hand began to feel like a space heater.

Finally, he placed it on my cheek and turned my face toward his. His kiss was firm and dry, like Duane himself. "I always dreamed of doing that, Jacy," he said finally. "I thought you'd never let me." To my immense surprise, I liked it. His lips were a little cracked, parched, like his voice; different from any man I'd ever kissed. He smelled of leather and tobacco—Texas-men smells I'd almost forgotten. Kissing him seemed perfectly right. An act of completion. For one moment, forty years' worth of simple affection was expressed in a simple way. It had never happened before; it would not happen again. But it was perfect for this moment: two fifty-something long-time friends acknowledging an old possibility that would never be fulfilled.

At dawn we stopped for scrambled eggs, something I never allow myself. But this was not an ordinary night; it was a night for breaking rules. As we pulled up in front of Daddy's house, Duane slipped off the silver saddle that held his bolo tie and placed it in my hand.

"For the first girl I ever loved," he said.

I stand here three years later pondering the infinite varieties of love, at once simple and complicated. An unfinished love, like that for Duane—and maybe a couple of other men in my life—remains for years, continuing to satisfy because it's never satisfied. It's a love that's always becoming, holding the tantalizing quality of eternal possibility. The opposite, I guess, of the love of Paola and Francesca, Dante's lovers doomed forever to a tight sexual embrace in a maddening swirl.

Eastern mysticism has something to suggest about the lasting enchantment of passion eternally suspended. I learned that from a professor once. And I really was in love with him, or thought I was. Thank god he was a grownup. I remember we talked about Jude the Obscure's *erotolepsy*—the human part of him being more powerful than the divine—and we opted for Zen and the Art of Behaving Yourself.

Deep love lightly held. Better than rum. Very different from the earthly variety I've shared exclusively with Marlboro for—what?— fifteen years? A love satisfying in every way. Better than rum *and* Dom Perignon.

Wouldn't you know I'd end up with someone who looked like the guy who sat tall in the saddle until he smoked himself to death?

My Marlboro has just enough of the good ole boy in him to qualify as a Texan a couple of times a year, and he doesn't smoke at all. He's about perfect, except, of course, he's still a nut about football, like all the old Texas jocks and Monday morning quarterbacks I couldn't wait to get away from in Thalia. Would you believe, he actually *watches* those things on TV—and even *cries* when they play "The Star Spangled Banner"? *And he wasn't even in the backfield!*

Which reminds me of the most important invitation I've ever had.

"Hi, this is Marlboro. The Reds are in town. I thought you might like to go."

"Do I know the Reds?"

"A famous baseball team. I have tickets and subway tokens."

"Do I know you?"

"We met at that editorial conference about a year ago. Why haven't you called?"

"I don't call boys."

"Other girls do."

"I'm not other girls. But oh, now I remember you. You sat next to me at a dinner that night. I was hoping you'd ask me out, but you didn't. I took a cab home. By myself. In the rain. It was dismal."

"I had my eye on another woman that night, and this was my chance. She lives out of town. You live here. I have a very busy social life. You're lucky your number came up at all. How come *you* never called?"

"It never occurred to me."

"Do you want to go or not? I've got somebody on hold."

"Well, what if I told you that when I've seen the Reds play before I've sat in a posh box where they serve gourmet finger food and cocktails. Can you top that?"

"No. I'll just show you how *real* people watch baseball. Bring your own hot dog."

"How do we do this? I mean do I wear a red dress and meet you at the subway station or what?"

"You can wear a red dress, but meet me at a bar called The Cowboy at 49th and Madison. It's owned by Clint Murchison. I remembered you were from Texas, so I had him put this bar up there just for you."

"You seem to remember a lot about me."

"I remember that you have auburn hair and very blue eyes. But you had on one of those pant things, and I don't like girls in those pant things."

"Hey, that's a great outfit, very stylish. I bought it at Barneys, that new store."

"I don't care where you bought it. Wear a skirt next time."

"Are you a male chauvinist pig?"

"I am male, and you'll have to find out the rest for yourself."

"Well, that's a challenge. The Cowboy, huh?"

"Early. Five o'clock. We've got to beat the crowd."

That evening stands out in the annals of first dates. For one thing, it was the first time I'd taken a subway to Shea Stadium, with the added attraction of standing up all the way, clinging to a pole while wannabe jocks yelled at each other and jostled me. And it was one of those Red—so to speak—letter nights (deep breath): *Pete Rose of the Cincinnati Reds broke the National League record of Tommy Holmes by hitting in his 38th consecutive game* (whew!).

Marlboro poked me in the ribs until I repeated that all the way home on the subway. I memorized it like I once memorized *the square of the hypotenuse of the right angle triangle is equal to the sum of the square of the other two sides*. I believe, however, that the hypotenuse equation has been more helpful in later life.

Also, I was a real wash-out of a date.

"Hey, girls don't shake my hand at the door. I'm single, employed, and straight. Not to mention presentable looking. You're supposed to fall at my feet."

"In another life. Thanks for the evening, though. It was fun."

"Well, see you around campus, as they say in the Ed Biz."

Our so-called relationship grew slowly, intermittently; like one of those evolutionary sleeps and leaps. We were both enjoying singledom after long years of marriage. Neither of us was looking to settle in with a partner, which only goes to show that when you're not desperate for something, more often than not you get it. (Isn't that right, Mother?) It's not fair, I know, but what can I say? For three years, though, whenever either of us wanted to scare up someone to impress a family member or an out-of-town friend, we scared up one another. That should have told us something.

I was in no hurry to marry. *Why do that?* I'd made a vow to myself that I wouldn't even consider marriage unless the man a) didn't want any more kids, b) had lived alone so he knew how to take care of himself, and c) was an orphan. As fate would have it, Marlboro rang the bell in all of the above: he had two kids, and that was enough; he'd been single five years; and both his parents were deceased. So when maintaining two apartments began to seem silly, since we were always in one or the other, we finally proposed to each other, taking turns doing the genuflecting. What we found though, was that mating is not easy in New York City. The good cheer of those seeking marriage licenses at the court house diminishes in proportion to the increasing length of the line. In Manhattan, you must also stand in line to get a blood test, but this test will allow you to get married even if you have rabies. The only information it gives you is that you don't (or heaven forbid, do) have syphilis.

We didn't, so we pledged eternal devotion at a small ceremony in a private club with a curving stairway for the bride to descend dramatically in her mail order dress from Neiman Marcus, where if you order from New York, you save the taxes. After the formal part, Marlboro's two lovely daughters sang the fight songs of every school in the Big Ten, plus Columbia (hers) and Harvard (his), led by Susan, Marlboro's beautiful and talented former wife, whom I might have married instead, had either of us been male.

At the Regency Hotel later that evening over Dom Perignon, Marlboro said, "From the very first, we were inevitable, you know."

"Of course. You look like Arthur Miller."

"Oh? Most of the girls say Omar Sharif."

My new life, however, couldn't keep me away from the computer for long. But now, instead of writing stories out of anger and frustration, as I had throughout the Keating years, I wrote about

HAPPY FAMILIES*

Three years ago in a modest ceremony in Manhattan, a Methodist from Texas married a Jew from Ohio. It was the second marriage for both. Both had lived and worked in the city for more than a dozen years. Both had happily stored Christmas tree balls and Hanukkah candles in the rarely opened little cabinets above their separate fridges.

Marriage, however, changes things. For one, the couple now have five children in five different colleges in five different states. For another, the one little cabinet above the fridge cannot accommodate the oft-discarded enthusiasms and fashion whims of five children who, though living in five states, have lots of stuff to store at home.

So the couple bought a house with a very large basement on Long Island. In it five children have five nests. None is empty.

For this group, the calendar holds only two mutually agreed upon holidays: Thanksgiving and the Fourth of July. The first celebrates the fact that even rebels from the crown can eat well, and the second celebrates total independence. If ever there were a family that needed to highlight these events, it is ours.

What may be unique to this grouping is that everyone likes everyone else quite a lot—at least on those two days. Liking, in our lexicon, is a step above loving, which is obligatory in families.

Surely there are differences among these young people, all in their twenties. Susie (his) may think Tommy (hers) could be more motivated, while Tommy may consider Susie judgmental. Dick (hers) may think Jane (his) is a space cadet, but Jane wonders why Dick doesn't just grow up. All think that Sally falls for every man she meets, while Sally considers the rest incapable of commitment.

So it goes. But on Thanksgiving and the Fourth of July, these differences are laid to rest. Probably because there are so many other differences to deal with—such as visitations from ex-spouses, ex-spouses' current mates, ex-spouses' parents and assorted other extended family.

Sometimes I wonder what my grandmother would make of it. If she were alive today, she would be nearly a century old. The family over which she presided was the product of one longtime husband. Each married someone "within the faith," from a neighboring town, settled down in the same state and remained married to the original spouse. Most have at least three children who have at least three children. Before my grandmother died in her eighties, she had to rent a large hall to get her family together for Thanksgiving Dinner. I am prematurely getting to the large hall stage. Sometime during the last decade my nuclear family exploded—some say from too much pressure—and the fallout lands each November in my dining room, where it deconstructs a turkey. But I love them all. I especially love my husband's former wife, who is invited because her children are here. Sometimes I think I may love her more than I do my husband, but then, maybe it's just that I identify with her more. We gossip, pass on family stories, and have sometimes been known to comfort each other when my husband and her man-friend huddle once too often before the TV ball game when the family is celebrating a holiday.

Then there are my husband's former in-laws, who are invited, of course, because their grandchildren are here. And my son's former girlfriend, who just broke up with her most recent boyfriend, and who seems lonely, so why don't we . . . and someone's hyperkinetic boss, who is as officious socially as otherwise, but who is alone today, so why not . . . and someone's roommate, and someone's international student, so just to be generous why don't we . . .

It gets hairy.

On this particular high holy day, this happy close-knit family group includes the following: nine Protestants, nine Jews, four Catholics, one mystic, and several undeclared. (I am the mystic. When it came to my attention many years ago that mystics do not have to bake cookies for church events or dress anyone as an angel once a year, I converted immediately. Since making this decision to let neither cookie nor angel come between me and the Lord, I have felt much more spiritual.) Four of my Thanksgiving crowd regularly go to church, three to Mass, and two to temple. The rest regularly sleep in on weekends, for want, most of them claim, of a clean shirt. (These claims are designed to make mothers and wives feel guilty. They just make me feel more mystic.)

I sometimes wonder what my grandmother would think of these scenes. I suspect that she would cluck her tongue over what the world is coming to, survey the room full of hungry people who have called a Thanksgiving truce, and then with something of the same amused resignation that I admit to, call for someone to come carve the turkey.

Happy families are all alike.

*This article originally appeared in *The New York Times*, November 15, 1987.

E·P·I·L·O·G·U·E

Miracles seem to rest, not so much upon faces or voices or healing power coming suddenly near to us from far off, but upon our perceptions being made so that for a moment our eyes can see and our ears can hear that which is about us always.
—Willa Cather

At my door, my shadow deserts me, following you down the sunny street.
—ME

I PUT DOWN my notebooks and jog myself out of my reverie. Marlboro will be home in a bit, after a week in California, and I want to finish planting the impatiens and the mandevilla. Early spring here evokes a frenzy of digging and roto-tilling even in those of us who assume that flowers grow primarily within our minds. I've planted pansies in the flower boxes; roses and begonias by the fence. I have a lot of Long Island earth underneath my nails, and I want to stop soon enough to dig it out, and to wash my hair and put on clean shorts, and make something nice for dinner, and change the bed.

When I'm away from home for a week or two, and can't wait to get back here, I can't tell you how great it makes me feel when Marlboro has thought to make things perfect for me when I return, to clean the fireplace and dump the ashes, to grind the coffee, and put the pot up, to change the bed, to stack my mail just so, and to take the interminable messages off my machine.

Something I've learned in my old age: little things mean a lot. Or was that a song Jacy sang in the fifties?

As I reach for my gloves, the FAX bell rings. I go to the machine and pick up the page: "Cece, this is frum Donnie, yur grandkid. This is a picshur of a squirel, a bird, and a rabbit playing hide an seek. Bethany is going to swimcamp. Momie fixed my bike. Love Donnie"

I wash my hair, clean up and head for the garden again. Again I am interrupted. This time by the phone. I sigh and pick it up.

"CC. Ellie. I'm sorry to have to call you with this kind of news. Unbelievable."

"What is it?"

"Logan. His neck is broken. He's in General."

"*What*?" My youngest brother.

"You know that wild little filly that he and Mills brought back from Montana? Well, Logan was trying to break her, and she threw him. He flew over her head and landed on the back of his neck."

"Oh my god! Is he going to be okay?"

"They're not sure right now. He was in a lot of pain, so he's knocked out. They're going to put a steel pipe-of-a-thing in his neck. His kids are here—Sherry and Cal are with him."

"I'll be right there. I can get a plane tonight."

"Wait till tomorrow, and let's see what happens. I'll let you know if you should come. Right now there's nothing you can do. Dad and I have been up there. Just keeping our fingers crossed. I'll call you tomorrow."

I hang up the phone, then as if on remote control go down to the kitchen, make a cup of tea and wander out to the garden. I am stunned; operating on default position.

I'll go down to thalia tomorrow and bail ellie out thats the least I can do with her living so close to the rest of the family they depend on her strength and sanity when theres a problem now that mothers gone and god this is not fair to logan the dearest man on earth kind gentle logan and damn that bitching filly for hurting him anyway so why do bad things happen to good people a dumb book probably but at least somebody tried like dostoyevsky years ago who couldnt answer that question either and I have spent my life trying to find answers to these things in books and maybe you cant do it through literature or philosophy or religion or any other way because the more people you love the more vulnerable you are and the more you grieve so maybe weve got it all wrong and should just go live in a cave by ourselves so nobody can hurt us but no no I swear I will be engaged and absorb the pain because in any case it tells you you are real flesh and blood alive and have a beating heart and are living breathing seeing the sun rise and set and watching the egrets when they come back home to hang in the trees yes and seeing the pond electric with fuzzy new ducklings and holding your lover yes and hugging your offspring are whats important and trying to answer things in a rational way is probably going to drive me mad because the way in is the way out the way up is the way down and yes mother you knew this all along and you didnt have to move out of little thalia to learn it did you . . . .

As I wander stupidly out the door, I look up, glancing toward my perennial garden. One luscious iris has burst into bloom. Suddenly. Instantly. It was not there less than an hour before, when I left. I walk toward it and bend to put my nose into its fragrant cup. Mother's velvety, purple iris from her own clump in Thalia that she helped me dig up and put in a plastic bag with moisture to take back on American Airlines to Long Island to plant in my own garden so I'd always have something of her with me. I sit down on the rock wall, teacup in hand, bending toward the bloom.

"He's going to be all right, isn't he?" I mutter. "Logan is going to get well. Please, God. Loggie will be all right."

The iris nods, and its petals flutter in the breeze.

When Marlboro returns an hour later, I am still sitting on the rock wall.

"What are you doing out there?" he calls.

"Talking to my flowers."

"Like the Prince of Wales, huh? And what are they telling you?"

"*Cum tacent clament.*"

"Oh, they speak Latin, then. Smart plants. Now tell me, what does that mean?"

"'Their very silence is a loud cry'—*Cicero.*"

"Oh, I see." Marlboro bends and kisses me. "Thanks for stacking my mail." Then he returns to the house in search of a sensible martini.